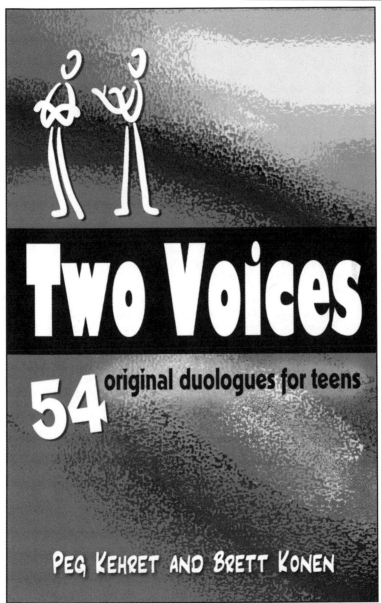

# Two Voices

## 54 original duologues for teens

### PEG KEHRET AND BRETT KONEN

MERIWETHER PUBLISHING LTD.
Colorado Springs, Colorado

**Meriwether Publishing Ltd., Publisher**
**PO Box 7710**
**Colorado Springs, CO 80933-7710**

**www.meriwether.com**

**Editor: Theodore O. Zapel**
**Assistant editor: Nicole Rutledge**
**Cover design: Jan Melvin**

Copyright © 2014 by Peg Kehret and Brett Konen
Printed in the United States of America
First Edition

**Library of Congress Cataloging-in-Publication Data**

Kehret, Peg.
 Two voices : 54 original duologues for teens / by Peg Kehret and Brett Konen. -- First edition.
      pages cm
  ISBN 978-1-56608-196-2 (pbk.)
 1. Dialogues. 2. Acting. I. Konen, Brett. II. Title.
  PN2080.K355 2014
  812'.54--dc23

                                        2014000344

            1    2    3          14    15    16

*For Brett, a terrific co-author and granddaughter.*
*You bring me joy.*

*— Peg Kehret*


*For Moonie, my co-author and all-star grandma,*
*from whom I've learned writing and so much more.*

*— Brett Konen*

# Table of Contents

## About the Authors

# Preface

The duologues in this book are intended for use in a wide variety of settings, from speech contests to auditions to class assignments to performance practice. Each scene presents distinctive viewpoints on issues ranging from simple to complex. All are meant to provoke thought and inspire discussion as well as to entertain.

Some scenes — "Pass the Peas," "Goody, Two Shoes," and "Two by Two" among them — play with language. Others — including "Goldilocks and the Three Court Charges" and "Parenting on Mt. Olympus" — are purely for fun. Several — like "North to Alaska" and "The Brit and the Yank" — are fictional portrayals of historic events. We also explore more serious topics: family relationships, immigration, preoccupation with weight, erosion of citizens' rights, consumerism, college decisions, and how to get a job.

We have assigned names and genders to some characters in this book, but the majority of the roles can be played by either a male or a female. Names may be changed as desired.

We hope that these duologues will inspire their audiences to laugh, think, and respond honestly.

— Peg Kehret and Brett Konen

# 1. Goldilocks and the Three Court Charges

**Cast:** GOLDILOCKS and ATTORNEY for the bears
**Setting:** Courtroom
**Props:** None

1 ATTORNEY: Your Honor, I will now present the charges
2     against Goldilocks.
3 GOLDILOCKS: Charges? What charges? I didn't do anything
4     wrong.
5 ATTORNEY: You are in big trouble, girl. You can't just stroll
6     into someone else's house uninvited and eat their
7     porridge and sit in their chairs and sleep in their beds.
8     What were you thinking?
9 GOLDILOCKS: I was lost in the woods! I knocked, and
10     nobody answered the door, so I went in to see if there
11     was a phone I could use. The battery on mine was dead.
12 ATTORNEY: Did you use the bears' telephone?
13 GOLDILOCKS: No. When I got inside, I saw the bowls of
14     porridge, and I was so hungry that I started to eat.
15     When I finally found a bowl that was the right
16     temperature, I gobbled it all up, even though it was
17     awfully bland. The bears really should add cinnamon
18     or raisins to their porridge. Brown sugar would be
19     good too, with a few walnuts. I wonder if the bears have
20     ever tried granola or a toasted bagel for breakfast.
21     Maybe I should send them my recipe for blueberry
22     bran muffins.
23 ATTORNEY: The bears don't need any recipes. Just answer
24     the questions, please. Why didn't you call for help after
25     you ate?
26 GOLDILOCKS: I was tired, and the warm porridge made me
27     so sleepy that I forgot all about being lost.
28 ATTORNEY: You also forgot that there are laws against

1      uninvited entry. **Papa and Mama Bear have accused**
2      **you of trespassing. This hearing is to determine if the**
3      **charges warrant going to trial.**
4      **GOLDILOCKS: Well, that is just about the meanest thing**
5      **I've ever heard. They're charging me with a crime?** *I*
6      **should be suing** *them!*
7      **ATTORNEY: For what?**
8      **GOLDILOCKS: Reckless endangerment! The first bowl of**
9      **porridge was way too hot. I burned my tongue! If I**
10      **had eaten it, my throat would be scalded. And that**
11      **third chair was a safety hazard. I'm lucky I didn't**
12      **break a bone when it collapsed under me.**
13      **ATTORNEY: You can't sue them for reckless**
14      **endangerment when you were in their house**
15      **uninvited. They are already suing you over the**
16      **broken chair. In addition to trespassing, you're**
17      **charged with destruction of private property.**
18      **GOLDILOCKS: You're kidding me, right? That piece-of-**
19      **junk chair was on its last legs already. I'll bet the**
20      **Salvation Army would have refused it as a donation. I**
21      **did those bears a huge favor by sitting on it before**
22      **one of them did. They should be giving me a reward**
23      **for saving them from serious injury.**
24      **ATTORNEY: Any judge will throw out your claim of**
25      **reckless endangerment. That chair was perfectly safe**
26      **for Baby Bear.**
27      **GOLDLOCKS: I can sue the bears for attempted**
28      **kidnapping! They chased me into the woods, and if**
29      **they had caught me, they would have taken me back**
30      **to their house against my will.**
31      **ATTORNEY: The bears chased you because they found you**
32      **asleep in Baby Bear's bed. They weren't trying to**
33      **kidnap you – they were pursuing the person who**
34      **trespassed in their home. They only wanted to catch**
35      **you and bring you to justice for stealing from them.**

1     Besides trespassing and destruction of private
2     property, the bears accuse you of petty theft.
3  GOLDILOCKS: Petty theft? I didn't steal anything! They
4     didn't have anything worth stealing. No iPods, no
5     computers, no DVD players. Nothing but honey pots.
6  ATTORNEY: What about their porridge? You've already
7     admitted to this court that you ate Baby Bear's
8     porridge.
9  GOLDILOCKS: OK! So I ate a bowl of crummy porridge.
10     That hardly seems like a criminal offense. They
11     didn't even have spoons. I had to use my fingers. And
12     it definitely needed dried cranberries or a sprinkling
13     of nutmeg.
14  ATTORNEY: The porridge may not have been to your
15     liking, but you cannot dispute the fact that it
16     belonged to the three bears. You had no right to eat it.
17  GOLDILOCKS: Had I known how selfish the three bears
18     would be, I would never have gone near their cottage.
19     Instead of chasing me away, they should have offered
20     to call me a cab or invited me to stay for dinner.
21     Although if their dinner was as unappetizing as their
22     breakfast, I wouldn't have wanted to eat it, anyway.
23  ATTORNEY: If someone you had never met came into
24     your home while you were gone and broke your
25     furniture and ate your food, and then you found that
26     person sleeping in your bed, would you invite her to
27     stick around?
28  GOLDILOCKS: When you put it that way, no, I don't
29     suppose I would. But I wouldn't file a bunch of
30     lawsuits, either. What a waste of time and money!
31     The bears are going to spend way more on legal fees
32     than it would cost to buy a new chair and more
33     porridge.
34  ATTORNEY: Shhhh! Don't let them hear you say that.
35  GOLDILOCKS: The three bears don't need you. All they

1    need is a lock for their door. *(She hollers toward Stage*
2    *Left.)* **Do you hear me, bears? Instead of hiring this**
3    **charlatan,    spend    your    money    on    something**
4    **worthwhile, like cable TV for your cottage!**
5    **ATTORNEY: If they drop their charges against you, would**
6    **you be interested in having me represent you in your**
7    **claim of attempted kidnapping?**
8    **GOLDILOCKS: No. I've decided not to sue the three bears.**
9    **ATTORNEY: Too bad. I guess I'll have to take the case of**
10   **Little Bo Peep versus The Department of Sheep**
11   **Health and Welfare.**

# 2. An Honest Holiday Letter

**Cast:** SISTER and BROTHER

**Setting:** No special set required.

**Props:** Both characters have a notebook and pencil or a laptop computer.

**Costume:** Sister wears a knit cap.

1 SISTER: I love holiday letters! It's so cool to read everything
2     that people have done all year, and now we get to write
3     one for our family. It's about time Mom and Dad let us
4     do it. They've written the holiday letter every year for
5     forever. It's usually all about us kids and our activities
6     anyway, so why not let us write it ourselves?
7 BROTHER: This is so stupid. Who wants to read every detail
8     of our boring lives? What a waste of time and paper.
9     Mom and Dad are making us do it this year because
10     neither of them can stand to write about our rotten
11     lives.
12 SISTER: How to begin? Oh, I know! *(Starts to write.)*
13 BROTHER: I have yet to read an interesting holiday letter.
14     The worst are the ones that start out by saying, "It's
15     that time of year again when we write to our family and
16     friends." I mean, we *know* it's that time of year or we
17     would not be reading holiday letters, right?
18 SISTER: *(Reads what she wrote.)* "It's that time of year again
19     when we write to our family and friends."
20 BROTHER: Then they go on to brag about all the wonderful
21     things that their family has done. Fabulous vacations.
22     New jobs with big salaries. Scholarships for the kids.
23     The dog won "Best in Show."
24 SISTER: *(Continues to write.)* "It's been a fantastic year for
25     our family, with lots of exciting news."
26 BROTHER: Well, Mom said I have to do this. *(Starts to write.)*

1 "Yo dudes! You are about to read the first-ever honest
2 holiday letter."

3 SISTER: "I'll start with my dad. After working hard all his
4 adult life, Dad got to enjoy an extended vacation this
5 year and a chance to follow his lifetime dream of
6 being a freelance writer."

7 BROTHER: "The year had a crummy start in January
8 when my dad got laid off. He'd worked at the
9 underwear factory for twenty-three years, so it was a
10 blow when the factory downsized and laid off fifty
11 workers."

12 SISTER: "It only took him six months to finish his book,
13 *The Insider's Guide to Underwear That Fits.*"

14 BROTHER: "Finding another job in our small town
15 proved impossible, especially when forty-nine other
16 people with his identical experience started looking
17 for work at the same time, so he decided to write a
18 book."

19 SISTER: "With his book done, he began the search for a
20 literary agent and a publisher. What a great learning
21 experience!"

22 BROTHER: "So far it has been rejected by twenty-seven
23 literary agents and forty-four publishers. The only
24 positive response he got was from a vanity press that
25 wanted him to pay them four thousand dollars to
26 print the book."

27 SISTER: "Watch for our holiday letter next year to see the
28 for-sale date of Dad's book. You'll want an
29 autographed copy. By then, we expect to announce
30 that the movie rights have also been sold. Rumor has
31 it that Tom Cruise is interested."

32 BROTHER: "Between losing his job and not selling his
33 book, Dad is none too perky these days. His new
34 hobby is watching golf on TV."

35 SISTER: "Now on to my mom. Mom decided this was the

1     year for our family to get organized. What a whiz she
2     is at cleaning out closets and tidying up shelves! We
3     expect to be featured in *Good Housekeeping* soon."
4  BROTHER: "With Dad moping around, Mom went into
5     overdrive. As soon as she got home from work every
6     day, she started going through closets and drawers,
7     looking for stuff to sell on eBay. She seemed to think
8     we could make up for Dad's loss of income with old
9     Beanie Babies."
10 SISTER: "Mom also started her own home business and
11     soon got the rest of us involved in helping her with
12     it."
13 BROTHER: "She nagged at me until I went through every
14     single item in my room and gave her all the old toys
15     and other things I don't use anymore. She even tried
16     to talk me into selling my baseball cards, but I drew
17     the line at that."
18 SISTER: "We decided to help the planet by going green!
19     Riding our bikes is great exercise and we are
20     reducing our carbon footprints."
21 BROTHER: "Our good car was repossessed in April. We
22     still have the clunker and Mom uses that to get to
23     work, but the rest of us either have to walk or ride
24     our bikes. One day, I had to ride my bike home from
25     school in a hailstorm."
26 SISTER: "It was a big year for me. I got what every
27     teenager waits for – my driver's license!"
28 BROTHER: "It's probably just as well we don't have the
29     good car anymore because my sister finally passed
30     her driver's test. It took her three tries, and even
31     then, she barely squeaked by. Dad says the only
32     reason she got her license was because the person
33     who gives the test got tired of riding with her. The
34     first day she had her license, she backed into the
35     mailbox at the end of our driveway. Now she isn't

1        allowed to drive the car unless Mom or Dad goes with
2        her.”
3 SISTER: “Of course, I don't drive much because we're
4        going green, but it's still exciting to have my license.
5        My other big news is that I have a new hair color.”
6 BROTHER: “The reason we are not including a family
7        photo this year is because my sister totally ruined her
8        hair trying to put in highlights. She did it herself and
9        got distracted talking on the phone. She left the
10        solution on too long and ended up with big patches of
11        hair that are this bilious yellow-green color.”
12 SISTER: “I had entered our town's Miss Preppy Pageant,
13        and I decided to experiment and go for a
14        nontraditional look.”
15 BROTHER: “She tried to lessen the damage by dyeing all
16        her hair blonde. It's the ugliest mess you ever saw.
17        She had to withdraw from the Miss Preppy Pageant
18        because she refuses to take her hat off.”
19 SISTER: “Did you know that knit caps are *in* this year? I'm
20        upholding my reputation as a trendsetter.”
21 BROTHER: “My year wasn't any better than the rest of my
22        family's. I tried out for the football team and didn't
23        make it. Then I tried out for soccer and didn't make
24        that either.”
25 SISTER: “My brother spent the fall months heavily
26        involved in school sports.”
27 BROTHER: “Since athletics weren't working for me, I
28        joined the debate club. The first topic they gave me
29        was, ‘Why School Sports Are Important.’ I wasn't very
30        convincing.”
31 SISTER: “Being the big brain that he is, Bro excelled at
32        debate. He even placed in his very first debate
33        tournament.”
34 BROTHER: “There were eight kids on the debate team. I
35        got eighth place.”

1    SISTER: "Many holiday letters include the family pet. We
2        are currently looking for the perfect pet to adopt and
3        can't wait to give a loving home to a needy animal."
4    BROTHER: "Besides losing Dad's job, the good car, the
5        debate tournament, and the Miss Preppy Pageant, we
6        also lost both our pets this year. Grungie the gerbil
7        somehow got out of his cage and the neighbor's cat
8        ate him. Tweety Bird fell victim to a tainted package
9        of birdseed."
10   SISTER: "That's all the news from here. I hope next year
11       is even better than this one was."
12   BROTHER: "This whole year was the pits, and I suspect
13       next year will be the same."
14   BROTHER and SISTER: *(Together)* "Happy holidays!"

# 3. Admit It, We're Lost

**Cast:** CAMERON and SKYLER

**Setting:** Front seat of a car. Two chairs face the audience as seats of the car.

**Props:** None

1   CAMERON: I think we're lost.

2   SKYLER: No, we're not.

3   CAMERON: Where are we, then?

4   SKYLER: We're nearly there.

5   CAMERON: I'm telling you, we're headed in the wrong

6       direction. I haven't seen anything familiar for miles.

7   SKYLER: I know where we're going.

8   CAMERON: We should have printed directions. I knew we

9       should have printed directions.

10   SKYLER: I have an internal compass. Directions slow me

11       down.

12   CAMERON: Had I searched the directions? Yes. Did I have

13       them pulled up on the computer screen? Yes.

14   SKYLER: Were you about to kill a tree and widen the hole in

15       the ozone layer by printing them? Yes.

16   CAMERON: I'm telling you, I read them. None of these street

17       names sound familiar. Do you realize you're on West

18       Cricket Chirp Lane? Doesn't exactly sound like a

19       thoroughfare, does it?

20   SKYLER: Of course not. It's a shortcut.

21   CAMERON: A shortcut! Do you remember the last time you

22       tried to take us on one of your "shortcuts"? We were

23       two hours late to the wedding!

24   SKYLER: I've said it before, and I'll say it again. Computer

25       directions are convoluted. Have you ever used them to

26       get home from somewhere? They take you miles off

27       course! MapQuest is probably sponsored by oil

28       companies who want you to burn through an extra

1     gallon of gas with every trip.

2  CAMERON: Oil companies are probably doubly delighted
3     every time you drive somewhere. We're going in gas-
4     guzzling circles. We've definitely passed that cow
5     mailbox before.

6  SKYLER: Just because you can't get anywhere without
7     your GPS talking at you the whole way doesn't mean
8     we're all directionally challenged. *(Mimics*
9     *robotically.)* "In a quarter-mile, take a left turn."

10 CAMERON: I'm going to buy you a GPS for Christmas.
11     They're miraculous.

12 SKYLER: It's going in the storage shed with the atlas you
13     bought me last Christmas. You don't mess with an
14     internal compass.

15 CAMERON: The lasagna is getting cold in the backseat. So
16     much for all the time I spent on a nice potluck
17     contribution. We'll be lucky to get dessert.

18 SKYLER: Please. Last time we got to your sister's house for
19     dinner, she hadn't even put the bread in the oven.

20 CAMERON: Yes, because we got there early. And as I
21     recall, I drove.

22 SKYLER: You mean your GPS drove. Siri interrupted us
23     the entire way.

24 CAMERON: Do you have maps on your phone?

25 SKYLER: Don't be ridiculous. Know what I use my phone
26     for? Phone calls.

27 CAMERON: Wait, there's someone walking up ahead! Pull
28     over. I'll ask him how to get back on the freeway if
29     you're too embarrassed.

30 SKYLER: Embarrassed! Of what?

31 CAMERON: Exactly. You shouldn't be embarrassed that
32     we're lost. It's only embarrassing if you refuse to
33     admit it – What are you doing? You passed him!

34 SKYLER: He looked clueless.

35 CAMERON: So do you. That doesn't mean I refuse to talk

1      to you.

2    SKYLER: If we're not there in five minutes we'll stop at a

3      gas station.

4    CAMERON: I haven't seen a gas station in ages.

5    SKYLER: Then I guess it's a good thing we won't need to

6      stop.

7    CAMERON: You're impossible. I'm starving, we're more

8      lost by the minute, and you'd rather imprison me in

9      this moving vehicle than let me ask someone for

10    help.

11  SKYLER: And get us even more lost?

12  CAMERON: Ha! So you admit it! You are lost!

13  SKYLER: If I'm not lost now, asking that man certainly

14     would have done the trick.

15  CAMERON: We might not see anyone else. It's getting

16     dark, and all I see are fields.

17  SKYLER: We're going as the crow flies, my dear. Cutting

18     past all the freeway traffic.

19  CAMERON: We're also cutting past all the roads we

20     recognize.

21  SKYLER: It's scenic.

22  CAMERON: Do you have any paper napkins? I'm going to

23     have a piece of lasagna.

24  SKYLER: If you're not going to wait for the dinner, maybe

25     we should just head back home now.

26  CAMERON: I'd like to see you try to get home from here!

27     Do you even know what town this is?

28  SKYLER: It's not the destination but the journey that

29     counts.

30  CAMERON: Can I see your non-mapping telephone? It's

31     time to call my sister.

32  SKYLER: Oh, ye of little faith.

33  CAMERON: Hey, wait. This street looks familiar. Doesn't

34     this street look familiar? Haven't we been by this

35     house before?

1   SKYLER: Ha! What did I tell you? Admit it, you were
2        wrong and I was right.
3   CAMERON: I've definitely seen that tree stump.
4   SKYLER: I have too. It's all coming back now.
5   CAMERON: We must be getting close! What does that sign
6       say?
7   SKYLER: Pah, signs. Who needs 'em?
8   CAMERON: Oh, good grief! We're back on Cricket Chirp
9       Lane!
10  SKYLER: Oh. Are you sure?
11  CAMERON: Agh! We'll never make it!
12  SKYLER: Jeez, what's the big deal? I'm just going to pull
13      over and ask that guy up there for directions.
14      Honestly, I think you'll have a conniption one of
15      these days.
16  CAMERON: I probably will, and when I do, I'd like
17      someone other than you to drive me to the hospital.

# 4. How Not to Get a Job

**Cast:** CARTER and SARAH

**Setting:** No special set required.

**Props:** None

**Costume:** Sarah is neatly dressed. Carter wears sloppy clothes and a dirty baseball cap.

1　SARAH: I got it! I got a job!

2　CARTER: What job? I didn't know you were applying for a

3　　　job.

4　SARAH: I've been looking for a summer job for weeks.

5　　　Yesterday I saw a "Help Wanted" sign in the window at

6　　　Jasper's Java, so I went in and asked about it. They gave

7　　　me an application to fill out and said the manager

8　　　wasn't there, but he'd be in today. I hung around

9　　　awhile and talked to a couple of the people who work

10　　　there, and I bought two different coffee drinks. I also

11　　　got the manager's name. Today I went back and asked

12　　　for Jasper Johnson, and he talked to me. He asked me

13　　　why I want to work there, so I told him I love the

14　　　friendly atmosphere at Jasper's Java and my favorite

15　　　drink is Jasper's Three Bean, and I got hired!

16　CARTER: Congratulations! When do you start?

17　SARAH: On Saturday. I'll work after school and on

18　　　Saturdays until school is out and then full time this

19　　　summer.

20　CARTER: I'm impressed. I know about a zillion people who

21　　　are applying for jobs, and you're the first one who

22　　　actually got hired. I've been applying myself, but so far

23　　　I haven't had any interviews.

24　SARAH: Where have you applied?

25　CARTER: Any place that runs a "Help Wanted" ad. I follow

26　　　Craigslist and the newspaper. I send my resume to all

27　　　of them, but I haven't heard back from anybody. I've

1          probably emailed thirty or forty resumes.

2  SARAH: Do you send a cover letter too?

3  CARTER: A what?

4  SARAH: A cover letter. You know, "Dear Mr. Bossperson, I

5          have been a customer of yours for a long time

6          because I love your products, and I'd like an

7          opportunity to work for you."

8  CARTER: I just say, "To Whom It May Concern: Please see

9          attached resume."

10  SARAH: That isn't very personal. You should at least use

11         the person's name.

12  CARTER: I don't know their names.

13  SARAH: Then you need to find out. You go to whatever

14         business it is and you tell them you want to apply for

15         a job and ask for the name of the person who handles

16         applications.

17  CARTER: Go there? You mean in person?

18  SARAH: Yes, in person. Get cleaned up and take a stack of

19         resumes and go from place to place.

20  CARTER: I have to get dressed up?

21  SARAH: You don't have to wear a suit and tie to apply at a

22         fast food restaurant, but yes, you would need to be

23         clean. You'd probably want to ditch the baseball cap.

24  CARTER: If I got hired, I'd wear clean clothes to work.

25  SARAH: How is the boss supposed to know that? If you

26         show up looking like a slob, he'll think you always

27         look that way.

28  CARTER: They should hire me for my skills, not because I

29         wear the latest fashions.

30  SARAH: What skills?

31  CARTER: The skills I'll learn on the job as soon as I get

32         hired. I'm a fast learner.

33  SARAH: You haven't learned much about how to apply for

34         a job. You need to look respectable and tell your

35         prospective employers what you can do that would

1      make you valuable to them.

2  **CARTER:** Like what?

3  **SARAH:** You have a computer, right?

4  **CARTER:** Yes.

5  **SARAH:** What programs do you know? Can you use Word?

6      Have you done any programming? Do you know how

7      to make a spreadsheet?

8  **CARTER:** I use Word. I haven't done a spreadsheet, but I

9      publish an online newsletter for a car club that I

10     belong to.

11  **SARAH:** That's perfect! Add that to your resume.

12  **CARTER:** The car club? What if the boss isn't into cars?

13  **SARAH:** It isn't the cars that matter, it's the fact that you

14     know how to do online publishing. What else to you

15     do in your car club?

16  **CARTER:** We get together and work on our cars. Or we go

17     for drives. Or we just hang out and talk, mostly about

18     cars.

19  **SARAH:** Is it an official club, with officers?

20  **CARTER:** Yeah. I'm the president.

21  **SARAH:** Great! Put that on your resume too. It shows that

22     you have leadership qualities.

23  **CARTER:** No it doesn't. It shows that nobody else would be

24     the president. I only got elected because I wasn't

25     there that night to say no.

26  **SARAH:** What kind of jobs are you applying for?

27  **CARTER:** Anything. I answer every ad.

28  **SARAH:** Where did you send your last application? What

29     company?

30  **CARTER:** It was a private party. They want a nanny for a

31     two-year-old and an infant.

32  **SARAH:** Do you have any experience with little kids? Do

33     you know how to give a baby a bath? Have you ever

34     changed a dirty diaper?

35  **CARTER:** No experience. No bath. And definitely no dirty

1     diapers.

2  SARAH: Do you *want* to do those things?

3  CARTER: Are you kidding? Who in their right mind would

4     *want* to change dirty diapers?

5  SARAH: Then why did you apply for the nanny job?

6  CARTER: It pays fifteen dollars an hour. Forty-five hours

7     a week. That's big bucks!

8  SARAH: That's a lot of dirty diapers. You would *hate* being

9     a nanny for those kids.

10  CARTER: I'd hate it, but I'd be rich.

11  SARAH: You'd be rich, frustrated, and bored. Why don't

12     you apply for a job working on cars?

13  CARTER: There aren't any "Help Wanted" ads from auto

14     shops.

15  SARAH: Go to the car places in person. Tell them you love

16     cars. Tell them you're president of a car club, and

17     then ask if you can leave a resume in case they ever

18     have an opening. Even if they aren't looking for help

19     now, someone might quit tomorrow and then they'd

20     remember you.

21  CARTER: Good idea. I'll do it right now.

22  SARAH: No! Go home and take a shower first, and put on

23     clean clothes.

24  CARTER: If I get hired to fix cars, this is what I'll wear. I'm

25     not getting grease all over my good clothes. My mom

26     would have a fit.

27  SARAH: You have to make a decent first impression.

28     Maybe they don't need a mechanic right now. Maybe

29     they need someone to greet the customers and find

30     out what service their car needs.

31  CARTER: Oh. It seems like a lot of trouble when they

32     aren't even running a "Help Wanted" ad.

33  SARAH: Jasper's Java didn't advertise anywhere either,

34     except for the sign in their window. Jasper told me he

35     wanted applicants who came to Jasper's Java because

1        they like the place and not just because they want a
2        job. I think I got hired because I said Jasper's Three
3        Bean is my favorite drink.
4  CARTER: I'm going to apply at every car repair shop in
5        town! Even if I don't get hired, it will be fun to check
6        all of them out.
7  SARAH: Good luck!
8  CARTER: Are you sure I can't wear my baseball cap?

# 5. In the Market

**Cast:** SALESMAN and CUSTOMER

**Setting:** A Persian market. Two chairs and a small tea table are Center Stage.

**Props:** A teapot and two cups, a sugar bowl, four larger bowls of different colors, and a piece of paper to serve as a receipt. The tea service is on the table. The bowls are nearby toward Stage Left. Salesman has the piece of paper in his pocket.

1     *(As scene opens, SALESMAN is Center Stage looking*
2     *around expectantly. CUSTOMER enters Stage Left*
3     *walking slowly, and pauses to look over the bowls.)*
4   **SALESMAN: Hello! You there!**
5   **CUSTOMER: What? Oh, hello.**
6   **SALESMAN: You like that bowl?**
7   **CUSTOMER: I'm just looking.**
8   **SALESMAN: Today is your lucky day, my friend, because it's**
9     **very affordable!**
10  **CUSTOMER: I'm not in the market for a bowl.**
11  **SALESMAN: But you are in the market! The Grand Sunday**
12     **Market!** *(Gesturing all around)*
13  **CUSTOMER: I mean, I'm here. But not for a bowl. For spices.**
14  **SALESMAN: Pah! Spices! You can get spices anywhere. The**
15     **bowls I have here are one of a kind.**
16  **CUSTOMER: I think I just saw some of these bowls a few**
17     **stands back.**
18  **SALESMAN: No, no, no, no, no. Not these bowls. There are**
19     **no others like them.**
20  **CUSTOMER: I guess I was confused.**
21  **SALESMAN: I can see that you don't believe me.**
22  **CUSTOMER: I've got to be going ...**
23  **SALESMAN: But you must join me for a cup of apple tea!**
24  **CUSTOMER: That's very kind of you. But I really need to be**

1     **going.**

2     **SALESMAN:** *(Offering a chair)* **Please, do sit down.**

3     **CUSTOMER: I appreciate it, but ...** *(Sits down reluctantly,*

4        *and the SALESMAN sits across the table from the*

5        *CUSTOMER.)* **I really don't like apple tea.**

6     **SALESMAN: Aha! But have you ever tasted *my* apple tea?**

7     **CUSTOMER: Well, no, but —**

8     **SALESMAN: Travelers come from miles around for my**

9        **apple tea.**

10   **CUSTOMER: I'm sure they do.**

11   **SALESMAN: You must try it. My son just made a fresh pot.**

12      *(Begins to serve tea.)*

13   **CUSTOMER: All right. Just a sip, and then I'll head out.**

14   **SALESMAN: Here we are. Sugar cube?**

15   **CUSTOMER: No, thank you.**

16   **SALESMAN: You must have a sugar cube. It is the only way**

17      **to drink the tea.** *(Adds sugar cube to teacup.)*

18   **CUSTOMER: OK.**

19   **SALESMAN: Now tell me, my friend, where are you from?**

20   **CUSTOMER: I'm from Washington.**

21   **SALESMAN: Ah, America! I love California. Do you know**

22      **my cousin? He lives in Texas.**

23   **CUSTOMER: Probably not.**

24   **SALESMAN: And what brings you to this market?**

25   **CUSTOMER: I'm on vacation with my family, and right**

26      **now I'm looking for spices. I need some cardamom.**

27   **SALESMAN: How much would you like to spend on a bowl?**

28   **CUSTOMER: I don't want a bowl. I have bowls.**

29   **SALESMAN:** *(Standing and returning with a bowl)* **This**

30      **bowl right here is the finest craftsmanship available**

31      **— made by hand by my brother. It is worth at least two**

32      **hundred dollars. I can sell it to you alone for the very**

33      **good price of one hundred dollars.**

34   **CUSTOMER: A hundred dollars! I would never spend a**

35      **hundred dollars on a bowl.**

1   SALESMAN: You won't find a better price anywhere.
2   CUSTOMER: I'm not looking for a better price anywhere.
3   SALESMAN: I can see you know the value of money. Very
4       well. I can offer this to you for the special, one-time-
5       only price of ninety dollars.
6   CUSTOMER: Come on. We both know this bowl isn't
7       worth half that. Look here – the paint's chipped.
8   SALESMAN: I see no chip. This one is from my uncle's
9       stand anyway. *(Hiding it underneath his chair)* I'll be
10      giving it back to him.
11   CUSTOMER: And anyway, it wouldn't match anything in
12      my house.
13   SALESMAN: *(Standing up and hurrying over to get another*
14      *bowl)* You like purple. I can tell when my customers
15      like purple. This here is a very beautiful purple bowl,
16      excellent craftsmanship –
17   CUSTOMER: Purple?
18   SALESMAN: *(Hurrying the bowl away)* I can't stand purple,
19      either. My uncle, all he sells are purple bowls.
20      Tasteless, I always tell him. You like yellow. I can tell.
21      *(Coming back with another bowl)*
22   CUSTOMER: My house is all green.
23   SALESMAN: *(Hurrying the bowl away and returning with*
24      *another)* I knew it! My friend, it is your lucky day.
25      This is my very finest bowl, this green one here.
26      Many people have tried to buy it – I will only part
27      with it for a good friend like you. I can offer you my
28      very lowest, secret price ... eighty dollars.
29   CUSTOMER: It's not worth forty.
30   SALESMAN: Oho! But you are talking insanity. Imagine,
31      parting with the finest of my wares for barely more
32      than pennies.
33   CUSTOMER: I'll bet you buy these for five bucks apiece. If
34      that!
35   SALESMAN: *(Affronted)* The hand-painted designs! The

1      meticulous craftsmanship! You know not what you
2      say, my dear friend. And yet, fool that I am, I will
3      humor you – do you promise not to tell? If you
4      promise not to tell my other customers how very
5      cheaply I am selling you this treasure, I will offer you
6      my very last price ... seventy dollars, no lower.
7   CUSTOMER: I'd like to see you try to get fifty for it.
8   SALESMAN: What a joker! Sixty-five, final offer.
9   CUSTOMER: If you think I'm spending more than fifty-
10      five on that bowl, you're out of your mind.
11  SALESMAN: My friend, you're going to haggle my family
12      out of house and home. All right. Sixty dollars, final
13      offer.
14  CUSTOMER: Done! Ha! One hundred dollars, indeed.
15  SALESMAN: *(Taking receipt quickly from pocket)* If you'll
16      just sign right here –
17  CUSTOMER: Wait a second. What am I saying? I don't need
18      a bowl! I need spices! *(Standing up)* I've got to go.
19  SALESMAN: All right, all right, I can see you're
20      determined to have my bowl for fifty dollars.
21  CUSTOMER: I'm sorry. I'm running late.
22  SALESMAN: *(Also standing)* I see! Very well! Forty dollars!
23  CUSTOMER: Thank you for the tea ... *(Starts to walk away.)*
24  SALESMAN: *(Walking after CUSTOMER)* Forty for two! Two
25      bowls!
26  CUSTOMER: Good-bye!
27  SALESMAN: And I'll throw in two teacups!
28  CUSTOMER: Have a good day!
29  SALESMAN: And this sugar bowl! *(CUSTOMER exits Stage*
30      *Right.)*
31  SALESMAN: OK. Come back next time! *(Throws up hands,*
32      *stops, and turns to look around.)* Why, hello! You there!
33      Do you like that bowl?

# 6. How Was Your Trip?

**Cast:** TRAVELER and PIONEER
**Setting:** No special set
**Props:** Backpack for Traveler
**Costume:** Pioneer is female. If desired, she can dress in costume from the 1840s.

1    *(As scene opens, TRAVELER and PIONEER enter from*
2    *opposite sides of the stage and stand beside each other.*
3    *TRAVELER is wearing the backpack.)*
4    TRAVELER: Flying is such a hassle. My flight was at six-
5        thirty in the morning, which meant I had to get up at
6        four to be at the airport on time. No one should have to
7        get out of bed at four in the morning.
8    PIONEER: Our wagon train will leave at first light tomorrow
9        morning. After all the planning and tearful good-byes,
10    we rode ten days to this rendezvous site in Missouri,
11    and then spent another six days loading our
12    provisions. Tomorrow, finally, we will be on our way
13    west.
14    TRAVELER: I double-checked my backpack to be sure I had
15    everything I needed. Phone, boarding pass, ID, wallet,
16    and a book to read on the flight.
17    PIONEER: The supply wagon is loaded with one hundred
18    and fifty pounds of flour, sixty pounds of rice, twenty
19    pounds of sugar, and some salt and pepper. A milk cow
20    will walk beside us.
21    TRAVELER: The line to get through security took forever.
22    It's amazing I didn't miss my flight while they made
23    sure I didn't have a bomb hidden in my underwear.
24    What a pain. Took off my shoes. Took off my jacket. Put
25    my watch in the little bin so the metal detector didn't
26    beep.
27    PIONEER: The trail is full of holes and littered with rocks.

1      After bouncing in the wagon for the first few miles, I
2      chose to ride one of the horses. Even riding
3      sidesaddle, as befits a proper lady, I am already so
4      sore that I doubt I'll be able to move tomorrow.
5    TRAVELER: Wouldn't you know it? My seat was in the
6      center. I requested a window or an aisle seat, but no.
7      I was stuck in the middle. I hate sitting in the middle.
8      There's no elbow space, and of course, leg room on a
9      plane is nonexistent no matter where you sit. The
10     man next to me was snoring. He got the window seat,
11     but instead of looking at the view, he fell asleep
12     before we took off.
13   PIONEER: The oxen move slowly, pulling their heavy
14     loads. I thought the day would never end, and after
15     we finally stopped for the night, I still had to gather
16     buffalo dung to use as fuel so we could cook our meal.
17   TRAVELER: I bought a sandwich at the airport to eat
18     during the flight, and when I opened the bag, I found
19     the wrong order. Instead of turkey on whole wheat
20     bread, I got roast beef on rye. I don't even like rye.
21     Instead of plain chips, I got barbecue, and they gave
22     me an apple instead of the chocolate chip cookie that
23     I ordered. I picked the meat out of the sandwich, ate
24     the chips, and tossed the apple.
25   PIONEER: Our meal was rice, beans, and pan biscuits. We
26     shared an apple, savoring it because once the fresh
27     fruit is gone, we'll have no more until we reach
28     California. We have no dishpan so we heated water in
29     the cooking pot to wash our dishes. It is only our first
30     night, and already I miss having a real bed. The
31     ground is hard. My bones ache.
32   TRAVELER: I had already seen the movie that they
33     showed. It was a stupid movie that I didn't like the
34     first time, and I sure didn't want to watch it again. I
35     didn't buy a headset, but even without sound, the

1        screen kept catching my attention.
2   PIONEER: The air is filled with gnats. Their bites are worse
3        than mosquitoes! The paste of vinegar and salt that we
4        made to repel them is not working. I wave my hands
5        around my face and neck constantly, but I still get bit.
6   TRAVELER: You want to hear the worst part? I had to go to
7        the bathroom. I meant to go in the airport right
8        before we boarded, but it took so long to get through
9        security that I didn't have time. I detest the
10       restrooms on airplanes. They are cramped and
11       stuffy, plus it was embarrassing because the
12       bathroom was occupied when I got there, so I had to
13       stand up in front and wait my turn while every
14       passenger in the coach section stared at me.
15   PIONEER: The worst part of this journey is the lack of
16       privacy. There are no trees on the prairie, just huge
17       open spaces as far as the eye can travel. When I need
18       to relieve myself, I have no shrub or tree to hide
19       behind; I must do my body's business where
20       everyone can watch. Of course, all the others have to
21       do that too, so we are courteous and try never to look,
22       but it is hard to lift my petticoats and pull down my
23       bloomers in full view of all.
24   TRAVELER: I was still in the bathroom when the captain
25       announced that we might experience some mild
26       turbulence and told everyone to buckle their
27       seatbelts. I hurried back to my seat, and the woman
28       on the aisle had to unbuckle and stand up to let me
29       back in. She didn't say anything, but I could tell she
30       was annoyed.
31   PIONEER: We crossed our first river today. The cold water
32       rushed by waist deep as we struggled to the far side.
33       One of the mules bolted and caused a wagon to tip
34       over. I saw that family's food supplies, so carefully
35       stored and rationed out, spill into the water. My papa

| | |
|---|---|
| 1 | grabbed a bag of flour and carried it to the far bank |
| 2 | for them, but it was tainted from the river water and |
| 3 | had to be thrown away. The rest of us will share our |
| 4 | food with this unfortunate family, but I fear what will |
| 5 | happen at future river crossings. |
| 6 | TRAVELER: The captain's idea of mild turbulence was not |
| 7 | the same as mine. My seat bumped and dipped as if I |
| 8 | were saddled to a bucking horse rather than strapped |
| 9 | into an airplane. I was afraid someone would get sick. |
| 10 | I saw the woman next to me check to see if she had a |
| 11 | barf bag. If she had used it, I'd probably have been |
| 12 | sick too from the smell. It was the worst flight I've |
| 13 | ever experienced. |
| 14 | PIONEER: Most days we travel between fifteen and twenty |
| 15 | miles. One of the children in the lead wagon, a boy of |
| 16 | seven years, has taken sick. We fear he might have |
| 17 | cholera. There is no doctor among us, and cholera is |
| 18 | usually fatal. I pray for this child to be healed, but as |
| 19 | the dust blows in my eyes and sweat trickles down my |
| 20 | neck, I wonder if anyone is listening. |
| 21 | TRAVELER: The turbulence ended with all barf bags |
| 22 | empty, and we made our final descent into the |
| 23 | airport twenty minutes late. I couldn't wait to get off |
| 24 | that plane! I'm already dreading the return flight. |
| 25 | PIONEER: We buried little Joseph on the prairie. His |
| 26 | distraught family did not want to leave him in this |
| 27 | desolate place, but there was no choice. We have |
| 28 | come less than two hundred miles of the two |
| 29 | thousand we will travel. I wish we could sprout wings |
| 30 | and fly like the birds. We could reach our destination |
| 31 | in a matter of hours, rather than months. But that is |
| 32 | not possible. |
| 33 | TRAVELER: Sometimes I think the good old days of |
| 34 | covered wagons and horseback were a better way to |
| 35 | travel. |

# 7. The Showdown

**Cast:** RILEY and RYAN. This duologue works best with players of the same gender.
**Setting:** A poker table. Two chairs are at the table.
**Props:** A deck of cards, poker chips, and a set of car keys.

1  *(As scene opens, RILEY and RYAN are seated facing each*
2  *other across the table, slouching as if they have been*
3  *playing for a while. Deck of cards is face down in the*
4  *middle of the table. Each player has a modest stack of*
5  *poker chips beside him. Keys are in RYAN's pocket.)*
6  **RILEY: Your deal.** *(RYAN picks up cards and begins to shuffle.)*
7  **What do you want to bet on this one?**
8  **RYAN: I dunno. Same as we've been doing?**
9  **RILEY: We've played like five games that way. Let's make it**
10  **interesting.**
11  **RYAN: What do you want to bet then?**
12  **RILEY: Let me think for a second.**
13  **RYAN: You're small blind no matter what. Post up.**
14  **RILEY:** *(Removes a few chips from his pile and places them in*
15  *the middle of the table.)* **You too. Big blind.**
16  **RYAN:** *(Stops shuffling to add a short stack of chips to the pile*
17  *RILEY has begun. He sets deck before RILEY, who knocks*
18  *once on the top of the deck. RYAN picks the cards up*
19  *again and begins to deal for Texas Hold'Em poker: two*
20  *cards facedown to each player. RYAN sets deck down*
21  *between them, and both look at their cards. RYAN looks*
22  *up at RILEY.)* **So, what's it going to be?**
23  **RILEY:** *(Still considering cards)* **How about that pint of**
24  **Chunky Monkey ice cream you've got in your fridge?**
25  **RYAN: No way, I want to eat that.**
26  **RILEY:** *(Grins.)* **Don't lose the game then.**
27  **RYAN: Why would I bet with stuff I already own? What do I**
28  **get if I win this round? The chance to eat my own ice**

1    cream?

2    **RILEY: If I lose, I'll buy you another pint.**

3    **RYAN: I don't want another pint of Chunky Monkey.**

4    **RILEY: What do you want, then?**

5    **RYAN: A pint of Cherry Garcia, I guess.**

6    **RILEY: Done. A pint of ice cream is on the table.**

7    **RYAN: Don't actually put it on the table. It'll melt.**

8    **RILEY: Don't worry. I want my ice cream kept nice and**

9        **cold until I'm ready to eat it. Which will be after this**

10    **round.**

11  **RYAN: Whatever, dude. I saw your pint of ice cream. Do**

12      **you want to check?**

13  **RILEY: Check.**

14  **RYAN:** *(Places — "burns" — one card from the top of the deck*

15      *facedown beside the deck, and then flips the next three*

16      *consecutive cards — the "flop" — face up between the*

17      *two players.)* **Good grief! Those are terrible.**

18  **RILEY: Speak for yourself!**

19  **RYAN: Would you like to bet another pint of ice cream?**

20  **RILEY: I'd like to bet one week of sitting shotgun on the**

21      **way to school.**

22  **RYAN: You're bluffing. You can't possibly have made**

23      **anything with this junk.**

24  **RILEY: Guess you're going to have to call me on it to find**

25      **out.**

26  **RYAN: Call you? I'll raise you a week's worth of the**

27      **answers to Mr. Vu's math homework.**

28  **RILEY: Those assignments are way harder than sitting in**

29      **the backseat of the carpool!**

30  **RYAN: Guess I'm a high roller. Does that mean you fold?**

31  **RILEY: No, it means I hope you know what you're getting**

32      **yourself into. I'll double your bet.**

33  **RYAN: Two weeks of math answers?**

34  **RILEY: That's right. Too rich for your blood?**

35  **RYAN: I'll call.**

1   **RILEY:** *(Raises an eyebrow.)* **Fine. Let's see the turn.**

2   **RYAN:** *(Burns one card face down on top of the first burned*

3        *card, flips a fourth card face up — the "turn" — and both*

4        *players glance back at the cards in their hands.)* **Well,**

5        **that changes things.**

6   **RILEY: Check.**

7   **RYAN: That's it? No Spanish homework you'd like to add**

8        **to the pot?**

9   **RILEY: I said check.**

10  **RYAN: Well, I'd like to raise you ...**

11  **RILEY: What?**

12  **RYAN: Never mind. I'll check too.**

13  **RILEY: Ha! You've got nothing!**

14  **RYAN: You don't know that. I don't have to go all in on the**

15       **turn.**

16  **RILEY: Hey, what is all in anyway?**

17  **RYAN: I don't know. This was your idea in the first place.**

18  **RILEY: I guess we'll have to wait and see. In the**

19       **meantime, I'll raise you —**

20  **RYAN: You can't raise yet! We just checked. We have to do**

21       **the river.**

22  **RILEY: Well, do the river then.** *(RYAN burns one more card*

23       *and flips a fifth card face-up on the table. RILEY sits*

24       *back to look at RYAN.)* **Well, how do you like that?**

25       *(RYAN is silent, staring at the card.)* **Shall I go ahead?**

26  **RYAN: You're up.**

27  **RILEY: I'd like to bet the keys to your car.**

28  **RYAN: What?!**

29  **RILEY: You heard me.**

30  **RYAN: What do you think you have? Pocket aces? I told**

31       **you, you can't bet my stuff.**

32  **RILEY: Then fold.**

33  **RYAN: And lose everything that's already in the pot? I'm**

34       **not going to do that just because you try to put my car**

35       **on the table!**

1    **RILEY: What do you want if I lose?**

2    **RYAN: You can't have my car!**

3    **RILEY: What do you want if I lose?**

4    **RYAN: This is stupid. Besides, you've got about an eight**

5        **percent chance of having the cards you're acting like**

6        **you have.**

7    **RILEY: Then you must think you can win. And there must**

8        **be something you want.** *(RYAN glares at RILEY.)* **What**

9        **do you want if I —**

10   **RYAN: I get to take Rebecca to prom.**

11   **RILEY:** *(Dumbfounded, then forces a laugh.)* **Yeah, right. I**

12       **think my girlfriend of two years is off-limits.**

13   **RYAN: Hey. This is a no-limits game.**

14   **RILEY: We decided that when we were playing with ten**

15       **dollars apiece! This is going too far.**

16   **RYAN: This is making things interesting. It's what you**

17       **wanted.**

18   **RILEY: Forget it. Forget the car. I'll go buy my own ice**

19       **cream.**

20   **RYAN: Play the game.**

21   **RILEY: Besides, it's not like you can gamble away a girl like**

22       **a piece of property. She's not a car, and she'll never go**

23       **with you.**

24   **RYAN: Maybe not, but I get to ask her. If she says yes, you**

25       **don't stop her. If she says no, I'll drop it.**

26   **RILEY: Your car is worth like a hundred bucks. It's falling**

27       **apart. That's not really comparable.**

28   **RYAN: If you're so sure Rebecca will never look twice at**

29       **me, then you have nothing to worry about. Apart**

30       **from my math homework.**

31   **RILEY: You're serious about this?**

32   **RYAN: Yes.**

33   **RILEY: And the car's on the table?**

34   **RYAN: That's right. And the homework, and the front seat,**

35       **and the ice cream. I'm all in.**

1    **RILEY: Are you secretly in love with my girlfriend or**
2         **something? Why do you want to take her to prom?**
3    **RYAN: This is poker, not twenty questions.**
4    **RILEY: For real though.**
5    **RYAN: Are you out or are you in? Look** — *(Fishes in his*
6         *pocket for car keys, and tosses them on the table with*
7         *the chips.)* **You said you wanted to play for the car.**
8    **RILEY: Yeah, but** —
9    **RYAN: Here's your chance.**
10   **RILEY: Yeah, but** — *(Shakes his head and checks cards one*
11        *more time.)* **Look, if Rebecca even *hints* at answering**
12        **"no," you'll leave her alone?**
13   **RYAN: I swear. We'll forget it ever happened.**
14   **RILEY: I guess we showdown then.**
15   **RYAN: I guess so.**
16   **RILEY: On three?**
17   **RYAN:** *(Takes a deep breath.)* **On three.**
18   **RILEY: And you're sure you want to do this? Winner take**
19        **all?**
20   **RYAN: I'm sure. Ready?** *(RILEY nods.)*
21   **RILEY and RYAN:** *(Together)* **One ... two ... three.** *(Both flip*
22        *cards face up on the table, look down at each other's*
23        *cards, and look slowly back up at each other, eyes wide.)*

# 8. Dear Sister

**Cast:** SISTER ONE and SISTER TWO

**Setting:** Two desks that are across the country from each other.

**Props:** A stack of blank paper and a pen or pencil for each desk.

1  (*As scene opens, the desks are set up across the stage from*
2  *each other, facing the audience. SISTER ONE sits Stage*
3  *Right and SISTER TWO at Stage Left. Both have a stack of*
4  *blank paper and their pen or pencil in front of them on*
5  *the desk. Both pantomime writing their lines throughout*
6  *the duologue. After each sister finishes her part, she folds*
7  *the "letter" into a paper airplane and sends it soaring*
8  *across the stage toward the other sister, who is already*
9  *"writing" her next part. This continues throughout the*
10  *duologue.)*
11  **SISTER ONE: Dear sister, How is boarding school? I see from**
12  **your pictures that you are pretending to have a good**
13  **time and make lots of friends. You're not fooling**
14  **anyone, you know. No school is fun without your dear**
15  **old favorite sister. On the other hand, Mom and Dad**
16  **have already forgotten you, and I'm planning to turn**
17  **your old room into my own personal massage salon,**
18  **complete with good-looking masseuse. Hope you didn't**
19  **want any of your furniture, because we are selling it all**
20  **at a garage sale tomorrow morning. Love, your favorite**
21  **sister.**
22  **SISTER TWO: Dear sister, How is boring old regular school?**
23  **I see from your pictures that you have helped yourself**
24  **to everything in my closet. Remember that just because**
25  **you look like me doesn't mean you are on the same**
26  **level of coolness. Try to contain your despair. Oh, and**
27  **don't forget to do all my chores while I'm away. And**

1     clean Humdum's litter box. Love, your bestest sister.

2   SISTER ONE: Dear sister, Do you have any attractive love

3     interests pestering you at your new school? If you do,

4     give me their mailing addresses, and I will send

5     them the photo of when you dressed up as a truly

6     horrifying clown for Halloween. I guarantee they

7     will not bother you again. Speaking of things dressed

8     up, I have enclosed a photo of Humdum disguised as

9     a ballerina. He really seems to be enjoying himself,

10    and I have him practicing his fouettés to show the

11    trick-or-treaters. Regards from your dearly beloved

12    sister.

13   SISTER TWO: Dear sister, Please and thank you for not

14    terrorizing my cat! He has mailed me a paw print of

15    distress, and I feel I must speak up on his behalf.

16    Rather than stuffing him into tutus, you should

17    spend your time being jealous of me because I get to

18    go to sunny Myrtle Beach for fall break, and all you

19    get to do is sit inside and make soup. Bummer about

20    rainy Washington. I'll mail you a postcard or a

21    picture of my tan lines if you are lucky. Kind regards

22    from the sister who loves you even though you are

23    oh-so-pale.

24   SISTER ONE: Dear sister, All the leaves are turning pretty

25    and falling off the trees. All of Dad's hair is turning

26    gray and falling off his head. Just kidding, but Mom

27    did make him let her cut it because she said it looked

28    scruffy. She really screwed up so we had to take him

29    to Great Clips to get it all buzzed off. Now I'm

30    knitting him a hat with that purple yarn you were

31    going to knit leg warmers from before you gave up.

32    Between Dad's new look and my new nose piercing,

33    you will hardly recognize the family! All the best

34    from your faraway sis.

35   SISTER TWO: Dear sister, I am coming to visit for

1     Thanksgiving. I bet you thought you were going to
2     borrow my gray winter dress and spill turkey all over
3     it. No can do. Instead, don't forget to plan a big party
4     for my arrival! I would prefer a safari theme but I
5     know you've been putting together a Viking bash in
6     your head since we watched that History Channel
7     documentary three years ago. Either way, I am your
8     eternally tolerant sister, and if need be, I will go
9     shopping for a Viking helmet. Please advise. Best
10    wishes from your sister.
11 SISTER ONE: Dear sister, Please don't come for
12    Thanksgiving. Your gray winter dress looks so good
13    on me. Besides, we have three inches of snow, which
14    you hate, as you ought to remember from the
15    tobogganing incident. Still, if you do come, bring
16    your best pillaging attire, because I have a party in
17    the works for your arrival night. The theme is a
18    surprise. Everyone's coming. See you soon! Best
19    regards from your infinitely more attractive sister.
20 SISTER TWO: Dear sister, What do you want for
21    Christmas? How about some nice flannel pajamas or
22    a bow tie or a school year planner? All with my
23    boarding school crest on them, of course, because the
24    school store is the only place I have time to shop
25    before I get home. Be sure to have Humdum freshly
26    brushed with a bow on his collar waiting to greet me.
27    In the meantime, I'm headed out to struggle through
28    an essay on the virtues of turn-of-the-century English
29    literature. Of which there are none. All the best from
30    the sister you get to see in forty-eight hours!
31 SISTER ONE: Dear sister, I am getting a job as a barista so
32    I can get super rich and buy a house in the south of
33    France. You can probably come visit as long as you
34    don't bring Humdum. Did Mom tell you he got scared
35    by the New Year's fireworks and shredded my

1     slippers? You owe me a pair. Preferably not with your
2     boarding school crest, like all the other clothes I now
3     own. Love from Mom and Dad's secret favorite.
4    SISTER TWO: Dear sister, I'm sitting in history class and
5     the substitute teacher is ignoring our upcoming unit
6     test and trying to teach us Russian. He looks a little
7     bit like Uncle Bob except with more teeth. How is
8     barista life? I'm thinking of getting a job at a local
9     cheese shop so I can buy a house bigger than yours.
10    You may come to my garden parties if you promise to
11    behave and not scarf all the macaroons like that one
12    time. Yours truly, sister. P.S. What do you need, a
13    personalized invitation? Come visit me already!
14   SISTER ONE: Dear sister, Exciting news! Skype me! Love,
15    sister.
16   SISTER TWO: Dear sister, I know! Mom told me! I can't
17    believe they got us tickets to California! Best birthday
18    present ever. I have written the California tourist
19    bureau to let them know that you are joining me on
20    the trip, and they say you can only come if I keep you
21    on a leash at all times. Don't worry. I'm sure we can
22    find one that matches your bathing suits. Love, your
23    caretaking sister.
24   SISTER ONE: Dear sister, May I have your nail polish
25    collection? Why, thanks! You are the most generous
26    sister a girl could ask for. This weekend we are taking
27    Dad skiing for his birthday. Oh yes, and Aunt Kath is
28    bringing her triple-chocolate cake with the mocha
29    fudge frosting. I guess I'll be stuck eating your piece.
30    Life here is hard. Sincerely, sister. P.S. Mom says I can
31    come visit you for spring break! Get your party pants
32    on! And I don't mean those eighties stretchy pants
33    that you stole from Mom's donation pile and use to
34    scare away potential new friends.
35   SISTER TWO: Dear sister, I hope you gain a thousand

| 1 | pounds from gobbling up my piece of cake. Why don't |
|---|---|
| 2 | you be a good sister and offer to mail it to me? You |
| 3 | clearly have my address, as evidenced by your |
| 4 | repeatedly sending me pictures of my costumed cat. |
| 5 | Yesterday my art history teacher told us a story about |
| 6 | the architecture at the Louvre, and I thought of the |
| 7 | time on vacation there when you tripped and almost |
| 8 | knocked over that bust of a philosopher. Naturally, I |
| 9 | told all my friends. They can't wait to meet you. Love, |
| 10 | your much more graceful sister. |
| 11 | SISTER ONE: Dear sister, Did I leave my really cool new |
| 12 | denim vest in your dorm room when I visited? If so, |
| 13 | you had better keep it safe and sound for me. I bet you |
| 14 | kept it on purpose just so you can sleep with it under |
| 15 | your pillow at night, because you already miss me so |
| 16 | much. Troll. Best wishes from your sister who got all |
| 17 | the good genetics from Mom and Dad. |
| 18 | SISTER TWO: Dear sister, I can neither confirm nor deny |
| 19 | that your denim vest is hanging in my closet. I would |
| 20 | never dream of touching it, of course. If it were |
| 21 | hanging there. Which I can't say that it is. Yesterday I |
| 22 | went to a Zumba class thinking I would get in good |
| 23 | shape for California's sandy beaches, but today I can't |
| 24 | move sans severe pain. Obviously I expect that you |
| 25 | will be a good sister and stop working out from now |
| 26 | on so that I can continue to be perceived as the more |
| 27 | attractive of us. Shouldn't be too hard, as Dad told me |
| 28 | you guys are re-watching all ten seasons of *Friends*. |
| 29 | Lucky couch potato. Love, your super sore sister. |
| 30 | SISTER ONE: Dear sister, Let the countdown begin! Two |
| 31 | weeks to California! I can't believe you have spent |
| 32 | almost a whole school year on the East Coast. |
| 33 | Humdum has forgotten what you look like, so I have |
| 34 | been putting your picture by his cat bed. He seems |
| 35 | uninterested. Oh, did I tell you he's coming with us to |

1    California? I'm packing lots of kibbles in my bag for
2    his unending appetite. And for yours. Very best
3    wishes from your sister.
4    SISTER TWO: Dear sister, Very funny. No one invited
5    Humdum. One week! My dorm room is almost all
6    packed up in boxes to ship home, and my teachers
7    say I haven't failed my finals too badly. Boarding
8    school's been worth a year, but I think it's time for
9    me to come back to regular school with you in the
10    fall. Just to keep you in check, of course. Because I'm
11    caring like that. But first, brush up on your Valley
12    girl phrases and get excited to see me! We are going to
13    have the best time. Love always, sister. *(Both SISTERS*
14    *stand and exit on their side of the stage.)*

# 9. Pass the Peas

**Cast:** PICKY and FOODIE

**Setting:** A table and two chairs. PICKY and FOODIE sit on the same side.

**Props:** Foodie carries a clipboard with paper and a pencil.

**Costume:** Foodie should wear green clothing.

1 FOODIE: Oh, good. We're having peas for dinner.

2 PICKY: Gag! Yuck! Not peas again.

3 FOODIE: Please pass the peas.

4 PICKY: I hate peas!

5 FOODIE: I love peas.

6 PICKY: Peas are little rotten marbles, green and mushy in
7      my mouth.

8 FOODIE: Peas are little soft pearls, tumbling off my fork.

9 PICKY: Ick!

10 FOODIE: Yum!

11 PICKY: Putrid peas. Poison peas.

12 FOODIE: Plump peas. Pretty peas.

13 PICKY: Pesky peas.

14 FOODIE: Precious peas.

15 PICKY: Party pooper peas!

16 FOODIE: Picture perfect peas!

17 PICKY: Peas are my pet peeve.

18 FOODIE: Peas are my passion.

19 PICKY: Peas are appalling.

20 FOODIE: I'm proud to promote peas.

21 PICKY: There's a plague of peas on my plate.

22 FOODIE: There's a preponderance of peas on my plate.

23 PICKY: I propose that peas be prohibited.

24 FOODIE: Would you sign my Pea Party petition? *(Offers pen*
25      *and clipboard.)*

26 PICKY: Say it isn't so! You've started a political Pea Party?

27 FOODIE: Our platform is "Eat Peas and Prosper!"

1    PICKY: Oh, please! With all the potential problems in the
2        world, why waste time and energy on peas?
3    FOODIE: *(Starts chanting.)* **Plant more peas! Plant more**
4        **peas!**
5    PICKY: You are going to be perceived as a pea-brained
6        nutcase.
7    FOODIE: *(Raises fist in air.)* **Power to the pea-ple!**
8    PICKY: What do peas have to do with politics?
9    FOODIE: It is our constitutional right to eat peas at every
10      meal.
11   PICKY: I don't recall any mention of peas in the Constitution.
12   FOODIE: It's at the beginning, where it says the Constitution
13      is meant to promote the general welfare.
14   PICKY: Eating peas does nothing to promote my welfare.
15   FOODIE: The Pea Party promises to make peas our
16      nation's number one priority.
17   PICKY: Peas should be purchased by prescription only.
18   FOODIE: Peas in every pot! Peas or perish!
19   PICKY: You are a peculiar, pathetic pest.
20   FOODIE: There's no need to get personal. I'm only
21      proclaiming my priorities.
22   PICKY: I am perplexed by your persistent preaching about
23      peas.
24   FOODIE: I am perturbed by your provocative protests.
25   PICKY: Peas are propagating everywhere.
26   FOODIE: Yes! A plethora of peas!
27   PICKY: It's a pea pandemic!
28   FOODIE: Peas are paradise! I prefer three course meals
29      with peas for every course.
30   PICKY: I'll skip dinner and just have dessert. Is there any
31      pecan pie?
32   FOODIE: No. There's a choice of pea parfait or pea pudding.
33   PICKY: Argh!
34   FOODIE: *(Holds up two fingers in a peace sign.)* **Peas,**
35      **brother. Peas!**

# 10. Parenting on Mt. Olympus

**Cast:** ZEUS and HERA

**Setting:** Mt. Olympus. No special set required.

**Props:** A book and a baby carrier with a baby doll in it for Zeus. Hera wears a watch.

**Costumes:** Togas are optional for both characters.

1 *(As scene opens, HERA stands Center Stage, tapping her*
2 *foot impatiently and checking her watch. ZEUS enters*
3 *with baby carrier and book.)*
4 **ZEUS:** Hera, honey, I'm home!
5 **HERA:** Zeus! There you are! I've been waiting all day for you.
6 Where have you been? Not out chasing other women, I
7 hope.
8 **ZEUS:** Of course not, love. Don't worry about me. My
9 brother was acting up in the underworld again. I had to
10 send a message and a few thunderbolts his way.
11 **HERA:** What are you carrying?
12 **ZEUS:** This is baby Hercules! Alcmene and I have joint
13 custody, and this is the first weekend I get to spend
14 with the tyke. Isn't he precious?
15 **HERA:** Zeus! How dare you bring another woman's child
16 into our home! Out with him!
17 **ZEUS:** Hera, please keep your voice down. The little angel is
18 sleeping.
19 **HERA:** He's no angel. He's half mortal, and he shouldn't
20 even be on Mount Olympus. In fact, he shouldn't have
21 been born at all.
22 **ZEUS:** You certainly did your best to prevent it. I can
23 understand why you're angry with me, sweetheart. But
24 my sinning days are over. I want my son to grow up in a
25 happy home.
26 **HERA:** He can grow up in a happy home, as long as it's not

1    ours.

2    ZEUS: I thought it would appease you to name him

3        Heracles in your honor. It's not my fault the other

4        gods called him Hercules and it stuck.

5    HERA: I don't care what he's named. I would rather die

6        than play stepmother to that brat. Immortality is

7        such a pain sometimes.

8    ZEUS: You're going to be a wonderful stepmother. And

9        look, I got us a book on rearing divine children!

10    HERA: I'm not interested. This is not my job.

11    ZEUS: *(Sets down baby carrier and reads from cover of*

12        *book.)* It's called *From Tots to Titans: Parenting on*

13        *Mount Olympus.*

14    HERA: Who publishes this trash?

15    ZEUS: Hestia wrote it. She's seen as something of an

16        expert in the field, from what I understand.

17    HERA: If I were goddess of hearth and home, I'd be busy

18        enough without churning out useless handbooks.

19        Does Hestia even have any children?

20    ZEUS: Well, no. But Leto raised Apollo and Artemis by this

21        book, and they've turned out splendidly.

22    HERA: I don't want to hear about Leto, or any of your

23        other exes. I hear enough through the grapevine.

24    ZEUS: Fine, but let's take a look at the book.

25    HERA: I thought you were going to take me for a chariot

26        ride! I'm the goddess of marriage, not of babysitting.

27        I want to go now.

28    ZEUS: I let Poseidon borrow the chariot for the afternoon.

29        Wouldn't you rather go at sunset anyway? Let's get

30        the baby settled first.

31    HERA: Settled! You mean you plan to keep it here too?

32    ZEUS: Of course! He needs a stable father figure, and I

33        intend to be just that.

34    HERA: You, stable? Ha! You're king of the gods for your

35        fury, not your family values.

1  ZEUS: **Maybe to the other Olympians, but at home all**
2  **that's going to change. This is a turning point in my**
3  **life, Hera. I want to be the best father I can be. And I**
4  **want you to love my son like he was your own.**
5  HERA: **One more wishy-washy word, and I'll walk out this**
6  **door.**
7  ZEUS: *(Opens book and reads.)* **"Chapter One: Child-**
8  **Proofing Mt. Olympus."** *(HERA wanders over to where*
9  *ZEUS has set Hercules' carrier. She peers down at baby*
10 *in disgust and gives the carrier a contemptuous nudge*
11 *with her foot.)*
12 ZEUS: **"Prior to arriving home with an infant, new parents**
13 **should make a thorough inspection of their living**
14 **space. Things like spare lightning bolts and tridents**
15 **should be picked up and stowed well out of reach." I**
16 **can't believe I didn't think of that! Look, there are**
17 **lightning bolts lying around everywhere. Careless of**
18 **me!** *(ZEUS turns his back on HERA and begins to*
19 *pantomime picking up lightning bolts and throwing*
20 *them Off-stage.)*
21 HERA: **You really need to pay more attention to your**
22 **child's well-being.** *(HERA looks to be sure that ZEUS's*
23 *attention is diverted, and then picks up the baby doll*
24 *from the carrier and begins swinging it pensively back*
25 *and forth by its ankle.)*
26 ZEUS: *(Straightening up)* **That's better. What's next?**
27 *(Reads.)* **"Parents should also be aware of the dangers**
28 **of Mt. Olympus's altitude. Gods and goddesses have**
29 **been known to throw one another from the**
30 **mountaintop in fits of anger and emotion."** *(HERA is*
31 *now swinging the doll around her head, as if to throw it*
32 *from the mountain.)*
33 ZEUS: *(Still not looking)* **Hera!**
34 HERA: *(Stops and quickly tosses doll back into carrier.)* **Yes,**
35 **dear?**

1  ZEUS: Come look at this illustration! Doesn't that look
2      like you throwing someone off the mountain?
3  HERA: Don't be ridiculous, Zeus.
4  ZEUS: Just a thought. Where was I? Ah, yes. "If your
5      offspring is part mortal, don't forget that a long fall
6      from Mt. Olympus could mean in a one-way ticket to
7      the underworld. It is best to take precaution against
8      this by procuring a winged horse or dragon. If loyal
9      and properly trained, these creatures can catch your
10     child should they take a tumble from the heights."
11  HERA: Now there's a good idea! I have a dragon that
12     Hercules could borrow.
13  ZEUS: The book says it needs to be loyal and well-trained.
14     Your dragon bites everything that moves.
15  HERA: Exactly.
16  ZEUS: I think I'll ask Poseidon if he'll let me borrow his
17     Pegasus instead.
18  HERA: You can't mollycoddle the child through life.
19     Imagine how the other immortal kids will bully him
20     at school! They'll say, "You can't even fend off a silly
21     old dragon."
22  ZEUS: We can't treat him like a normal immortal. It's
23     hazardous to his health.
24  HERA: Natural selection is the spice of life.
25  ZEUS: Moving on to "Chapter Two: Know Your Arch-
26     Enemies."
27  HERA: Let's skip that section. I can't think of anyone who
28     would harm such a precious little creature.
29  ZEUS: Sometimes I think Hades is jealous of my heirs.
30  HERA: I always liked your brother Hades. It's no wonder
31     he's jealous. How would you like to rule the
32     underworld?
33  ZEUS: I'm not saying I blame him. All the same, I think I'll
34     ask Hermes to double-check any mail he sends. I
35     don't want malevolent baby gifts.

1 HERA: Speaking of gifts, what happened with that nice
2     pair of snakes I sent Hercules?
3 ZEUS: Hercules strangled them with his own two fists!
4     He's such a clever little thing. And strong like his
5     papa!
6 HERA: Strangled them! Those were my prize serpents!
7     Medusa herself bred them for me. They were very
8     valuable.
9 ZEUS: They were very venomous. You really need to be
10     more mindful of the baby, Hera. Snakes are not a safe
11     gift.
12 HERA: So sue me. I'm used to shopping for immortals.
13 ZEUS: Now don't get defensive. It's just something to work
14     on.
15 HERA: When's the chariot coming back? I'm sick of this
16     book, and your baby is starting to stink.
17 ZEUS: Oh, I forgot! Do you know how to change diapers?
18 HERA: There's no way I'm getting near that mess.
19 ZEUS: I don't know how, either. Maybe I should get Hestia
20     to babysit while we go out. She's a much better
21     caregiver than we are.
22 HERA: Why don't you go ask her and leave Hercules with
23     me? I'll take good care of the little gemstone.
24 ZEUS: You just refused to change his diaper! How do I
25     know you'd lift a finger if something went wrong?
26 HERA: You don't, I guess.
27 ZEUS: I'll take him with me to Hestia's now.
28 HERA: Nobody ever trusts me.
29 ZEUS: I'll be back soon.
30 HERA: You'd better be baby-free.
31 ZEUS: Come on Hercules, let's go see Auntie Hestia. *(He*
32     *picks up carrier and exits. HERA crosses arms and*
33     *makes a face after them.)*

# 11. Best Little Town in Montana

**Cast:** ALEX and KERRY

**Setting:** A train. Two chairs, side by side, function as train seats.

**Props:** Two backpacks

1 *(As scene opens, KERRY sits with his backpack at his feet. ALEX*
2   *enters with the other backpack.)*
3 **ALEX: Can I sit here?**
4 **KERRY: Sure.**
5 **ALEX: Thanks.** *(Sits and drops backpack at his feet.)*
6 **KERRY: Yeah.** *(Brief pause)* **Where you headed?**
7 **ALEX: Worst place ever.**
8 **KERRY: Really?**
9 **ALEX: Yeah. My parents sent me the ticket. It's the last place**
10   **I want to go.**
11 **KERRY: That sucks. Where?**
12 **ALEX: You've never heard of it. It's the world's tiniest town**
13   **and it's in the middle of nowhere. No one in their right**
14   **mind goes to this place.**
15 **KERRY: Why not?**
16 **ALEX: Because there is literally nothing to do. I mean, I**
17   **could spend the whole week I'm there sitting around**
18   **staring at a wall and it would be more exciting than**
19   **what goes on in town.**
20 **KERRY: What are you going for, then?**
21 **ALEX: My family reunion.**
22 **KERRY: Won't you have fun with your family at least?**
23 **ALEX: Yeah, it will be good to see them. But we'll probably**
24   **be sitting around talking the entire time. I wish we**
25   **were going somewhere entertaining. I proposed**
26   **Hawaii, but no. We go to the same place every year.**
27 **KERRY: At least you know where you're going. My friend**

1        **told me how to get where I'm supposed to be headed,**
2        **but I kind of forgot.**
3   **ALEX: Do you know anything about the place? I might be**
4        **able to help you; I've ridden this train a million times.**
5   **KERRY: Well, I'm headed to a huckleberry festival, but I**
6        **can't remember the town name. I'd recognize it if I**
7        **heard it.**
8   **ALEX: Mountainside?**
9   **KERRY: No.**
10  **ALEX: Ketchison?**
11  **KERRY: No.**
12  **ALEX: Are you meeting anyone there that you can call?**
13  **KERRY: I'm meeting my friend there for a random**
14        **adventure, but his phone's dead.**
15  **ALEX: I've never heard of any huckleberry festival around**
16        **here. What does it involve?**
17  **KERRY: I know they've got a pie-eating contest and a rodeo**
18        **and a Huckleberry Fun Run. From what the website**
19        **said, they've got a pretty good lineup of bands playing**
20        **too. Plus, there's a huckleberry jam-making contest**
21        **with some crazy-cool prizes. Actually, I think the**
22        **grand prize is a trip for two to Hawaii. I've got a huge**
23        **jar of jam in my bag. I'm going to enter and hope for**
24        **the best.**
25  **ALEX: You're joking. Sign me up for wherever you're**
26        **going! Maybe I can skip my reunion and come with**
27        **you and your friend.**
28  **KERRY: If you can't make it this weekend, you should**
29        **definitely try to go some other time. Apparently the**
30        **town has the longest glow-in-the-dark mini golf**
31        **course in the world. And of all things, it's the only**
32        **town in Montana with a camel sanctuary!**
33  **ALEX: Are you sure you're on the right train?**
34  **KERRY: I hope so. I've been waiting for this trip for**
35        **months. We got a reservation at the weirdest hotel,**

1   too. It's built to look like everything in it is upside
2   down! There's a bunch of odd furniture bolted to the
3   ceilings, and the windows are set low in the walls so
4   it looks like the whole building got flipped over.
5   ALEX: Dang. Maybe if I tell my family about that place, we
6   can go there next year.
7   KERRY: Or maybe you guys can take a day trip. There's a
8   swimming hole on the river with a giant rope swing
9   over it. I can't wait to take an inner tube down the
10  river. Either that or go whitewater rafting.
11  ALEX: I bet my family would go for that. I wonder how far
12  of a drive it is from where we're staying. Probably at
13  least an hour. Our cabin is in the absolute boonies.
14  We usually only make it into town for a midweek
15  grocery run. To the most boring grocery store ever.
16  KERRY: That's too bad. It seems like the rest of Montana
17  has so much going on.
18  ALEX: Yeah, I guess it does. Maybe someday I'll get to see
19  the good parts of it.
20  KERRY: Yeah, you don't want to miss that golf course.
21  ALEX: That sounds amazing. Well hey, this is my stop. It's
22  been fun hearing about your adventure. Have so
23  much fun wherever you're going, OK?
24  KERRY: Wait, I'm getting off here too.
25  ALEX: This is your stop? Are you sure?
26  KERRY: Yeah, I recognize the name now that they said it
27  over the intercom. Troutsville, right?
28  ALEX: This is the Troutsville stop, but that can't be right.
29  Nothing ever happens in Troutsville.
30  KERRY: Apparently a huckleberry festival does.
31  ALEX: And glow-in-the-dark mini golf? You're positive
32  you're not thinking of somewhere else?
33  KERRY: Positive. There's my friend on the platform!
34  ALEX: Where?
35  KERRY: The one with the life vest. Looks like we're going

1   rafting!
2  ALEX: I had no idea there was so much to do around here!
3   I'm going to grab my cousins and find that swimming
4   hole you were talking about. This is going to be the
5   best reunion ever.
6  KERRY: You guys should enter the jam contest too! Maybe
7   you'll win that Hawaiian vacation you wanted.
8  ALEX: Pfft — Hawaii. I'm staying in Troutsville. This place
9   is awesome!

# 12. The Alibi

**Cast:** CARVER and BEN

**Setting:** Outside a courthouse. No special set required.

**Props:** None

1   CARVER: What were you thinking?
2   BEN: I don't want to talk about it.
3   CARVER: We have to talk about it. You sat in the courtroom
4        and lied under oath!
5   BEN: I didn't have any choice.
6   CARVER: You could have told the truth.
7   BEN: I told the police the truth the first time they
8        questioned me, and the second time. They didn't
9        believe me. If they had believed me, I wouldn't have
10       been subpoenaed to testify in court today.
11  CARVER: Just because they wanted to question you again
12       doesn't mean they didn't believe you. You were free to
13       leave. You weren't charged with any crime.
14  BEN: They had better not charge me, because I didn't
15       commit any crime! Why can't they leave me alone?
16  CARVER: The way they were leaving me alone until you lied
17       and said you were with me when Rachel was
18       murdered. Now you've dragged me into this mess.
19  BEN: The reason they kept questioning me was because I
20       didn't have an alibi. I figured if I said I was with you,
21       that would satisfy them and they'd quit bothering me.
22  CARVER: What about me? Did you stop to think what this
23       does to me?
24  BEN: I knew you'd back me up. I saw you sitting in the
25       courtroom, and I knew if you heard me testify that I
26       was with you on the night of the murder, you'd say it
27       was true.
28  CARVER: Why should I commit perjury just to cover up for
29       your lie?

1 BEN: Because we're friends! You know I'd do the same for
2      you if our positions were reversed.
3 CARVER: Did it not occur to you that I might prefer not to
4      be involved in this? Rachel and I dated for six
5      months. This murder has not been easy for me, you
6      know.
7 BEN: It's been worse for me.
8 CARVER: How could it be worse for you? You had only
9      been dating her for — what? Two weeks?
10 BEN: That's right. I didn't ask her out until after she broke
11      up with you. I wanted to ask her sooner, but I didn't
12      want to hurt your feelings.
13 CARVER: My point exactly. I have ten times more
14      memories of Rachel than you have, so it will be ten
15      times as painful for me to be interrogated by the
16      police.
17 BEN: Maybe they won't bother to talk to you.
18 CARVER: Are you kidding? When the prime suspect says
19      he spent the night of the murder with me, you know
20      they're going to check me out.
21 BEN: So you tell them where you were and say I was with
22      you.
23 CARVER: Where were you when it happened? Why do you
24      need me for an alibi?
25 BEN: I was in the library. I had my history final the next
26      day, so I was cramming like crazy, trying to make up
27      for all those assignments I never read.
28 CARVER: Were you with someone?
29 BEN: I was alone.
30 CARVER: Someone must have seen you there. Did you talk
31      to anybody?
32 BEN: No.
33 CARVER: So you really can't prove you were there?
34 BEN: If I could prove I was at the library, I wouldn't have
35      had to say I was with you.

1 CARVER: Since you told them that you were at the library,
2     and now you say you were with me, I'll have to say I
3     was at the library too. Are you positive nobody saw
4     you that night?
5 BEN: Why are you asking me all these questions? Surely
6     you don't think I had anything to do with Rachel's
7     murder.
8 CARVER: The boyfriend is always a suspect until proven
9     innocent.
10 BEN: I thought everyone was innocent until proven guilty.
11 CARVER: Under the law, yes. In reality, the cops always
12     check out husbands and boyfriends first because the
13     odds are high that they did it.
14 BEN: What if the victim was a man?
15 CARVER: Then they question his wife or girlfriend.
16     There's no sexual bias, if that's what you're
17     wondering.
18 BEN: They need to quit bothering someone who loved her
19     and start trying to track down the person who killed
20     her. They found her body down by the lake. Why
21     aren't they questioning the people who live in that
22     area?
23 CARVER: Maybe they already did.
24 BEN: Is that old boathouse still down there? You know,
25     the one where your family used to keep that
26     rowboat?
27 CARVER: It's still there. So is our boat. I took Rachel
28     fishing in that boat many times. She loved going out
29     on the lake. She used to pack us a picnic lunch, and
30     we'd drift for hours.
31 BEN: Where were you on the night she was killed?
32 CARVER: At the library. With you.
33 BEN: No you weren't. *(Through the next several lines it*
34     *gradually dawns on BEN that CARVER might be the*
35     *killer. He is more and more horrified.)*

1 CARVER: Of course I was. You just testified under oath
2     that we were there together.
3 BEN: I was lying, and you know it. I never saw you that
4     night.
5 CARVER: Neither did anyone else. You got lucky when you
6     named me as your alibi because nobody can prove
7     that I wasn't with you at the library.
8 BEN: Why won't you tell me where you were that night?
9 CARVER: It's better that you don't know. That way we keep
10     our stories straight. We were at the library together.
11 BEN: Were you with Rachel? Did you get back together and
12     not want me to find out?
13 CARVER: We did not get back together.
14 BEN: You only answered one of my questions.
15 CARVER: You're very observant.
16 BEN: You were with her, weren't you?
17 CARVER: You're guessing.
18 BEN: You went to the old boathouse together.
19 CARVER: Let it go, Ben. Nobody saw me that night. Your
20     alibi will hold.
21 BEN: You were angry because she dumped you, so you
22     lured her to the boathouse.
23 CARVER: I didn't have to lure her. She loved the boat, and
24     she loved me.
25 BEN: You killed her, didn't you? You killed Rachel!
26 CARVER: How could I have killed Rachel? I was at the
27     library with you.
28 BEN: *(Starts to exit.)* You won't get away with this. I'm
29     telling the police!
30 CARVER: Do that. Change your story again! First you told
31     them you were alone at the library. *(BEN stops and*
32     *turns back.)* Then you swore under oath that you were
33     with me. Now go tell them that you weren't really
34     with me, that you lied about it in court. If they didn't
35     have cause to arrest you and charge you before, this

1     should give them what they need.

2   BEN: How could you? Rachel was the sweetest, most

3     beautiful —

4   CARVER: Most two-timing girl in the world. She vowed

5     she would love me forever. She swore that she'd be

6     loyal and true. We were going to get married in a

7     couple of years.

8   BEN: No way! She loved me!

9   CARVER: Then why did she agree to meet me at the

10     boathouse and go for a moonlight ride on the lake?

11   BEN: You're lying.

12   CARVER: That makes two of us, doesn't it?

13   BEN: They'll catch you. You can't prove you were at the

14     library.

15   CARVER: Of course I can. You testified under oath that I

16     was there. And when the police question me, I'll tell

17     them that you were there too, except for about half

18     an hour between seven-thirty and eight when you

19     left to get a bite to eat. At least that's what you told me

20     you were doing.

21   BEN: The time of death was between seven-thirty and

22     eight.

23   CARVER: I know.

24   BEN: You killed her and you're going to put the blame on

25     me.

26   CARVER: Thanks for the alibi.

# 13. North to Alaska

**Cast:** EDDIE and WILL

**Setting:** A Seattle tavern, 1898. A table and two chairs are on the stage.

**Props:** Two mugs

1   *(As scene opens, EDDIE is sitting slouched at the table*
2   *with a mug. WILL enters from Stage Left with a mug and*
3   *looks around curiously. EDDIE sees WILL.)*
4   **EDDIE: You've come for gold, haven't you, son?**
5   **WILL:** *(Startled, looks over at EDDIE.)* **How did you know, sir?**
6   **EDDIE:** *(Chuckles.)* **I've seen that look before. What's your**
7   **name, son?**
8   **WILL: William Nordheim, sir. But everyone calls me Will.**
9   **EDDIE:** *(Extends his hand. WILL shakes it.)* **Pleased to meet**
10   **you, Will. My name is Edward Gresham. You can call**
11   **me Eddie. Have a chair. Let's hear your story.**
12   **WILL:** *(Sits across table from EDDIE.)* **My story, sir?**
13   **EDDIE: Where you're from, where you've been, how you**
14   **came to be going where you are.**
15   **WILL: I'm not from much, sir. I was born in Sweden but**
16   **raised in New York City. We immigrated in 1880 when I**
17   **was a year old. My father makes a humble living as a**
18   **baker and raised me to follow in his trade. But about a**
19   **year ago, I saw the first headlines about the miners**
20   **who struck gold. Sixty-eight rich men arrive on the**
21   **steamer *Portland!* Pockets and satchels filled with**
22   **gold! I knew then that my fortune was waiting for me**
23   **in the Yukon, if only I could get there. I saved every**
24   **penny I earned to buy a ticket west. I arrived this**
25   **evening by the Great Northern Railway.**
26   **EDDIE: How did you decide to come to Seattle? Why not**
27   **Portland or Vancouver?**
28   **WILL: I saw a full-page newspaper ad in *The New York***

1     *Times.* Everyone says Seattle is the Queen City of the
2     Pacific and the gateway to the Klondike.
3  EDDIE: So they say, but Vancouver or even Victoria would
4     be closer.
5  WILL: They would?
6  EDDIE: The Klondike gold fields are in Canada. It's a long
7     trip from here.
8  WILL: Really? I thought they were quite close.
9  EDDIE: That's the impression promoters want you to get.
10     The Yukon is nearly two thousand miles to the far
11     North. No one is allowed through Canadian customs
12     without a year's worth of supplies. An outfit won't be
13     cheap.
14 WILL: I have a little cash with me.
15 EDDIE: A little can go a long way, but only if you learn to
16     differentiate between important tools and the many
17     gadgets of fictional utility.
18 WILL: I was going to hire an outfitting agent to get me the
19     best prices.
20 EDDIE: I strongly recommend that you don't. Most agents
21     out there are looking no further than to make a
22     quick buck. They take top dollar, buy rock-bottom
23     merchandise, and by the time the miner finds out
24     about it, he's hundreds of miles away.
25 WILL: Where do you suggest I outfit?
26 EDDIE: Start with the Seattle Woolen Company for
27     blankets and clothes. Nothing's more important than
28     keeping out the cold. You'll need a good tent and
29     stove too.
30 WILL: I hope I don't get Klondicitis.
31 EDDIE: What?
32 WILL: You know, Klondicitis. Gold miners' disease. I've
33     seen lots of advertisements warning about it.
34 EDDIE: Who publishes them?
35 WILL: A local doctor's office, I think. Why?

1   EDDIE: Dr. Lowden, I'll wager. Don't trust a thing he puts
2       out.

3   WILL: Is he a known liar?

4   EDDIE: He's a known capitalist. If you've seen adverts for
5       "Yukon bicycles" and "frost extractors," don't waste
6       your money on those either. And don't buy any
7       Aleutian dogs from Barney McGovern. He sold me a
8       pair of lame ones as part of my team.

9   WILL: You were a miner too?

10   EDDIE: I was. One of the first to leap onto a vessel bound
11       for the north. It was only a few weeks after the
12       steamer *Portland* docked along the wharf. I saw those
13       miners disembark, laden with gold, before my very
14       eyes. They were like gods. I bought my outfit the next
15       morning. I wasn't alone, either. There were hundreds
16       of men clamoring along the docks, looking for any
17       halfway seaworthy vessel to carry them north. I was
18       one of the lucky ones. An old friend of mine ran a
19       fishing boat north along the coast every month. He
20       took me as far as Victoria, and I caught a ship there
21       more easily.

22   WILL: What did you find?

23   EDDIE: I found a vast barren landscape of ice and snow
24       and a footpath north littered with broken equipment
25       and the bodies of sick pack animals. My wagon broke
26       down, and I was forced to abandon much of the
27       equipment that I had spent my own life savings on.
28       Still, I was undeterred. I arrived in the Yukon and
29       spent eleven months slaving away along Rabbit
30       Creek. The gold seemed so close! But by the end of my
31       time there —

32   WILL: Do you mean you never found any?

33   EDDIE: Never more than dust. And believe you me, a flake
34       was enough to keep me panning the creek for
35       another month. But in the end, I came home empty-

1     handed.
2     WILL: What did you do?
3     EDDIE: What could I do? Without the money for so much
4        as a train ticket, I sold the last of my salvaged
5        equipment and rented a room at a local boarding
6        house. I found a job selling tents for a man named
7        Helmer. But I realized that the real profits were right
8        here where I started from. Will, if you could only see
9        how this city has changed since I first came through
10       it a year ago! On my return I hardly recognized it for
11       all it's grown. Sailing out of Elliott Bay, I remember
12       looking back on hardly more than a few stumpy
13       buildings erected on swamplands. And now, eight-
14       story structures scrape the sky! People of every
15       ethnicity roam the business district by day and the
16       entertainment district by night. Vice is matched by
17       vigor. More trade comes through Seattle's docks than
18       anywhere else on the coast, excepting perhaps San
19       Francisco. I've never seen New York, but surely even
20       you won't deny that this city is a sight to behold.
21    WILL: It's true. The *Post-Intelligencer* is calling the rush
22       one of the greatest migrations in the history of the
23       world. A hundred thousand people headed north!
24       And almost all of them coming through Seattle. I'll
25       admit I've never seen a city quite so dynamic and
26       expectant as yours when I stepped off the train today.
27       It's gripping.
28    EDDIE: Will, listen to me. Your fortune isn't waiting for
29       you in the north. The fortunes to be made from the
30       gold rush are here, at its very doors. Miners come
31       through our metropolis for their outfits and every
32       possible supply they could expect to want. And on the
33       off chance that they come home rich, where's the
34       first place they stop to spend their newfound wealth?
35       Right where they left from. It's unmatched business.

1  WILL: I know what you're saying makes sense, sir. But
2      with all due respect, my fortune is in gold. I can feel
3      it. It might seem crazy, but I just know it's out there.
4  EDDIE: That doesn't seem crazy. It sounds familiar. I
5      heard the same call. But mark my words: a year from
6      now you'll be right back in this tavern, wishing you
7      had stayed and made ten times what you'll find in the
8      Klondike.
9  WILL: I hope I'll be living on the top floor of the Grand
10     Pacific Hotel, a wealthy and respected man.
11 EDDIE: Then take up a trade. You ought to be my partner,
12     Will. You strike me as a smart young man, and I could
13     use someone like you. I'm looking to start my own
14     business selling tents. Or if tents don't appeal to you,
15     open a restaurant or gambling house or saloon. Sell
16     outfits. Breed sled dogs. The real market is right here,
17     waiting to be mined.
18 WILL: I appreciate the offer, sir. But I can't turn my back
19     on my destiny. I was born to strike gold.
20 EDDIE: Then I wish you the best of luck. Look me up when
21     you come back through. My offer for a business
22     partnership still stands.
23 WILL: *(Stands, and they shake hands.)* Thank you, sir. Best
24     of luck to you as well. *(He exits Stage Left.)*

# 14. When You Walked Out

**Cast:** ROWAN and MORGAN. ROWAN works best as male, MORGAN as female.

**Setting:** No special set required.

**Props:** None

1  *(As scene opens, MORGAN and ROWAN stand Stage Right*
2  *and Left respectively, facing the audience to recite their*
3  *letters. Over the course of the duologue, actors may stand*
4  *still, pace, or turn to face each other depending on*
5  *personal preference.)*
6  **MORGAN: Dear Rowan.**
7  **ROWAN: Dear Morgan.**
8  **MORGAN: I've wanted to write you for a long time. For**
9  **about ten years, to be exact.**
10 **ROWAN: I got your letter yesterday. After all these years, I**
11 **couldn't believe my eyes.**
12 **MORGAN: One of the old neighbors sent your address to me,**
13 **but I was afraid to give you back the power to break my**
14 **heart again. I'm not sure what to say to you, but I've**
15 **started writing now, and I may as well put everything**
16 **I've been thinking and feeling for a decade down on**
17 **paper. I guess I'll decide whether to send this when I**
18 **get to the end of the page.**
19 **ROWAN: I can't tell you how glad I am that you sent it. I'd**
20 **wished you'd written a hundred times, but of course**
21 **it's easy to say that now.**
22 **MORGAN: Here's what I really need to say: nobody's ever**
23 **hurt me like you did. When you walked out, you**
24 **dragged my heart with you over cold, rough ground for**
25 **miles on end. Or at least that's what it felt like for a long**
26 **time.**
27 **ROWAN: I am so truly sorry for hurting you like that. I never**
28 **should have walked out in the first place, and when I**

1       realized my mistake, I should have come right back,
2       begging your forgiveness. But I was a coward. And
3       when I finally got up the courage to try to contact you
4       again, you were gone without a trace.
5 MORGAN: I tried to move on with my life, but our
6       relationship was a big piece to be missing. Still, I
7       leaned on my friends and went back to my old
8       pastimes.
9 ROWAN: I went up and down our old street, leaving my
10      address with every neighbor, asking them to please,
11      please tell you I was looking for you. I looked on
12      Facebook, but your profile wasn't listed. For years I
13      scanned the newspapers for any mention of your
14      name, but I had no idea where you were until I got
15      your letter. For all I knew you'd gone across the
16      country. You'll never know how many times I've
17      thought about you since I left.
18 MORGAN: Eventually I got into a routine. I found a new
19      normal, and one day I realized I was happy again.
20 ROWAN: Even now, ten years after the fact, hardly a day
21      has passed when I haven't seen your face in my
22      mind's eye. But I went back to living on my own, and
23      I pulled my life together. I got a new job, put a deposit
24      on an apartment, made new friends, and kept busy.
25      Everything in my life was coming together.
26 MORGAN: Happy doesn't necessarily mean complete,
27      though. I recently began to think that no matter how
28      happy my mother was to see you go, maybe I still need
29      you. I didn't know how or in what capacity exactly,
30      but to this day, life feels wrong without you. You don't
31      know how many times I've imagined you calling me
32      up out of the blue one day or calling to me across a
33      city park.
34 ROWAN: Everything was coming together, that is, except
35      for you. I couldn't find you to tell you I was sorry, and

1   it was killing me. I had visions of glimpsing you
2   across a crowded street, of calling out to you and
3   seeing your face for the first time in years.
4   MORGAN: We would approach each other like old friends,
5   then get gelato and catch a bus downtown, retelling
6   the stories of all our favorite adventures. Remember
7   the time we buried treasure at Pirate Creek? Or the
8   time you almost fell in the seal tank at the aquarium?
9   ROWAN: I thought we would take the day off and see the
10   city sights together, eat junk food for lunch and
11   dinner, and walk along the waterfront. We would
12   play board games and laugh like we used to
13   whenever either of us got bumped home in *Sorry*. I
14   would tell you how beautiful you looked even though
15   you would ignore me.
16   MORGAN: I kept promising whoever's up there listening
17   that if we had another chance, I would be patient
18   with you and listen when you asked me to do
19   something differently. I was young and naïve back
20   when you left, and I thought I had it all figured out.
21   Turns out, relationships take more compassion and
22   patience than I knew how to give. I know better now,
23   but I can't swallow the feeling that I'm the one who
24   made you leave in the first place.
25   ROWAN: But Morgan, you could ignore everything else I
26   ever say as long as you hear this: never, ever think
27   that you made me walk out. Leaving you was *my*
28   mistake, and the biggest mistake I've ever made.
29   MORGAN: No matter whose fault it was, I often wonder
30   what you've been doing. Maybe if you wanted to, we
31   could start over from square one. Please write back.
32   ROWAN: If you'd like to, could I take you out to lunch
33   sometime? Nothing fancy, maybe grab sandwiches
34   and soda and take them with us to watch the boats. If
35   not, I can understand. There's nothing to account for

1    my stupidity and a decade of lost time between us.
2    But I'd love to try again from square one. Please write
3    back.
4  MORGAN: With love, your daughter Morgan.
5  ROWAN: Love always from your dad, Rowan.

# 15. Prince Not-So-Charming

**Cast:** Two females, BETH and SUZIE
**Setting:** No special set required.
**Props:** None

1

2 SUZIE: I wish I were a princess. I want to be exactly like
3     Cinderella.

4 BETH: Be careful what you wish for. That whole princess gig
5     isn't all it's cracked up to be.

6 SUZIE: I get goosebumps when I think about her dancing
7     with the prince at the ball, losing her glass slipper, and
8     having him search the whole country to find the
9     owner. And then, when the slipper fit only Cinderella,
10     he asked her to marry him.

11 BETH: What a ridiculous reason to get married. Just
12     because she has small feet doesn't mean she's someone
13     you want to spend the rest of your life with. Did he ask
14     her if she wants to have kids? Did he learn if she's a
15     good money manager? What if she has enormous
16     student loans and is crushed with credit card debt and
17     she ends up bankrupting the kingdom?

18 SUZIE: Where is your sense of romance? The Cinderella
19     story is not about student loans or credit card debt. It's
20     about love!

21 BETH: Did they discuss getting a pet? What if he's absolutely
22     crazy about cats and she's allergic to animal fur?

23 SUZIE: He knew from the first second he saw her that she
24     was the only woman for him, and when the glass
25     slipper fit her, he lifted her onto his white horse and
26     they rode off to the palace.

27 BETH: Right. He didn't give her time to pack, so she arrived
28     at the palace without any of her clothes. She didn't
29     even have a toothbrush.

1    SUZIE: Her clothes were rags. She wouldn't have wanted
2    to take them. The prince bought her all new beautiful
3    clothes. He probably bought her an electric
4    toothbrush too.
5    BETH: That's the crux of Cinderella's problem right there.
6    The prince bought her clothes. Would you want some
7    guy picking out all your clothes for you?
8    SUZIE: Maybe he had catalogs and let her choose. Maybe
9    they shopped online together.
10   BETH: What if she likes L.L. Bean and he likes Victoria's
11   Secret? That would be a problem.
12   SUZIE: That's a hypothetical problem that might not even
13   exist.
14   BETH: What about the king and queen? They exist. Where
15   were they when all of this was going on? Prince
16   Charming is still only a prince, which means the king
17   and queen are in charge. Cinderella not only got
18   dragged off to that palace with none of her own jeans
19   and hoodies, but she had to live with her in-laws.
20   SUZIE: You don't know that for sure.
21   BETH: Of course I know it. Where else would the king and
22   queen live besides the royal palace?
23   SUZIE: Royal palaces are big. Huge! Probably Cinderella
24   and the prince have their own separate living area
25   with dozens of rooms separating them from his
26   parents.
27   BETH: I certainly hope so. Of course, she still wouldn't
28   have any privacy, what with all the maids and the
29   ladies-in-waiting. Frankly, I don't know how she
30   could stand it. One day nobody paid any attention to
31   the rags she wore to scrub the kitchen or clean out
32   the fireplace, and the next day, she had complete
33   strangers helping her get dressed.
34   SUZIE: I wouldn't mind having a maid or two at my place.
35   They could start by scrubbing the tile in the shower.

1 BETH: The maids and ladies-in-waiting are the least of
2     Cinderella's problems. The word from the palace is
3     that once they tied the knot, the prince was less than
4     charming.
5 SUZIE: What do you mean? What happened?
6 BETH: Well, for one thing, he insisted on having bacon
7     and fried eggs for breakfast every day.
8 SUZIE: What's wrong with that?
9 BETH: Nothing for him. But he started to make Cinderella
10    eat bacon and fried eggs too when she preferred thin,
11    watery gruel. She was used to gruel. She had thin,
12    watery gruel for breakfast every day of her life until
13    she married the prince, and it always helped her
14    keep her girlish figure. If she scarfs down bacon and
15    eggs every morning, she won't be able to fit into her
16    new gowns.
17 SUZIE: You're right. She'd better watch it, or the glass
18    slippers will be too tight.
19 BETH: Breakfast is only the beginning of the day's
20    troubles for that girl. I've heard some truly shocking
21    stories, let me tell you.
22 SUZIE: Don't repeat unfounded rumors. There's no
23    reason to besmirch Prince Charming's reputation.
24 BETH: They are not unfounded rumors. They came
25    straight from Cinderella's serving wench. I
26    happened to sit next to her at the rally for "Voting
27    Rights for Peasants." But if you don't want to hear
28    the latest news from the castle, I'll keep it to myself.
29 SUZIE: Well, if it's true, I suppose you can repeat it.
30 BETH: Far be it from me to spread malicious gossip, even
31    when it does involve Prince Not-So-Charming.
32 SUZIE: What did he do?
33 BETH: You're right. There's no reason to besmirch the
34    prince's reputation, especially since none of his loyal
35    subjects would ever guess his secret.

1   SUZIE: What's his secret? I promise it will be safe with me.

2   BETH: I'm warning you, you'll be shocked.

3   SUZIE: Has the prince been cheating on Cinderella?

4   BETH: Not that I know of, although it wouldn't surprise

5       me if that happens next.

6   SUZIE: Did he get caught stealing gold from the royal

7       coffers and gambling it away on jousting matches?

8   BETH: Worse than that.

9   SUZIE: Worse? What? Tell me!

10   BETH: The prince doesn't like football.

11   SUZIE: No! Every red-blooded prince likes football.

12   BETH: He spent Super Bowl Sunday reading a book.

13   SUZIE: That's scandalous! How can he lead his kingdom if

14       he doesn't like football?

15   BETH: Poor Cinderella. She had bet three gold coins in the

16       palace football pool, and she never found out if her

17       numbers won because the prince didn't want the TV

18       on when he was trying to read.

19   SUZIE: No! If that becomes common knowledge, there

20       could be a feudal uprising.

21   BETH: I say Cinderella should cut her losses and leave.

22       Take her fancy new clothes and hit the road.

23   SUZIE: Where would she go? She won't want to return to

24       the cruel stepmother and stepsisters. How would she

25       support herself? Even thin, watery gruel costs money.

26   BETH: That's easy. She'll write a book!

27   SUZIE: I don't think Cinderella knows how to write a

28       book.

29   BETH: That won't matter. She's a celebrity. She'll write an

30       exposé about life in the palace, and the publishers

31       will scramble to buy it.

32   SUZIE: You mean reveal the prince's secret? That seems

33       like a dirty trick after he rescued her from her

34       miserable life and bought her an electric toothbrush.

35   BETH: Do you have a better suggestion?

1   SUZIE: She could stay and co-author a book with Prince
2        Charming. She can convince him that he will save
3        the kingdom if he can get the serfs to read instead of
4        watching football all the time. When they work
5        together on their book, Cinderella and the prince
6        will become true partners, and he'll quit bossing her
7        around and let her buy her own clothes and eat what
8        she wants.
9   BETH: That just might work.
10  SUZIE: Imagine being married to a handsome prince and
11       living in a palace *and* being a published author. I
12       wish I were a princess. I want to be exactly like
13       Cinderella.

# 16. Hitchhikers

**Cast:** DRIVER and DRIFTER

**Setting:** Front seat of a car on the highway. Two side-by-side chairs facing audience serve as car seats.

**Props:** Backpack for Drifter. Frisbee, small hoop, or similar is optional as a steering wheel. Otherwise, Driver may pantomime.

1 *(As scene opens, DRIFTER is standing to one side of the*
2 *stage with backpack on and thumb up. DRIFTER is*
3 *looking forward to where DRIVER is sitting in driver's*
4 *seat, holding steering wheel, and having presumably just*
5 *coasted to a stop. DRIFTER puts thumb down and jogs*
6 *over to stop next to passenger-side chair. He bends down*
7 *to talk to DRIVER as if through a car window.)*
8 **DRIFTER: Thanks for stopping, man!**
9 **DRIVER: Not a problem. Where you headed?**
10 **DRIFTER: Anywhere. Anywhere at all.**
11 **DRIVER: West, I presume?**
12 **DRIFTER: Works for me.**
13 **DRIVER: Hop in.**
14 **DRIFTER:** *(Pantomimes opening car door and sits down in*
15 *passenger seat, reclosing door.)* **Thanks again, man. I**
16 **appreciate it.**
17 **DRIVER: Sure thing.** *(Looks over left shoulder as if merging*
18 *back onto the road.)* **It looks too hot to be standing out**
19 **there.**
20 **DRIFTER: You're right about that.**
21 **DRIVER: Where are you coming from?**
22 **DRIFTER: My last stop was in Salina.**
23 **DRIVER: So where are you from originally?**
24 **DRIFTER: From everywhere. From nowhere.** *(Pauses.)* **I'm**
25 **kidding, I just like the sound of that. I was born in**
26 **upstate New York.**

1  DRIVER: You must have grown up there, then.

2  DRIFTER: That's right.

3  DRIVER: How long have you been on the road?

4  DRIFTER: A few weeks. I had to get out of New York. There

5      wasn't anything for me there.

6  DRIVER: You can't be more than seventeen or eighteen,

7      can you?

8  DRIFTER: I'm seventeen.

9  DRIVER: So where have you been since you left home?

10  DRIFTER: From my hometown I got a ride with a friend's

11      brother as far south as Philly. The brother goes to

12      college there, and I ran around town with him for a

13      few days. Then I caught a ride with a trucker headed

14      to Chicago. I meant to head out of Chicago pretty

15      soon after I got there, but I bumped into an old

16      friend who I hadn't seen in nearly ten years, and I

17      ended up staying with her for about a week. From

18      there I've been bumming rides: Chicago to

19      Indianapolis, Indianapolis to St. Louis ...

20  DRIVER: And somehow you found yourself in the dead

21      center of Kansas.

22  DRIFTER: Yep. A girl named Audrey gave me a ride from

23      Lawrence to Salina. Then I got a short ride from the

24      outskirts of Salina to wherever we are now. And now

25      here I am.

26  DRIVER: Here you are. We're headed out of Hays. Ever

27      seen this part of the country before?

28  DRIFTER: Nope. I've never been farther than New

29      England.

30  DRIVER: Don't your parents travel?

31  DRIFTER: They used to, but now they're homebodies. We

32      live in Oneonta, they've got a summer place in

33      Maine, and between the two, they're content to stay

34      where they are.

35  DRIVER: It's a beautiful region.

1 DRIFTER: I know, but I want to see the world. I figured I'd
2     start with the U.S.
3 DRIVER: I was the same way when I was your age. Do your
4     parents know where you are?
5 DRIFTER: Well, they don't know I'm in Kansas
6     specifically. I did write my mom a long note
7     explaining what I was doing before I left. She'd be a
8     nervous wreck if I didn't.
9 DRIVER: She's probably a nervous wreck anyway.
10 DRIFTER: I promised her I'd call when I got to California.
11     I was even going to call sooner, but I forgot my phone
12     charger at home the night I left. It's been kind of nice,
13     to be honest. Being unreachable, I mean.
14 DRIVER: Don't you kids have Facebook nowadays? Get on
15     any computer, post a picture, say where you are, and
16     the whole world sees it. My daughters do that. I can't
17     understand how it works, but they're always showing
18     me links from their friends and tagging this and that.
19 DRIFTER: That's part of the reason I wanted to get out and
20     go where no one knew me. I felt like I knew every
21     little detail about my friends, and they never did
22     anything unexpected. I wanted to be surprised.
23 DRIVER: Have you been?
24 DRIFTER: Yeah. I've met some fantastic people. Been
25     taken in and cared for by complete strangers. I've
26     heard some great stories from people who have
27     picked me up on the road, too. But it's harder than I
28     expected to get a ride sometimes.
29 DRIVER: Times have changed. It used to be that you could
30     get anywhere in the United States in a day or two
31     thumbing rides. Now we're barraged with news
32     stories about kidnappings and assaults because that's
33     what sells papers, and suddenly everyone we see on
34     the street is suspect. I'm not saying there's no reason
35     to be careful, but most people are overly afraid.

1   DRIFTER: But you picked me up.
2   DRIVER: What goes around comes around. I thumbed a
3       fair share of rides in my day.
4   DRIFTER: How far are you driving?
5   DRIVER: I can take you as far as Pueblo. You'll have to
6       make your way southwest from there.
7   DRIFTER: That's great. I can do that.
8   DRIVER: It's funny you should be headed to California.
9   DRIFTER: Why's that? I want to surf San Diego and see
10      San Francisco. Maybe work on an organic farm.
11      Whatever comes up. I know it sounds stereotypical,
12      but —
13  DRIVER: It's not that. It's funny because when I was
14      seventeen years old, I left California to hitch my way
15      up to New York.
16  DRIFTER: No way! Are you kidding?
17  DRIVER: Nope. I left home with my best friend. I can
18      remember my mother crying on the front lawn, but
19      we jumped in the back of our friend's pickup truck
20      and waved as we drove away.
21  DRIFTER: Why would you want to go to upstate New York?
22  DRIVER: For Woodstock.
23  DRIFTER: You were there? What was it like?
24  DRIVER: It was the festival of a generation. Everything
25      was happening right there before our eyes, and we
26      really believed that we could change the world. It was
27      muddy and crazy and the music was unreal.
28  DRIFTER: That's so amazing that you actually lived
29      through that.
30  DRIVER: That was all the way back in 1969. Sometimes it
31      seems like yesterday.
32  DRIFTER: What did you do after the festival?
33  DRIVER: I left New York and traveled, first with my best
34      friend, then with people I met along the way. I took
35      odd jobs and settled down for a few months at a time,

1      sometimes longer. I lived in Beaufort, North Carolina
2      for almost a year. I had a girlfriend there, and we
3      lived on the beach.
4  **DRIFTER:** And then?
5  **DRIVER:** The girl and I broke up, and I rode a three-speed
6      bicycle all the way home. That was four years after I
7      first left. I was broke and technically homeless, with
8      a pair of sandals and two T-shirts to my name. I rode
9      into the front yard with hair halfway down my back
10     and the worst sunburn of my life, and my own
11     mother barely recognized me.
12  **DRIFTER:** What did she say?
13  **DRIVER:** Nothing. She grabbed me by the arm, marched
14     me inside, sat me down at the kitchen table and made
15     me chicken fried steak and the biggest plate of
16     mashed potatoes I've seen in my life. I had three
17     slices of peach pie for dessert, went to bed, and slept
18     for twenty-eight hours straight.
19  **DRIFTER:** You lived through one of the best times in
20     history. I wish I'd been there. No one lives like that
21     anymore.
22  **DRIVER:** Are you kidding? You're living through a
23     generation where culture, technology, and the world
24     are changing faster than they ever have in the course
25     of human history. No one knows what your legacy
26     will be yet, just like we never knew then what the
27     sixties would come to mean. We still don't fully
28     understand. Your job is to get out there and live your
29     life. You won't find out your legacy until later. Maybe
30     you never will. But you won't make history by
31     wishing you'd been part of something else. (*Looks*
32     *over at DRIFTER.*) Enough of my rambling, son. You
33     look like you haven't slept in days.
34  **DRIFTER:** It has been awhile.
35  **DRIVER:** Go ahead and sleep now. It's still five hours until

1      Pueblo. When we get there I'll take you to the best
2      breakfast place in town and tell you the wildest
3      beaches to surf in San Diego. And you can call your
4      mother to tell her you're alive.
5  DRIFTER: OK. If you insist.
6  DRIVER: I insist. From personal experience. Now enough
7      sermons from me. Sleep well, my friend. *(DRIFTER*
8      *slumps down in seat and closes eyes.)*

# 17. Goody, Two Shoes

**Cast:** SHOE ONE (left) and SHOE TWO (right)
**Setting:** No special set required.
**Props:** None
**Costumes:** *Dressing up as shoes, e.g. using string tied as laces, is optional.*

1  (As scene opens, SHOE ONE sits Stage Left and SHOE
2  TWO sits Stage Right.)
3  SHOE ONE: Oh, good grief. Where are we going today?
4  SHOE TWO: I think we're going hiking!
5  SHOE ONE: Hiking? I hope you heard wrong.
6  SHOE TWO: You know I'm always right.
7  SHOE ONE: Tell me you're joking, then. I'm in no shape to
8  go hiking.
9  SHOE TWO: We're the same size. And you always manage to
10  keep up with me.
11  SHOE ONE: I don't think you're in any shape to go hiking
12  either. Look at you.
13  SHOE TWO: What's that supposed to mean? I'm rugged. I'm
14  ready.
15  SHOE ONE: You're filthy.
16  SHOE TWO: So? Doesn't affect my hiking.
17  SHOE ONE: It affects my wanting to be seen with you.
18  SHOE TWO: Well, you don't have much choice, do you?
19  SHOE ONE: (Snorts.) No.
20  SHOE TWO: That's what I thought.
21  SHOE ONE: And you're seriously excited about this?
22  SHOE TWO: It's going to be awesome!
23  SHOE ONE: We haven't been hiking in ages. We'll start
24  chafing before we make it a mile.
25  SHOE TWO: No way. A couple feet and we'll fall right back in
26  step.
27  SHOE ONE: You go. I might hide in the closet.

1  SHOE TWO: Stop it. I obviously can't go without you.
2     Anyway, someone will find you there.
3  SHOE ONE: It's worked before. Remember when they
4     wanted to take us camping?
5  SHOE TWO: Yes. You made me miss the whole weekend.
6  SHOE ONE: They weren't even going to let us stay in the
7     tent!
8  SHOE TWO: Probably because you smell.
9  SHOE ONE: Whoa there. Who smells? You're no
10     midsummer night's rose yourself.
11  SHOE TWO: *(Sniffs, then shrugs it off.)* We've been lying
12     around here for days. Don't you feel kind of useless?
13  SHOE ONE: I feel relaxed. You should try it sometime.
14  SHOE TWO: We're young! We're strong! We should be out
15     roaming the world, not sitting around inside!
16  SHOE ONE: I'm worn out.
17  SHOE TWO: Don't act all holey. I've been through as much
18     as you have.
19  SHOE ONE: I don't want to go.
20  SHOE TWO: You're sole-less.
21  SHOE ONE: That's not my fault. It was that dumb
22     backpacking trip that you made me go on —
23  SHOE TWO: Shhhh, hold your tongue! The counselor's
24     coming. You always rub him the wrong way.
25  SHOE ONE: All right, fine. I guess I have no choice. Don't
26     get your laces in a knot.
27  SHOE TWO: *(Ecstatic)* I knew you'd come! And I'll be by
28     your side every step of the way.
29  SHOE ONE: Here we go again.
30  SHOE TWO: We're a perfect pair, you and I.
31  SHOE ONE: Shoo! Stop following me.

# 18. No Solicitors

**Cast:** JOHN and BRITNEY

**Setting:** No special set required.

**Props:** Two phones

1  *(As scene opens, JOHN and BRITNEY should be standing*
2  *apart from each other facing the audience and should not*
3  *acknowledge each other's physical presence. JOHN dials*
4  *his phone and holds it to his ear.)*
5  **BRITNEY:** *(Picks up her phone.)* **Hello?**
6  **JOHN: Hello. May I please speak with Miss Coleman?**
7  **BRITNEY: This is she. May I ask who's calling?**
8  **JOHN: This is John Anderson calling with Hypotenuse Cable**
9      **Corporation. We're conducting a survey of potential**
10     **customers, and we're hoping you'll take five minutes to**
11     **answer a few questions regarding —**
12 **BRITNEY: John?** *The* **John Anderson? John, I can't believe**
13     **it's really you! Do you remember me?**
14 **JOHN: I beg your pardon. I'm not sure I know who this is.**
15 **BRITNEY: But you just said my name, John. It's me! Britney**
16     **Coleman! You must remember me. We went to**
17     **elementary school together. It** *is* **you, isn't it?**
18 **JOHN: I'm not sure I'm the person you're thinking of ...**
19 **BRITNEY: Of course it's you! I'd recognize your voice**
20     **anywhere. I can't believe you called! How have you**
21     **been?**
22 **JOHN: Well, I'm doing just fine. But are you sure you aren't**
23     **confusing me with another John Anderson? I can't**
24     **recall any Britney I attended elementary school with.**
25 **BRITNEY: You always were coy, John. I know you know me.**
26     **We dated for half of second grade.**
27 **JOHN: We did?**
28 **BRITNEY: Yes. You carved our initials on the maple tree in**
29     **the middle of the playground.**

1   JOHN: I'm sure I've never done that.
2   BRITNEY: I watched you. Do you know I went back a year
3       ago to see that tree again? I can still see a faint "J.A.
4       loves B.C."
5   JOHN: We'll have to agree to disagree. Are you willing to
6       answer a few questions today?
7   BRITNEY: Sure, but tell me ... what are you doing
8       nowadays?
9   JOHN: I'm a telemarketer, ma'am.
10  BRITNEY: Please, call me Britney. I never thought I'd hear
11      you say my name again. Are you back in the area?
12  JOHN: I'm not at liberty to discuss my physical location.
13  BRITNEY: Still playing hard to get, I see. Just like when
14      you moved away. You broke my heart. Did you know
15      that, John? You really broke my heart.
16  JOHN: I've only got three questions for you. Shall I go
17      ahead?
18  BRITNEY: Why ask? You know I'd do anything for you.
19  JOHN: Question One: Are you satisfied with your current
20      cable service?
21  BRITNEY: Here I am getting ahead of myself. I half
22      thought you were going to ask me to dinner, even
23      after all these years. No, I'm actually not satisfied
24      with my cable service. It's outrageously expensive. I
25      dread getting the bills every month.
26  JOHN: Would you consider switching cable companies
27      today if you were offered a competitive rate?
28  BRITNEY: Yes, I guess I would consider it.
29  JOHN: What would you say to an all-inclusive rate of forty
30      dollars per month?
31  BRITNEY: Forty a month! John! You don't have to do that
32      for me.
33  JOHN: I'm just doing my job, ma'am. We can have a new
34      dish installed tomorrow morning.
35  BRITNEY: You are truly the sweetest. Are you sure it

1      wouldn't be too much trouble?

2  JOHN: It's no trouble at all. Shall I sign you up?

3  BRITNEY: Oh, yes! That would be amazing.

4  JOHN: Wonderful. May I please have your current
5      address?

6  BRITNEY: It's 721 Valencia Street. Maybe now you can
7      send me all those love letters you promised me when
8      you left.

9  JOHN: That's highly unlikely. But I will send someone over
10     to install your new cable dish first thing tomorrow.
11     You'll be able to take care of all the necessary
12     paperwork then.

13  BRITNEY: Are you sure you can't come yourself?

14  JOHN: Unfortunately, I'm not involved in the installation
15     process.

16  BRITNEY: That's a shame. But you'll call me again, won't
17     you?

18  JOHN: You'll receive periodic calls from us. Is this the best
19     number to reach you at?

20  BRITNEY: Yes, it is.

21  JOHN: That's great. We'll call back in six months to ensure
22     your complete satisfaction with our service. Our
23     customers are very important to us.

24  BRITNEY: Six months! Well, I'll be counting the days. I
25     knew I was still important to you.

26  JOHN: You can also reach us online or by using the phone
27     number listed on our website.

28  BRITNEY: Is that the best way to contact you?

29  JOHN: No, that number will send you to our electronic
30     service center.

31  BRITNEY: I guess I'll just have to wait to hear from you
32     again. Don't make me wait too long, John.

33  JOHN: Do you have any questions for me?

34  BRITNEY: Just one question, John. Do you believe in fate?
35     Because I do. And this is proof that fate exists. I'm so

1    glad you called.
2    JOHN: So am I! Thank you for signing up with Hypotenuse
3    Cable, and have a great day!

# 19. Cutesy-Wutesy Doggie-Woggie

**Cast:** DORA and SYLVIA
**Setting:** A street corner
**Props:** Stuffed dog and blanket for Dora. Sylvia wears a watch.

1  *(As scene opens, SYLVIA is pacing and looking at her*
2  *watch. DORA enters, carrying a blanket and a stuffed*
3  *dog.)*
4  **DORA:** Hi! Sorry I'm a few minutes late. I had to wait for
5   Foo-Foo to go potty.
6  **SYLVIA:** I thought we were going to a movie.
7  **DORA:** We are. That's why we're here, right? We were
8   supposed to meet and go together.
9  **SYLVIA:** What about your dog?
10 **DORA:** This is Foo-Foo. Isn't she the most adorable thing
11  you've ever seen? *(Nuzzles the dog.)* Say hello to Auntie
12  Sylvia, Foo-Foo.
13 **SYLVIA:** What are you going to do with Foo-Foo while we're
14  in the theater? It's too hot to leave her in the car.
15 **DORA:** She'll go with us. *(To stuffed dog, in baby talk)* Foo-Foo
16  loves movies, don't you, sweetums? *(Back to Sylvia)* Her
17  favorite is *101 Dalmatians.*
18 **SYLVIA:** Are you sure they allow dogs in the theater? Most
19  places like that don't, unless it's a service dog.
20 **DORA:** Why would anyone object to Foo-Foo going to a
21  movie?
22 **SYLVIA:** Some people are allergic to animal fur and can't be
23  in the same room with a dog or cat. Also, the theater
24  manager might worry about cleanliness.
25 **DORA:** Foo-Foo is clean. She had a bath yesterday in lilac-
26  scented doggie shampoo. Smell her! *(Holds dog toward*
27  *SYLVIA.)*
28 **SYLVIA:** No, thanks. I believe you. There's also a liability

1      issue. What if Foo-Foo bites someone?
2      DORA: Are you kidding? Foo-Foo wouldn't bite anybody.
3      She is the sweetest, most good-natured dog ever.
4      Don't you like dogs?
5      SYLVIA: I like dogs. I have a dog of my own, Beastie. He's
6      part collie and part German shepherd.
7      DORA: Ooooh, we should plan a play date for Foo-Foo and
8      Beastie. We could meet at the dog park and let them
9      run around together.
10    SYLVIA: Beastie is a lot bigger than Foo-Foo. Wouldn't Foo-
11    Foo be intimidated?
12    DORA: No way. Foo-Foo is small, but she's feisty. Last week
13    she attacked a Great Dane that tried to jump on me.
14    The dog was being friendly, but Foo-Foo didn't know
15    that.
16    SYLVIA: What happened?
17    DORA: The Great Dane's person intervened. He actually
18    yelled at me to call my dog off. Then he started in
19    about obeying the leash laws. As if I would ever put
20    Foo-Foo on a leash. Leashes are demeaning. How
21    would you like to have a strap hooked on to your
22    collar and be dragged around whether you wanted to
23    go or not?
24    SYLVIA: I wouldn't like it, but I'm not a dog. And I don't
25    attack Great Danes.
26    DORA: Are you saying you think leashes are a good idea?
27    SYLVIA: If the dog is out in public, then yes, I think it
28    should either be leashed or completely under
29    control.
30    DORA: Foo-Foo was not out of control. She was simply
31    defending her person. *(To dog)* Weren't you, my
32    cutesy-wutesy doggie-woggie?
33    SYLVIA: Why do you have that blanket? It's eighty degrees
34    out.
35    DORA: The theater might be air-conditioned.

1   SYLVIA: I hope it is.

2   DORA: Sometimes air conditioning is too cold for Foo-Foo,

3        so I carry a blanket to wrap her in. *(To dog, in baby*

4        *talk)* I wouldn't want my snooky-wooky to catch a

5        nasty old coldy-woldy.

6   SYLVIA: *(Copying DORA's babyish tone)* She might sneezey-

7        weezy some snotty-wotty.

8   DORA: Oh, look! She's wagging her tail at you. She likes it

9        when you talk baby talk to her.

10  SYLVIA: So you plan to hold your dog through the whole

11       movie?

12  DORA: If there's an empty seat beside me, I might let Foo-

13       Foo sit in her own space.

14  SYLVIA: What if she barks?

15  DORA: Why would she bark?

16  SYLVIA: Maybe she'll get excited if there's some loud

17       action, or maybe there's a dog in the movie and she'll

18       see it or hear it.

19  DORA: Foo-Foo understands the difference between a real

20       dog and a pretend dog.

21  SYLVIA: *(Barks loudly at stuffed dog.)* Woof! Woof, woof,

22       woof! *(They both stare at the stuffed dog.)*

23  DORA: As you can see, Foo-Foo is not excitable.

24  SYLVIA: Well, if we're going to be there in time for the

25       main feature, we'd better get started.

26  DORA: I have to make one quick stop on the way to buy a

27       doggie snack for Foo-Foo. She needs to eat every two

28       hours or she gets cranky.

29  SYLVIA: You plan to feed her during the movie?

30  DORA: Just a few peanut butter crackers or maybe some

31       chicken jerky.

32  SYLVIA: Can't she eat popcorn? You can get that at the

33       theatre.

34  DORA: It's too salty. I'm very fussy about Foo-Foo's diet.

35       *(To dog, in baby talk)* We wouldn't want our doggie-

1      woggie to get an upset tummy-wummy, would we?
2  SYLVIA: *(Exasperated)* **Heaven forbid. She might pukey-**
3      **yukey on the seaty-weaty.**
4  **DORA: Never.**
5  **SYLVIA: Let's go.** *Attack of the Killer Strawberries* **starts in**
6      **twenty minutes.**
7  **DORA: I thought we were going to see** *Dogs Rule: The*
8      *Sequel.*
9  **SYLVIA: No way. I saw the original** *Dogs Rule* **and could**
10    **barely stay awake. I left partway through.**
11  **DORA:** *Attack of the Killer Strawberries* **will be too scary**
12    **for Foo-Foo.**
13  **SYLVIA: It's an animated film. It's rated G.**
14  **DORA: I'm sorry, but I'm very fussy when it comes to Foo-**
15    **Foo's movies.**
16  **SYLVIA: And I'm fussy when it comes to my movies. I'm**
17    **not paying money to watch** *Dogs Rule: The Sequel.*
18  **DORA: I guess we aren't going to a movie then.**
19  **SYLVIA: I'm still going.**
20  **DORA: You'd go without me? After we had agreed to see a**
21    **movie together?**
22  **SYLVIA: You can come.**
23  **DORA: No. It's more important to be a responsible parent**
24    **than it is to have a couple of hours of entertainment.**
25    *(To dog, in baby talk)* **Isn't it, lovey-dovey?**
26  **SYLVIA: Maybe we can go to a movie some other day.**
27  **DORA:** *(Walks off baby-talking to dog.)* **It's OK, sweetsie-**
28    **poo. I'll still buy some treats for you. You're my**
29    **cutesy-wutesy dumpling-wumpling.**
30  **SYLVIA: I think I'm going to be sicky-wicky.** *(Exits opposite*
31    *direction.)*

# 20. The Ballad of Lewis and Clark

**Cast:** LEWIS and CLARK
**Setting:** The untamed Pacific Northwest, 1805.
**Props:** None
**Costumes:** Both should wear furs, large backpacks, and any other primitive outdoor gear.

1  *(As scene opens, LEWIS and CLARK are trudging wearily*
2  *in place, facing the audience. This continues throughout*
3  *the duologue.)*
4  LEWIS: *(Groans.)* Clark. This is exhausting. Are we there yet?
5  CLARK: Don't ask me. You think I know how to read a map?
6    Sacagawea's the only one keeping us from being
7    completely lost in the wilderness.
8  LEWIS: You can't read a map? How did you even get to come
9    on this expedition?
10  CLARK: You nominated me.
11  LEWIS: Oh. Well, I thought you knew cartography.
12  CLARK: What does it matter? We'll never reach the Pacific
13    Ocean. I'm starting to think it isn't out there.
14  LEWIS: Of course it is. Jefferson knows. He has the world's
15    largest collection of Northwest geography materials.
16  CLARK: So why didn't he take this trip himself?
17  LEWIS: He's busy being president, or so he says. Honestly,
18    though, how hard can that be? All I see him doing is
19    lounging around talking politics with James Madison.
20    His job is definitely not as tough as our trek.
21  CLARK: I just wish we had some way to distract ourselves.
22    Every time I see another Douglas fir tree, I want to
23    shoot myself in the foot.
24  LEWIS: I concur! These mountains are killing me. Why
25    didn't LePage's account of the transcontinental voyage
26    say anything about them? They're gargantuan! Twelve

1      thousand feet, I'd wager. I thought we'd be able to
2      carry our boats to the Columbia no problem.
3  CLARK: Instead, we can barely carry ourselves, and I'm
4      sweating through my deerskin pants.
5  LEWIS: Do you know any marching songs?
6  CLARK: Nah. And anyway, I can't sing.
7  LEWIS: What about rhymes?
8  CLARK: What do you mean, rhymes?
9  LEWIS: You know, poem-type things that could go along
10     with a beat, such as the rhythm of our footsteps.
11  CLARK: I can't say I know any of those, either.
12  LEWIS: Clarky, we should make one up.
13  CLARK: Meriwether, you have the strangest ideas.
14  LEWIS: Clark! As your captain, I command you to humor
15     me. I can't listen to myself think anymore because all
16     I think about is strangling Jefferson for sending us
17     on this abominable misadventure.
18  CLARK: All right, captain, we can try to make up a rhyme.
19     How do we go about it?
20  LEWIS: Firstly, we've got to step in time. *(LEWIS and*
21     *CLARK begin stepping to the same deliberate beat.)*
22  CLARK: Left ... left ... left, right, left ...
23  LEWIS: OK, I'll start. "It's Captain Meriwether Lewis and
24     Captain William Clark ... "
25  CLARK: Go on. Lots of things rhyme with my name.
26  LEWIS: Um. "We're trekking in the daylight 'cause we'd
27     get lost in the dark."
28  CLARK: Good one, captain!
29  LEWIS: Thank you, Clarky. And now it's your turn.
30  CLARK: Me, sir?
31  LEWIS: Yes, Clarky.
32  CLARK: OK, let me think ... How about, "The Oregon
33     country is hotly disputed.
34     It's not our property yet, so we might well get looted."
35  LEWIS: You're a natural!

1 **CLARK: You try it again.** *(From here on out LEWIS and*
2 *CLARK rap their lines in time with their march. They*
3 *get progressively more enthusiastic with each delivery.)*
4 **LEWIS: "The Corps of Discovery is certainly the best.**
5 **We're roaming in the untamed Pacific Northwest."**
6 **CLARK: "There are thirty-three of us, and we left from**
7 **Camp Dubois.**
8 **The winter wind was nasty and our noses red and**
9 **raw."**
10 **LEWIS: "The first one to desert the corps was Mr. Moses**
11 **Reed.**
12 **He told us he forgot his knife but fled with shocking**
13 **speed."**
14 **CLARK: "Then Sergeant Charles Floyd got acute**
15 **appendicitis.**
16 **He died, but we won't miss him, 'cause he tended to**
17 **deride us."**
18 **LEWIS: "Private Field was first to kill a bison with a gun."**
19 **CLARK: "Then we sent a prairie dog to Jefferson for fun."**
20 **LEWIS: "The Spaniards heard about us, and they tried to**
21 **intercept us ... "**
22 **CLARK: "But we are movin' faster, and we think they'll**
23 **never catch us."**
24 **LEWIS: "By now we're rocking fox furs and coonskin caps**
25 **... "**
26 **CLARK: "We're stepping in time as we're making up raps."**
27 **LEWIS: "We need to find a water route direct to the**
28 **Pacific,**
29 **So we can trade materials and make the states**
30 **terrific."**
31 **CLARK: "Thomas Jefferson gave us lots of books to carry.**
32 **They're useful but they're heavy, and they make the**
33 **West sound scary."**
34 **LEWIS: "If we're being honest, he gave us too much stuff."**
35 **CLARK: "On the bright side, when we get back we'll be**

1   buff."
2   LEWIS: "Those solid silver Peace Medals were really not
3   light.
4   We left them all behind, even though they're pretty
5   tight."
6   CLARK: "The American Philosophical Society
7   Is giving us our funding, quelling much of our
8   anxiety."
9   LEWIS: "But still we feel unprepared 'cause we don't have
10  good maps ... "
11  CLARK: "We're afraid that this will cause unfortunate
12  mishaps."
13  LEWIS: "I shot a big bison by myself the other day,
14  But then a bear got angry, and she chased me far
15  away."
16  CLARK: "We made a good friend when we met Sacagawea.
17  She helped us when we showed some early signs of
18  giardia."
19  LEWIS: "On the other hand, then she had to go and have
20  a son.
21  Now he cries a whole lot, and it isn't any fun."
22  CLARK: "We might leave her behind if she weren't
23  translating,
24  But her skills are pretty useful, so we really can't be
25  hating."
26  LEWIS: "Helpful as she is, though, this journey's never-
27  ending.
28  On and on and on we go, upwardly ascending."
29  CLARK: "We've learned about the plants and animals
30  across the region.
31  We're writing more essays than your average
32  collegian."
33  LEWIS: "We've established good relations with at least
34  two dozen tribes.
35  We're spreading U.S. influence and power

1     nationwide."
2 CLARK: "We didn't have the best of luck meeting with the
3     Sioux.
4     There was very nearly fighting, and we weren't sure
5     what to do."
6 LEWIS: "The Mandan were nice to us and kept us from
7     starvation.
8     We smoked the peace pipe with them, to their
9     appreciation."
10 CLARK: "Once we cross the Continental Divide, we'll
11     make history.
12     Our names will be in textbooks, and our feet will be
13     all blistery."
14 LEWIS: "But at the moment, we're still scaling this
15     humungous peak.
16     There isn't enough food for us, and we are getting
17     weak."
18 CLARK: "If we ever make it over this infernal hill,
19     They ought to put our faces on a ten-dollar bill.
20     In the meantime, Meriwether, just pretend we're
21     famous."
22 LEWIS: "Clark, I hope we are someday — and really, who
23     can blame us?"
24 CLARK: "If we don't make it as explorers, maybe we'll be
25     rappers."
26 LEWIS: "It seems at least as lucrative as working as fur
27     trappers!" *(LEWIS and CLARK nod in agreement. They*
28     *continue nodding to the beat as they march off the*
29     *stage.)*

# 21. Yard Sale Treasures

**Cast:** HARLEY and PEYTON
**Setting:** No special set required.
**Props:** None

1  *(HARLEY and PEYTON stroll onto the stage together.)*
2  HARLEY: *(Points.)* Wow! Look at all this stuff! Mom is really
3      ready for her yard sale.
4  PEYTON: I guess she was serious about getting the whole
5      house organized.
6  HARLEY: Once the sale is finished, we might even be able to
7      get the car in the garage again.
8  PEYTON: Did you clean out your room yourself, or did she
9      help you?
10 HARLEY: I meant to, but I got busy with other stuff and
11      Mom ended up doing it for me.
12 PEYTON: Me too. I feel kind of guilty because she asked me
13      a zillion times to sort through my things and set aside
14      stuff I don't need anymore, but I never got around to
15      doing it. She must have done it while I was at play
16      rehearsal.
17 HARLEY: There are so many things for sale out here that I
18      wonder what's left in the house.
19 PEYTON: I don't see any furniture, so I guess we still have
20      beds and a couch.
21 HARLEY: Wait a minute! *(Pretends to pick up an item.)* This is
22      the ceramic paperweight I made in second grade.
23 PEYTON: That ugly blob is a paperweight? I always
24      wondered what it was.
25 HARLEY: Ugly blob! This is not a blob. It's a work of art! I
26      painted it by hand.
27 PEYTON: *(Pretends to look at the paperweight.)* Apparently
28      you were in a black and purple phase. I'm glad you only
29      painted a paperweight and not your bedroom.

1　HARLEY: Mom can't sell this valuable paperweight!
2　PEYTON: Valuable? You're kidding, right?
3　HARLEY: It's loaded with sentimental value.
4　PEYTON: When did you last use it?
5　HARLEY: I don't know. I haven't seen it in years. I had
6　　　totally forgotten about it.
7　PEYTON: If you forgot about it for years, you won't miss it.
8　HARLEY: I want to save it. Someday I'll pass it on to my
9　　　son.
10　PEYTON: If you ever have a son, he'll make his own awful
11　　　second-grade projects.
12　HARLEY: You don't recognize quality when you see it.
13　PEYTON: Oh, no! Look! *(Points.)* That's my Cinderella
14　　　costume from fourth grade when I won the
15　　　Halloween costume contest. *(Pantomimes holding up*
16　　　*costume.)* Mom must have put this out here by
17　　　mistake.
18　HARLEY: I hate to be the one to break it to you, but you no
19　　　longer fit into that Cinderella costume. There's not
20　　　much point in keeping it if you can't wear it.
21　PEYTON: That costume contest was so great! Lila May
22　　　Snobface bragged for weeks about her Spider Woman
23　　　outfit and how she was sure to win first prize, which
24　　　was a ten-dollar certificate for the ice-cream store.
25　　　She asked me what my costume was, and when I told
26　　　her I was going to be Cinderella, she laughed and said
27　　　Cinderella costumes were for kindergarten babies.
28　　　After I won the contest, she got so mad she stomped
29　　　out of class and went to the bathroom and bawled.
30　HARLEY: And you, being the kind-hearted and empathetic
31　　　person that you are, went after her and consoled her
32　　　and told her you would share the prize with her?
33　PEYTON: Are you kidding? I laughed myself silly. Then I
34　　　went into the bathroom with Vicki, and while Lila
35　　　May hid in a stall, Vicki and I discussed which flavors

1      of ice cream we were going to get with my prize.

2    HARLEY: No wonder you want to keep the costume since

3      it brings back such loving and tender memories.

4    PEYTON: Hey, Lila May was the biggest bully in the whole

5      school. She made my life miserable for years, and

6      that contest was the only time I ever got the better of

7      her. Maybe it wasn't my finest moment, but she had

8      it coming.

9    HARLEY: Oh, no. This is going too far! *(HARLEY points.)*

10    Mom plans to sell the Kitty Hawk model that I made.

11    PEYTON: No, she doesn't.

12    HARLEY: Yes, she does. It's right there in that box.

13    PEYTON: That's the "free" box.

14    HARLEY: What? She's giving away my Kitty Hawk model?

15    PEYTON: She can't sell it. It only has one wing.

16    HARLEY: It had two when I built it.

17    PEYTON: What else is in that "free" box?

18    HARLEY: Some stained T-shirts, a Barbie doll with no

19      hair, and some other junk.

20    PEYTON: My Barbie's in there? I am *not* getting rid of

21      Barbie.

22    HARLEY: Seriously? You still want to play with Barbie?

23    PEYTON: Of course not, but Barbie was my friend. If I'm

24      not going to keep her, I should dispose of her in a

25      respectful way, not toss her in a "free" box.

26    HARLEY: You could have a funeral and bury her in the

27      backyard. Put some flowers on her grave.

28    PEYTON: That might be going a little too far.

29    HARLEY: What happened to her hair?

30    PEYTON: I shaved it off. I got in big trouble for wrecking

31      Dad's electric razor.

32    HARLEY: I have a brilliant idea. I'm going to buy your

33      Cinderella costume and take your free Barbie.

34    PEYTON: What?

35    HARLEY: And you are going to buy my paperweight and

1        take the free Kitty Hawk model.

2      **PEYTON:** I don't want your paperweight or your model.

3      **HARLEY:** I don't want a Cinderella costume and a Barbie

4        either. But I do want great gifts to give you for

5        Christmas. I never know what to buy, and I never

6        have any money for presents.

7      **PEYTON:** You are a certified genius! We'll have perfect

8        Christmas gifts for each other, and we each only have

9        to spend twenty-five cents! *(HARLEY and PEYTON*

10     *high-five.)*

11  **HARLEY and PEYTON:** *(Together)* What a great yard sale!

# 22. The Choice

**Cast:** KELLY and TAYLOR

**Setting:** No special set required. One chair is on the stage.

**Props:** Notebook and pen for Taylor

1　*(As scene opens, KELLY is standing and pacing. This*
2　*continues throughout. TAYLOR enters.)*
3　**KELLY:** *(Agitated)* **Thank goodness you're finally here! Will**
4　　　　**you help me make a pros and cons list? I'm freaking**
5　　　　**out right now. I have to send in my college acceptance**
6　　　　**letter by tomorrow.**
7　**TAYLOR: Whoa! Deep breath, OK? I can definitely try. Do**
8　　　　**you want me to write the list?** *(KELLY nods frenetically.)*
9　**TAYLOR:** *(Sits and opens notebook.)* **OK. Try to relax, Kelly.**
10　　　　**Let's start at the beginning. What are the schools again?**
11　　　　**The U and ...**
12　**KELLY: Lodine College.**
13　**TAYLOR:** *(Writes.)* **OK. Where is that?**
14　**KELLY: Way out in the middle of nowhere. It's some tiny**
15　　　　**rural town about an eight-hour drive from here.**
16　　　　**There's seriously nothing near it. I had to look it up on**
17　　　　**the map.**
18　**TAYLOR: OK, so that's one con. Do you think you could**
19　　　　**spend the next four years there?**
20　**KELLY: I don't know! I've never lived outside of a city. At**
21　　　　**first I thought it sounded horrible. They say that being**
22　　　　**in a small town means there's always something fun**
23　　　　**happening on campus, though, because there's**
24　　　　**nowhere else to go. Plus, it'd be easier to focus on**
25　　　　**studying. So maybe it's a pro. How am I supposed to**
26　　　　**know?**
27　**TAYLOR: Studying! Yeah, right. Those good intentions**
28　　　　**always disappear the first week of school.**
29　**KELLY:** *(Shrugs.)* **I know. The classes at Lodine actually look**

1        interesting, though. There's one called "Sociology of
2        Hipsters." Isn't it crazy what we can study in college?
3   TAYLOR: No way! Are you going to take it?
4   KELLY: No idea. I still don't even know what I want to
5        major in! I swear everyone in our class except me has
6        their entire career path figured out. How am I
7        supposed to know what I want to do for the rest of my
8        life?
9   TAYLOR: For one thing, not everyone has their careers
10       figured out. I still don't know what I'm going to study.
11   KELLY: You're so good at science, though. You'll do cancer
12       research or chemical engineering or something. I
13       have no applicable skills.
14   TAYLOR: That's the whole point of going to college! If you
15       already knew how to change the world, we wouldn't
16       be having this conversation. Anyway, you can always
17       double major if you can't pick just one.
18   KELLY: That's true.
19   TAYLOR: Is there a school you're leaning towards?
20   KELLY: I guess I always assumed I'd go to the U. I know the
21       area so well, and my entire family went there. We've
22       had season tickets to the football games since before I
23       was born. My parents and sisters bleed blue and gold.
24       I'd be the only one not to go there if I chose Lodine.
25       They might disown me.
26   TAYLOR: That's very true. Plus, a lot of your friends will
27       be at the U. That's a pro too. *(Starts to write.)*
28   KELLY: Is it, though? What if I never meet any new people
29       because of it? I've already spent eighteen years in the
30       same place. What if I get stuck here?
31   TAYLOR: Well, you're going to college to have more
32       opportunities in the future. What're four more years
33       around here? If you get tired of this place by
34       graduation, you can pick up and move anywhere you
35       like.

1   KELLY: Look at last year's class, though. All the cliques
2       from high school moved on to college together, and
3       their lives haven't changed a bit. And the kids who
4       have already graduated from there got jobs right
5       back in town. College is supposed to be a clean slate,
6       you know?
7   TAYLOR: Do you know anyone going to Lodine?
8   KELLY: Not a single person.
9   TAYLOR: Should I put that under pros or cons?
10  KELLY: I don't know. I could be anyone I wanted ...
11  TAYLOR: A pro then.
12  KELLY: But what if I don't make any friends? Lodine is
13       tiny. Like, smaller than our high school.
14  TAYLOR: Seriously? Is there anything to do on campus?
15  KELLY: There's so much! I looked on the website and
16       they've got about a hundred clubs. It might be too
17       much. I have no idea how I'd juggle all the things I'd
18       want to join.
19  TAYLOR: *(Writing that down)* What about sports? Do they
20       have good teams?
21  KELLY: No teams to watch and cheer for on TV, if that's
22       what you mean. Their teams are mostly walk-ons
23       because Division Three schools aren't allowed to give
24       sports scholarships.
25  TAYLOR: They're not? But what about soccer? You've got a
26       scholarship offer from the U, haven't you? And you're
27       considering a school that can't even match that?
28  KELLY: *(Guiltily)* I might not want to play soccer next year.
29  TAYLOR: Not play soccer? But you're our top scorer! You
30       could play anywhere you wanted. I know people who
31       would give anything to be able to play like you.
32  KELLY: I met with the coach at the University. They
33       practice six days a week for four hours a day. And
34       there are two-a-days every day of spring break. How
35       would I have time to be a normal college student?

1    TAYLOR: I can't imagine you not playing soccer.

2    KELLY: To tell you the truth, neither can I. But I am kind

3        of ready for a break. I was looking at Lodine's page on

4        intramural sports and I started thinking about it. I

5        could still play intramural soccer, and it would be

6        strictly for fun. And I might try Ultimate Frisbee!

7    TAYLOR: Backtrack for a second. Is this Lodine place

8        expensive?

9    KELLY: Um, yeah. Actually, it's really expensive. But they

10    do have some financial aid.

11    TAYLOR: You should probably stop and ask yourself how

12    much you're willing to rack up in student loans over

13    the next four years. Your parents aren't paying for

14    this, are they?

15    KELLY: No, they're not. I'll have to get an on-campus job to

16    offset the cost of tuition. Even then, I'll be paying bills

17    long after I graduate.

18    TAYLOR: Big con. The U would be so much cheaper. You

19    can even come home on the weekends to do your

20    laundry.

21    KELLY: If I did that, how would I learn to live on my own?

22    Isn't that what college is supposed to teach you more

23    than anything? If I could come home on the

24    weekends and see all my old friends and do the same

25    things I've always done living here, how would I learn

26    anything new about myself?

27    TAYLOR: *(Closing the notebook)* Listen, Kelly. Forget this

28    list. It's all scribbly and full of arrows anyway. You're

29    going to have a fantastic time no matter where you

30    choose. You know that, right? *(KELLY nods, lost in*

31    *thought.)* It seems like you might have an idea of what

32    you really want to do, though. Am I right about that?

33    *(KELLY nods again, slowly.)* That's what I thought.

34    KELLY: I think I know what I'm going to do.

35    TAYLOR: I think I know too.

1    **KELLY: You're the best, Taylor. Want to come with me to**
2    **the post office? I need to go mail that letter!** *(TAYLOR*
3    *stands, and they exit enthusiastically.)*

# 23. Runaway Slave

**Cast:** SLAVE and FARMER. If Farmer is female, change "sir" to "ma'am" in Slave's speeches.

**Setting:** Farmer's home, 1861. A small table and plain chair are Center Stage.

**Props:** A glass of water and a piece of bread wrapped in cloth are on the table.

**Costumes:** Slave's clothing is ragged and he/she is barefoot.

1   *(As scene opens, FARMER is standing Stage Right. SLAVE*
2   *enters Stage Left and stops after a few paces. He crouches*
3   *as if ready to run, then knocks on the floor. Farmer walks*
4   *toward SLAVE, stops a few feet in front of SLAVE, and*
5   *pretends to open a door.)*
6   **FARMER: You're a runaway?**
7   **SLAVE: Yes, sir.**
8   **FARMER: Welcome. Come in.** *(SLAVE hesitates, looking*
9   *around as if fearful that this is a trap.)* **Hurry now, before**
10   **you're seen.** *(SLAVE steps forward. FARMER "closes"*
11   *door.)* **You'll be in this room. It's dark because there are**
12   **no windows, but you'll be safe here. There's water for**
13   **you, and bread.**
14   **SLAVE:** *(Takes a drink.)* **Thank you.** *(Sits wearily in chair.)*
15   **FARMER: You're young to be traveling the Underground**
16   **Railroad by yourself.**
17   **SLAVE: My mam and pap were with me when we left, but**
18   **the soldiers caught them. I saw them ride up in their**
19   **gray clothes and bright brass buttons. Pap heard the**
20   **horses' hooves coming and told me to hide.**
21   **FARMER: Where did you hide?**
22   **SLAVE: There was an old clay pit dug into a high bank.**
23   **That's where we got clay to mix with hog hair to make**
24   **chinking for log houses. That's what Pap and the other**
25   **men built for the master. I ran and hid way back in that**

1  old clay pit. I heard the soldiers shouting, and I knew
2  they'd caught Mam and Pap. I never came out 'til it
3  was dark. By then the soldiers were gone, and so
4  were my mam and pap.
5  FARMER: Do you want to tell me about your mam and
6  pap? Sometimes it's less lonely if you talk about those
7  you love.
8  SLAVE: My mam, she's a seamstress. She has a spinning
9  wheel and a loom. She makes the cotton cloth for all
10 the slaves' clothes. Mam's cloth is mighty fine.
11 FARMER: What about your pap?
12 SLAVE: Pap plants cotton and hoes cotton and picks
13 cotton. Dem cotton baskets weigh seventy-five or a
14 hundred pounds, but my pap, he lifts 'em right up.
15 He says a slave is the same as a mule to de master,
16 'cept mules sometimes get fed good, and we slaves is
17 half-starved.
18 FARMER: The bread is for you. I'll give you food to take
19 with you when you leave, too.
20 SLAVE: I thank you. *(Nibbles on bread.)*
21 FARMER: Did you work too?
22 SLAVE: Oh yes, sir, I been workin' since I was six years old.
23 I tote wood and feed the hogs and do odd jobs.
24 FARMER: Do you have sisters and brothers?
25 SLAVE: I gots one brother, but I don't know where he is.
26 He's older than me, a big husky boy. Master sold him
27 for four hundred dollars, and he got took away to
28 Alabama. 'Fore he left, he told me to go north first
29 chance I got. He said people in the north don't have
30 slaves. He said he was goin' to run north too, and
31 maybe we would find each other someday.
32 FARMER: I hope you do.
33 SLAVE: His name is Thomas. If a Thomas stops here one
34 day, and he's a big husky boy, you tell him I went
35 north looking for him.

1   FARMER: I'll do that.

2   SLAVE: My name is —

3   FARMER: No! Don't tell me your name. If the vigilantes

4       come looking for you, I want to be able to say I never

5       knew anyone with that name.

6   SLAVE: Are you a church-goin' person? You seem to have a

7       good heart. My mam took me to the Baptist church

8       every Sunday and told me if I was goin' to be a good

9       person, I needed to walk with the Lord.

10  FARMER: What about your pap?

11  SLAVE: Pap said he'd go to church when he could sit

12       wherever he wanted, 'stead of all the slaves on one

13       side and all the white folk on the other. Said when the

14       Lord let him read God's word in the Bible for himself,

15       he'd start to pay attention.

16  FARMER: Smart man, your pap.

17  SLAVE: Mam said for Pap to keep his ideas to hisself or

18       he'd get a whipping. Pap said he'd walk with the Lord

19       when the Lord decided to let him walk anywhere he

20       chose.

21  FARMER: After you left the clay pit and were all by

22       yourself, how did you know to come here?

23  SLAVE: 'Fore we left home, Pap showed me a map.

24  FARMER: Do you know how to read?

25  SLAVE: Oh no, sir. We wasn't allowed to have lessons. If

26       you was caught doin' learning, you was whipped. The

27       master once saw Mam peeking at the preacher's

28       Bible, and he was mad as a hive of bees. Told her

29       books warn't meant for her kind. He didn't whip her,

30       though, 'cause she was the best seamstress.

31  FARMER: But if you can't read, how did the map help you?

32       How did you find my house?

33  SLAVE: It warn't a paper map. Pap drew the directions in

34       the dirt. Told me I needed to know where we was

35       headed, in case we got separated. After me and Mam

1      studied that map, Pap scraped his foot across the dirt
2      'til the map was gone. But I 'membered how it
3      looked.
4   FARMER: I should let you rest. You're probably tired, and
5      you have another long journey ahead of you yet
6      tonight. You'll arrive at the next resting place before
7      daylight. It's right on the Ohio River, so you'll be
8      crossing that tomorrow night.
9   SLAVE: How'm I gonna walk clear to the Ohio River by
10     tomorrow night? These legs are strong, but ...
11   FARMER: You won't be walking. You'll be riding in a
12     wagon with two other runaways. You'll have baskets
13     of eggs, and if anyone stops you, you say you're
14     delivering eggs for your master. First you'll need to
15     change your clothes.
16   SLAVE: I have no other clothes.
17   FARMER: I have clothes for you. My neighbors collect
18     money to help with this work, and I use it to buy food
19     and clothes. Many people believe slavery is wrong,
20     and they're willing to contribute to this effort.
21   SLAVE: Mam told me not to accept charity.
22   FARMER: This isn't charity. This is giving you a better
23     chance to escape. As you are now, in ragged clothes
24     and unwashed, you look like a runaway. When you
25     leave here in clean clothes and shoes and with your
26     face washed, you won't call attention to yourself.
27   SLAVE: *(Fingers the bottom of shirt he's wearing.)* My mam
28     made this shirt. She wove the cotton and sewed the
29     seams. Wearing this shirt feels a little as if my mam
30     is still here with me.
31   FARMER: I'll wash your clothes and pack them away and
32     save them for you. Someday, when the people of the
33     South have accepted that slavery can no longer exist,
34     you can come back here as a free person and get your
35     clothes. You can walk down my path in daylight and

1      not care who sees you. When you knock on my door, I

2      will open it and cry, "Welcome!" and not worry who

3      might hear me.

4      SLAVE: *(Stands.)* You really think that will happen?

5      FARMER: It will happen. It *must* happen. It may take

6      longer than we'd like, and we may end up fighting

7      our brothers in order to achieve it, but it's the only

8      way for our country to survive.

9      SLAVE: You are brave to help me. Many won't, even if they

10      believe slavery is wrong. My brother told me they fear

11      retaliation. And many cling to the old ways, whether

12      those ways was right or not.

13      FARMER: You're the one with courage. I'm privileged to

14      help you on your path to freedom.

15      SLAVE: I hope my mam and pap will run away again.

16      Maybe next time they'll make it.

17      FARMER: Sleep now, my friend. I'll wake you in an hour so

18      you have time to wash and change clothes before you

19      leave.

20      SLAVE: I know not how to thank you.

21      FARMER: Someday, after you are free, you will have an

22      opportunity to help someone who needs assistance.

23      When you give that help, think of me. *(FARMER offers*

24      *his hand; SLAVE shakes it.)*

25      SLAVE: I'll be back when I can come in daylight, to collect

26      the clothes my mam made me.

27      FARMER: And I will welcome you.

# 24. Too Tall, Too Short

**Cast:** TALL person and SHORT person
**Setting:** No special set required.
**Props:** None

1  TALL: I'm the tallest person in my class. Every year when we
2      get a class picture taken, I have to stand in the back
3      row. All through elementary school when we lined up
4      to go anywhere, I was the last kid in line.
5  SHORT: I'm the shortest kid in my whole school. People
6      who don't know me sometimes think I'm in third
7      grade.
8  TALL: Every chance I get I drink coffee, because Grandma
9      says coffee will stunt my growth. So far it hasn't
10     worked.
11  SHORT: I take a multivitamin pill every day. I avoid sugar
12     and eat lots of salads. I even eat cauliflower, which is
13     my least favorite food in the whole world. Maybe if I get
14     healthy enough, I'll have a growth spurt.
15  TALL: I should have started drinking coffee when I was in
16     kindergarten. My parents should have filled my baby
17     bottles with coffee instead of milk. Even if I stunt my
18     growth now, it's too late.
19  SHORT: I can't reach the top shelves in any of the grocery
20     stores. Yesterday I had to ask a stranger to hand me a
21     box of cat litter.
22  TALL: People ask me, "How's the weather up there?" Ha, ha.
23     Very funny. I've only heard that about six hundred
24     times.
25  SHORT: I am so sick of being called Shrimp or Shorty.
26  TALL: They call me Giraffe or Bean Pole and think it's the
27     cleverest joke in the universe. I try to be a good sport,
28     but it isn't easy.
29  SHORT: Why is it considered impolite to comment on

1       another person's weight, but it's OK to discuss their
2       height? Both are personal matters.
3    TALL: If I weighed too much, I could diet. If I was too thin,
4       I could eat more. But I can't do anything about how
5       tall I am, so why do people have to make a big deal of
6       it?
7    SHORT: I know! It isn't fair that people make fun of
8       something we can't control.
9    TALL: I'm always bumping my head on low entryways.
10   SHORT: When I go to a movie, I can never see over the
11      person in front of me.
12   TALL: A regular twin bed is too short for me. I have to keep
13      my knees bent, and I wake up in the morning all stiff.
14   SHORT: Every time I buy a pair of pants, I have to hem
15      them.
16   TALL: Don't get me started on buying clothes. I have to get
17      the "Tall" size, and it always costs about five dollars
18      more than the same thing in a regular size.
19   SHORT: I love to play sports, but being short is a handicap
20      in everything except gymnastics. I tried doing
21      gymnastics, but I get scared on the balance beam.
22   TALL: My dad says maybe I can be a professional
23      basketball or volleyball player. Then my height would
24      be an advantage. The trouble is ... I'm not that good at
25      sports. I'm tall, but I'm not fast, and I have terrible
26      coordination.
27   SHORT: I can't even reach some of the kitchen cupboards
28      in my own house. And forget about trying to take a
29      sweater off the shelf in my bedroom closet.
30   TALL: If a genie came along and granted me one wish, I
31      would wish to be six inches shorter.
32   SHORT: If I could have one wish granted, I'd wish to be six
33      inches taller.
34   TALL: I wonder what other kids would wish for, kids who
35      are an average height.

1   SHORT: I know one kid who would wish for different
2        blood. He goes to my cousin's school, and he has a
3        rare blood disease. The people in his school and
4        community hold fundraisers to help pay for his
5        medical expenses. My cousin's been working at car
6        washes and bake sales to raise money.
7   TALL: A rare blood disease makes being too tall or too
8        short seem trivial, doesn't it?
9   SHORT: Even with treatment, the outlook is not good for
10       him. He'd probably trade places with me in a
11       heartbeat, even if it meant he would never be more
12       than five feet tall.
13   TALL: He'd trade with me too, even if he got called Giraffe
14       for the rest of his life.
15   SHORT: I think I'll change my wish and ask the magic
16       genie to grant good health to all kids everywhere, no
17       matter how short they are.
18   TALL: Or how tall.

# 25. Surviving the Ferris Wheel

**Cast:** RORY and AVERY

**Setting:** A large waterfront Ferris wheel. Two chairs serve as seats.

1 **Props:** None

2

3 *(As scene opens, the chairs are Center Stage and side by*
4 *side, facing the audience. RORY and AVERY stand behind*
5 *them.)*
6 **RORY:** *(Looking up)* **Wow! That is the tallest Ferris wheel I've**
7 **ever seen. Five stories high!**
8 **AVERY: I didn't expect it to be quite so big. Are you sure it's**
9 **safe? Those glass buckets look kind of flimsy.**
10 **RORY: This is going to be so cool. What a view we'll have!**
11 **We'll soar above those buildings and out over the water.**
12 **AVERY: Heights make me dizzy. I can't stand by the window**
13 **in a tall building.** *(Starts to turn away.)* **Maybe we can get**
14 **our money back.**
15 **RORY:** *(Grabs AVERY's arm and pulls him/her back.)* **We can't**
16 **leave now. It's almost our turn.**
17 **AVERY: You go without me. I'll wave at you.**
18 **RORY: Once we get on, you're going to love it.**
19 **AVERY:** *(Points up.)* **See how those buckets are swinging**
20 **back and forth?**
21 **RORY: Cool!**
22 **AVERY: Not cool! Terrifying! This whole idea was a horrible**
23 **mistake.**
24 **RORY: I think we're going to have a bucket all to ourselves.**
25 *(Both walk toward seats.)*
26 **AVERY: Good. If I throw up, I won't humiliate myself with**
27 **anyone but you.**
28 **RORY: Hop in! Do you want to face forward or backward?**
29 **AVERY: It doesn't matter. My eyes will be closed anyway.**

1    *(RORY and AVERY sit down.)*

2  **RORY:** Here we go!

3  **AVERY:** What was I thinking? I could have gone to a movie.

4       I could have stayed home and played solitaire. But

5       no, I had to let you talk me into riding the world's

6       tallest Ferris wheel.

7  **RORY:** Whoa! *(Rocks forward and back.)* Feel that? It really

8       sways when they stop for the next bucket to fill.

9  **AVERY:** I will not get off this alive. I can see the headline

10       now: "Student Dies of Fright on Ferris Wheel."

11  **RORY:** Are you OK? You look a little pale.

12  **AVERY:** *(Grips the seat of the chair.)* There's no seatbelt, no

13       guard rail, nothing to hold on to. I have to dig my

14       fingernails into the seat and brace my feet to keep

15       from falling out. No, I am *not* OK!

16  **RORY:** You can't fall out. These buckets are as sturdy as a

17       piece of plywood. Look. *(Starts to push against the side.)*

18  **AVERY:** Don't demonstrate! I'll pretend to believe you!

19  **RORY:** Just relax. Enjoy the view. If you look straight

20       down, you can see the top of that seafood restaurant.

21  **AVERY:** I would rather be *in* the seafood restaurant.

22       Instead of spending twelve bucks on this oversize

23       wheel, we could be eating fish and chips!

24  **RORY:** You can eat those any time. How many chances do

25       you get to experience this?

26  **AVERY:** One too many.

27  **RORY:** Oh, look! We're higher than that little floatplane!

28  **AVERY:** *(Eyes closed)* If I survive this, I will never be mean

29       to my brother again. I will do the dishes without

30       being asked. I will be kind to animals and patient

31       with that old woman who fumbles for her change at

32       the grocery store.

33  **RORY:** *(Turns from side to side, looking down.)* It's like

34       flying. It's *better* than flying! Whoosh! Up, up, up, up,

35       and now dowwwwn. Open your eyes — we're almost

1      down to the platform again.
2   AVERY: Sit still! Every time you lean toward the window,
3      you make the bucket jiggle.
4   RORY: I wonder how many times we'll go around.
5   AVERY: Once. Please, please only go around once.
6   RORY: For the price of the tickets, they should take us up
7      and around for at least half an hour. Maybe ten times.
8   AVERY: Oh!
9   RORY: Maybe even more. Yeah! Here we go, up again!
10  AVERY: The tickets should come with a warning: "This
11     ride may cause nausea, terror, heart attack, or
12     death."
13  RORY: You are perfectly safe.
14  AVERY: What's that sound? That whooshing noise?
15  RORY: I think the wind is picking up.
16  AVERY: Oh, great. Next the lightning will start.
17  RORY: Up and down, around and around.
18  AVERY: *(Opens eyes to glare at RORY.)* If you say one more
19     word, I will take great pleasure in barfing on your
20     shoes.
21  RORY: Oh, no. We're slowing down already. We've only
22     been around twice, and they're stopping and putting
23     new people on.
24  AVERY: *(Eyes closed again)* Maybe I can make it. If the
25     bucket doesn't move too much when we stop, I might
26     actually keep my dinner down.
27  RORY: Rats. They're unloading the one ahead of us. We'll
28     be next.
29  AVERY: Yes. Yes!
30  RORY: The eagle has landed. You can open your eyes.
31  AVERY: *(Opens eyes and lets go of chair, raising arms in*
32     *victory.)* I have survived the worst twenty minutes of
33     my life! *(RORY and AVERY stand and step away from*
34     *the chairs.)*
35  RORY: That was awesome! Do you want to go again?

# 26. Wedding Plans

**Characters:** JANE and LAURIE
**Setting:** No special set required.
**Props:** Each girl carries a purse. Laurie has a cell phone.

1  *(As scene opens, JANE and LAURIE enter from opposite*
2  *sides of stage and meet in the middle.)*
3  LAURIE: Jane! Hi!
4  JANE: Hey, Laurie! I haven't seen you since we graduated.
5      How are you? What are you doing these days?
6  LAURIE: I'm getting married!
7  JANE: So am I! When's your wedding?
8  LAURIE: June thirtieth. When's yours?
9  JANE: July second. I assume you're marrying Richard?
10 LAURIE: Richard and I broke up. I met Steve about a week
11      later through an online dating service.
12 JANE: That's a surprise! Didn't you and Richard date all
13      through high school?
14 LAURIE: I got tired of Richard. Who are you marrying?
15 JANE: His name is Jackson. I met him at the U when he was
16      the professor's assistant for a psychology class that I
17      took. He's in grad school now.
18 LAURIE: Where's your wedding going to be?
19 JANE: We're having a small informal ceremony in my
20      grandparents' backyard. It'll be just our families and a
21      few close friends. And my dog Lucy's going to be the
22      ring bearer. We're tying the rings to her collar.
23 LAURIE: Mine is going to be in the main sanctuary at the
24      Cathedral on the Beach.
25 JANE: Wow! I went there once as part of a local tour. It's
26      huge.
27 LAURIE: I've always wanted a big wedding. We've invited
28      over three hundred guests, so we need a big space.
29      Today I'm meeting with two of my bridesmaids to tie

1     the bows.

2  JANE: Bows?

3  LAURIE: My colors are blue and silver, so we're using wide
4     blue and silver ribbon to make these huge bows.
5     There'll be one on the end of every pew, all the way
6     down the center aisle. The same ribbons will
7     decorate all the baskets of flowers that we're having
8     at the front of the sanctuary. White roses and blue
9     delphinium.

10  JANE: It sounds lovely.

11  LAURIE: What kind of flowers are you having?

12  JANE: Whatever is in bloom in Grandpa's garden that day.
13     He grows snapdragons, zinnias, daisies, geraniums,
14     and lots of others. I'm sure it will be colorful. He told
15     me he fertilized everything a month in advance.

16  LAURIE: What about your bouquet?

17  JANE: Just before the ceremony, we'll cut a few fresh
18     flowers for me to carry. We want to keep the costs
19     down because we need the money for next year's
20     tuition.

21  LAURIE: You're still at the U?

22  JANE: Yes. I'm going to summer school too, although I'm
23     not taking a full course load this summer because I'm
24     working part time in the University library.

25  LAURIE: I don't see how you have time for school and a
26     job. I dropped out of school as soon as I got engaged,
27     and I have spent every day this summer working on
28     the wedding. You can't imagine how long it took to
29     make three hundred little bags and fill them with
30     birdseed so each guest can have some to throw. And
31     the table decorations took weeks! I made these
32     adorable little bride and groom figures out of pipe
33     cleaners and then glued a picture of Steve's face on
34     all the grooms and a picture of my face on all the
35     brides. I still have to make little white dresses for the

1    brides. I finished the tiny tuxes for the grooms last
2    night.
3  JANE: Jackson and I took an interesting prenuptial class
4    at the U. It was only two nights, but it covered a lot of
5    topics and really got us talking. They give it every
6    Tuesday and Thursday. You guys might want to do it.
7  LAURIE: What kind of topics? Like what's the best music
8    for a wedding?
9  JANE: It was things like how you intend to handle your
10    finances. Separate accounts or all together? Who
11    balances the checkbook?
12  LAURIE: Oh, I never try to balance the checkbook. Steve
13    can handle that.
14  JANE: The class also had us discuss kids.
15  LAURIE: Kids! You aren't pregnant, are you?
16  JANE: No. This discussion was about if we want them.
17    How many? When? If it should turn out that we can't
18    have kids, how do we feel about adoption or being
19    childless? It was a good talk to have.
20  LAURIE: We can talk about stuff like that later on, after
21    the wedding. Right now I'm focused on making
22    bows, and we still have to choose between white cake
23    and chocolate cake. We've been buying both from
24    every bakery in town and sampling them. If we don't
25    decide soon, I won't fit into my wedding dress. What
26    kind of cake are you having?
27  JANE: My sister's going to bake applesauce cupcakes.
28    Jackson and I both love Amy's applesauce cupcakes
29    with caramel frosting.
30  LAURIE: That doesn't sound very fancy. Wedding cakes
31    are usually at least three tiers with roses made of
32    icing.
33  JANE: Amy will arrange the cupcakes on a tiered plate and
34    put some fresh flowers in between them. It will be
35    great. It's going to be an informal event, so cupcakes

1     are perfect.

2     LAURIE: It will make the cake cutting part easy, that's for

3     sure. Do you mind if I ask you something personal?

4     JANE: Go ahead.

5     LAURIE: Where did you get your loan?

6     JANE: Loan?

7     LAURIE: To pay for all the wedding stuff. We need to

8     borrow twenty-seven thousand dollars.

9     JANE: We're paying cash for everything. Our only

10     expenses are the officiator's honorarium and our

11     rings. Oh, and a new collar for Lucy. Her old one was

12     all frayed.

13     LAURIE: What about your dress? My dress cost almost

14     three thousand dollars. It's gorgeous!

15     JANE: My mom and I sewed my dress. I wanted something

16     I could wear for other occasions, and we had fun

17     making it together. Jackson's wearing his suit.

18     LAURIE: Have you hired caterers? Are you serving food

19     afterwards?

20     JANE: My aunts and Jackson's two sisters are bringing

21     salads and casseroles for the lunch. Grandma already

22     had a big coffee urn, and our wedding gift from my

23     brother was a case of champagne, plus he'll be the

24     waiter. So we're all set.

25     LAURIE: We'll be making payments for years, but it will be

26     worth it. It's going to be a fabulous wedding.

27     JANE: It sounds like exactly what you want. Have you and

28     Steve talked about your lives after the wedding?

29     LAURIE: Of course! We're going to Oahu for our

30     honeymoon.

31     JANE: I mean long term. You really should look into that

32     pre-marriage class. Probably the best part for us was

33     when we talked about our families. One question

34     was, "Is there anyone in your family that you have not

35     told your fiancé about? If so, why?" It turned out

1     Jackson has an uncle who's in prison! He's so
2     ashamed of his uncle that he had never told me
3     about him. He said it was a big relief to get that out in
4     the open.
5   LAURIE: What did his uncle do that landed him in prison?
6   JANE: He was an alcoholic, and he was driving drunk. He
7     hit a car head-on, and the other driver died. Jackson's
8     uncle was convicted of second degree manslaughter.
9     He sobered up in prison and goes to an AA group and
10    swears he'll never touch a drink again.
11   LAURIE: I wonder if Steve has any family members that
12    he hasn't told me about. Probably not.
13   JANE: You should ask him.
14   LAURIE: You know, maybe I should. *(She takes out a cell*
15    *phone and makes the call.)* Hi, sweetie. I have a
16    question for you. *(Pause)* No, not about the cake. Do
17    you have any family members that you haven't told
18    me about? *(Pause. LAURIE's jaw drops.)* What?! How
19    old is she? Who's the mother? Do you ever see her? Do
20    you pay child support? *(Pause)* We need to talk, Steve.
21    Tonight. I know I said I was going to be busy making
22    bows, but this is more important. And don't plan
23    anything for next Tuesday and Thursday. There's a
24    class we have to take together. *(She hangs up looking*
25    *dazed.)*
26   JANE: Steve has a secret?
27   LAURIE: He has a daughter and an ex-wife. He wanted to
28    tell me but he was afraid if I knew this wasn't his first
29    wedding, it would spoil my excitement.
30   JANE: I need to get to work. It was nice to see you, Laurie.
31    Good luck with the wedding ... and I'm glad you're
32    going to take that class.
33   LAURIE: Me too. I wonder what else we need to talk about.

# 27. Now Hiring

**Cast:** EMPLOYER and APPLICANT
**Setting:** An office. Two chairs face each other over a desk.
**Props:** A clipboard and a pen for Employer
**Costumes:** Both players should dress in professional attire.

1  (As scene opens, EMPLOYER and APPLICANT sit facing
2  each other with the desk between them. EMPLOYER has
3  clipboard ready to take notes.)
4  EMPLOYER: I want to start off by thanking you for coming
5  in today. Can you tell me a little bit about yourself?
6  APPLICANT: Certainly, and thank you for having me. Where
7  to begin? Let's see. I was born eighteen years and three
8  weeks ago, at 12:34 a.m. on February second. It was in
9  a car going seventy miles per hour. My dad was
10  speeding to the hospital, because my mom started
11  hollering in the middle of dinner that she was about to
12  have the baby, and my dad didn't know what to do. So
13  my whole family hopped in the car and we were
14  speeding down Highway 99 when —
15  EMPLOYER: (Clears throat.) I'm sorry to interrupt, but
16  would you mind starting a bit more recently than that?
17  APPLICANT: Sure thing! How about high school?
18  EMPLOYER: That'd be great. Go ahead.
19  APPLICANT: High school was when I really started
20  developing my unique skill set. I beat my brother's
21  high score on Dance Dance Revolution when I was still
22  in ninth grade! My brother is three years older than I
23  am, by the way. I also started competing in local Rock-
24  Paper-Scissors tournaments. I've been to Rock-Paper-
25  Scissors regionals twice since I started, and I'm
26  training for nationals this year.
27  EMPLOYER: That's interesting. You would certainly bring
28  diversity to our staff. Have you been involved in any

1     more organized extracurricular activities? Held any
2     leadership positions?
3 APPLICANT: Definitely. I co-founded the SAHA club at my
4     school.
5 EMPLOYER: I've never heard of that. What does SAHA
6     stand for?
7 APPLICANT: Student Anti-Homework Alliance. It's a
8     national movement. We're a very active chapter.
9 EMPLOYER: I see. Anything else?
10 APPLICANT: I'm the teacher's assistant for our school's
11     detention program.
12 EMPLOYER: That seems like a group that must take some
13     skillful leadership. Were you nominated for that
14     position?
15 APPLICANT: In a manner of speaking. I had been in
16     detention so often that I started coming out of habit.
17     Mr. Farrington suggested to the principal that they
18     make me his assistant so he didn't have to keep
19     kicking me out when I wasn't in trouble.
20 EMPLOYER: Let's move on to the questions I have for you.
21 APPLICANT: Sounds good.
22 EMPLOYER: Question One: Honesty and integrity are
23     very important to our company. Can you give me an
24     example of a time that you maintained your honesty
25     in the face of opposition?
26 APPLICANT: One time a girl in our class wore this weird
27     rainbow tunic to school. It was hideous. Everyone
28     else kept smiling and saying it looked good on her,
29     even though we all knew it didn't. I was the only one
30     willing to stand up and tell her that her tunic was
31     horrible.
32 EMPLOYER: OK. Next question: Almost everything we
33     accomplish here is done in small teams assigned to a
34     particular task. Have you ever worked effectively as a
35     part of a team?

1   APPLICANT: Of course! This one time I was playing a huge
2          game of capture the flag. I was on the green team. We
3          were amazing! We brought Super Soakers from home
4          and ran straight through enemy territory to find the
5          flag. No one even tried to tag us.
6   EMPLOYER: Well, that does sound like you were thinking
7          outside the box. How about question three: Tell me
8          about a time you were faced with a stressful
9          situation, and explain how you handled it.
10  APPLICANT: A few weeks back I had two essays due
11         Friday, and I left them until Thursday night. I was
12         freaking out, so I went to QFC and bought two pints
13         of Ben & Jerry's. While I took a study break to eat
14         them, I remembered advice I'd once received: "Don't
15         sweat the small stuff."
16  EMPLOYER: And that helped calm you down?
17  APPLICANT: Definitely. I resolved to do better next time
18         and went to bed.
19  EMPLOYER: And you didn't ... Well, never mind. How
20         about an example of a time that you were
21         resourceful?
22  APPLICANT: Oh, that's easy! On the way here I got pulled
23         over for speeding. Luckily I had a box of Krispy
24         Kreme donuts on the passenger seat that I was going
25         to bring to butter you up. I thought fast and gave
26         them to the officer in exchange for getting away with
27         a warning.
28  EMPLOYER: I don't mean to be rude, but that's not exactly
29         the answer we're looking for.
30  APPLICANT: I'm sorry, that wasn't the best example to
31         use. You're hungry for donuts now.
32  EMPLOYER: That's not what I meant, but let's move on. In
33         our line of work, you'll need to be capable of
34         demonstrating a high degree of professionalism in
35         interacting with our customers. What would you do if

1      a customer became frustrated with the service you
2      were providing?
3  APPLICANT: I would thank them for expressing their
4      frustrations and point them politely in the direction
5      of the door.
6  EMPLOYER: Please keep in mind that our customers are
7      the number-one reason for our success as a business.
8      Would you like to change your answer?
9  APPLICANT: I guess I would give them a free keychain on
10     their way out.
11  EMPLOYER: We don't provide complimentary keychains.
12  APPLICANT: A pen, then.
13  EMPLOYER: We don't provide complimentary pens
14     either. Is there anything else we should know about
15     you in considering you for hire?
16  APPLICANT: I'd be happy to be in charge of getting
17     company keychains made! I did that for SAHA — they
18     were a huge success.
19  EMPLOYER: That's good to know. I think we'll wrap
20     things up there. Do you have any questions for me?
21  APPLICANT: Do employees get paid time off? I'm kind of
22     prone to strep throat.
23  EMPLOYER: We decide that on a case-by-case basis.
24     Anything else?
25  APPLICANT: When should I call you back?
26  EMPLOYER: Please don't trouble yourself. We'll call you.
27  APPLICANT: Are you sure?
28  EMPLOYER: Very sure.
29  APPLICANT: OK. *(Stands up and starts for the door.)* Thank
30     you for your time!
31  EMPLOYER: *(Smiles and waves.)* Thank you so much for
32     coming in.

# 28. Dear Crabby

**Cast:** CRABBY, an advice columnist, and STENO, Crabby's assistant

**Setting:** Crabby's office. One small table is Center Stage.

**Props:** A stack of letters to Crabby are on the table. Steno has a tablet and pen to pretend to write down Crabby's answers.

1 CRABBY: I hope we have some interesting letters today. I'm
2     tired of the same old problems. I never knew so many
3     kids needed a cure for acne or help getting a date for
4     the prom.
5 STENO: When you write an advice column for teens, you're
6     bound to hear from people who worry about acne and
7     prom dates.
8 CRABBY: Acne and prom dates. *(Sighs.)* OK, let's get started.
9 STENO: *(Picks up letter and pretends to read.)* "Dear Crabby:
10     Are you aware that it is more than a year since you gave
11     your assistant a pay raise? I think someone who is
12     talented and hard-working should be rewarded with – "
13 CRABBY: Wait a minute! You're making that up. Come on,
14     read one of the real letters.
15 STENO: It was worth a try. *(Picks up the next letter and reads.)*
16     "Dear Crabby: My history teacher says we have to use at
17     least one original source for our term paper project. I
18     am writing about beer brewing, so I need to go to a
19     local brewery to interview the owner and try some
20     samples. The trouble is, I'm sixteen, and it isn't legal
21     for me to drink beer. I asked my mom to make an
22     appointment for me, but she won't do it. She says I
23     should pick a topic I know about. I can't tell her I
24     already know a lot about beer because she'd have a cow.
25     Will you call the brewery manager and offer to
26     mention his beer in your column in exchange for

1 giving me an interview? I've enclosed his name and
2 phone number. You would be helping to further my
3 education. Signed, Too Young."
4 **CRABBY:** *(STENO pretends to write this down.)* **Dear Too**
5 **Young: Are you crazy? There is no way I would**
6 **further your education at a brewery. Get real. I**
7 **happen to like my job and do not intend to get fired**
8 **for helping some underaged kid get sloshed. Choose**
9 **another topic for your term paper.**
10 **STENO:** *(Reads next letter.)* **"Dear Crabby: Your replies are**
11 **stupid. Why do you give dumb answers that don't**
12 **solve the problem? Signed, Disgusted."** *(STENO*
13 *hands the letter to CRABBY.)*
14 **CRABBY:** *(Looks at the letter and then speaks. STENO writes.)*
15 **Dear Disgusted: I recognize your handwriting. I take it**
16 **you didn't like my advice to forget about getting**
17 **revenge on your biology teacher by spray-painting his**
18 **car. As for this letter, my mother said if you can't say**
19 **anything nice, don't say anything at all. I suggest you do**
20 **what Mama said. Please don't write again.**
21 **STENO:** *(Picks up another letter and reads.)* **"Dear Crabby: I**
22 **am seventeen and I've been dating my boyfriend Joe**
23 **for three years. We'll both graduate from high school**
24 **soon. I'm going to a state college and have rented an**
25 **apartment near the campus. Joe wants to share the**
26 **apartment. He says he really loves me, and we'll be**
27 **able to get married sooner if he can save his money**
28 **instead of paying rent. One thing worries me. Joe**
29 **says if he moves in, my dog has to leave. I adopted**
30 **Maxie at the animal shelter when I was six. She is**
31 **well-behaved, friendly, and sleeps on my bed every**
32 **night. Joe says he won't share our home with a dog.**
33 **What should I do? Signed, Dog Lover."**
34 **CRABBY: Well, this one is easy.** *(STENO writes.)* **Dear Dog**
35 **Lover: You don't need a boyfriend who hates dogs**

1    and expects you to pay his rent. Keep Maxie and

2    dump Joe.

3  STENO: *(Reads next letter.)* "Dear Crabby: My best friend has

4    become a vegan. That would be OK, except now she

5    wants everyone in the world to quit eating meat and

6    dairy products. We always sit together in the school

7    cafeteria, but every time I have a ham sandwich or a

8    cheeseburger, she starts quoting statistics about how

9    the meat industry is one of the most significant

10    contributors to serious environmental problems. She

11    says that refusing to eat meat or dairy is the single most

12    effective thing you can do to reduce your carbon

13    footprint. I want to be a good citizen and help the earth,

14    but do I really have to give up cheeseburgers? Signed,

15    Bacon Lover."

16  CRABBY: *(STENO writes.)* Dear Bacon Lover: According to

17    the Environmental Protection Agency, runoff from

18    factory farms pollutes our waterways more than all

19    other sources combined. Your friend is right, but

20    trying to bully her classmates into eating her way is

21    wrong. Sit with someone else at lunch, but also learn

22    how your food is supplied. It takes more than 2,400

23    gallons of water to produce one pound of meat, but

24    only 25 gallons of water to grow one pound of wheat.

25  STENO: No kidding? I thought vegetarians and vegans cut

26    out meat or dairy for humane reasons, not to help the

27    environment. I mean, we all know about the animal

28    cruelty, but we choose to ignore it.

29  CRABBY: Not all of us do.

30  STENO: Are you saying you don't eat meat?

31  CRABBY: That's right.

32  STENO: I didn't know that. I didn't know about the

33    pollution, either.

34  CRABBY: Keep reading "Dear Crabby" and you'll learn a

35    lot. We aim to educate, except when it comes to under-

1     age beer drinkers.

2     STENO: *(Reading another letter)* "Dear Crabby: Are you still

3          alive? If you are, please answer my letter right away.

4          If you have already died, have someone close to you

5          write back because I really, really need advice.

6          Signed, Desperate."

7     CRABBY: *(STENO writes.)* Dear Desperate: I'm alive, but

8          it's hard to give advice when you never told me what

9          the problem is. However, I have figured it out. You

10         are in need of a brain transplant. I'm sorry that I

11         can't help you.

12    STENO: *(Reading another letter)* "Dear Crabby: I have a

13         problem with my grandma. She steals things. When

14         we go grocery shopping, she slips small items into

15         her coat pockets. I've seen her take cans of tuna,

16         candy bars, and a bottle of vitamins. Yesterday I saw

17         her put a carton of yogurt in her purse. When we

18         were waiting in the checkout line I said, "Grandma,

19         don't forget the yogurt that's in your purse." She got

20         really angry and told me to be quiet. When we got out

21         to the car, she said the big stores make a huge profit

22         while senior citizens pinch pennies. She told me the

23         store would never notice a carton of yogurt. That is

24         probably true, but I still think it's wrong to take

25         something without paying for it. What do you think?

26         Signed: Honest Olivia."

27    CRABBY: Dear Honest Olivia: If the store's security guard

28         catches your grandma shoplifting, she could be

29         arrested. Next time, she should be more careful! Your

30         job is to make sure Granny has a good lawyer.

31    STENO: I don't think we can publish that.

32    CRABBY: Maybe not. I'm running out of good advice.

33    STENO: OK. Last letter for today. *(Reads.)* "Dear Crabby:

34         My twin sister and I are adopted. A year ago we

35         decided we wanted to know who our birth parents

1     are. Mom and Dad are wonderful parents, so it isn't
2     like we wanted to escape or anything. We were just
3     curious. We decided to search secretly so we didn't
4     hurt Mom and Dad's feelings. After six months of
5     hitting dead ends, my sister gave up and said she
6     really didn't care if she ever found out or not. I kept
7     searching, and last week I found my birth mother. I
8     was shocked to learn that she is an alcoholic and drug
9     addict who lives on the streets. I saw a photo of her,
10     but I have not gone to the town where she lives. I can't
11     imagine anything good coming from a meeting with
12     her. I don't know if I should tell my sister what I
13     found out or if I should forget it. What should I do?
14     Signed, Sorry I Searched."
15 CRABBY: *(STENO writes.)* Dear Sorry: My criteria for giving
16     out information is to ask three questions: Will it help
17     someone if you tell? Will it make the person you tell
18     happier? Will it serve some useful purpose? I think you
19     would have to answer no to all three of those questions,
20     so my advice is to keep quiet about what you learned. If
21     your sister decides she wants to search again in the
22     future, you can tell her then what you found out.
23     Meanwhile, this would be a good time to tell your
24     adoptive parents how much you love them.
25 STENO: That's all the letters for today.
26 CRABBY: What a pleasant surprise! There wasn't a single
27     plea for an acne cure, and no problems with a prom
28     date.
29 STENO: There were, actually. I tossed those out before you
30     got here so you wouldn't have to deal with them.
31 CRABBY: You screened the letters?
32 STENO: There were four acnes and six prom date
33     problems.
34 CRABBY: You are the best assistant I've ever had! You
35     deserve a raise.

# 29. The World's Finest Cutlery

**Cast:** SALESPERSON and CUSTOMER

**Setting:** Customer's home. A table and two chairs are Center Stage.

**Props:** Three forks, three knives, and three spoons, all wrapped in a cloth and carried in by Salesperson. Sheet of paper and pen are carried by Salesperson with the cutlery.

1   *(As scene opens, SALESPERSON enters and pretends to*
2   *knock on a door. CUSTOMER enters from opposite side of*
3   *stage and pantomimes peering out peephole and opening*
4   *door.)*
5   **SALESPERSON:** Good morning, Mrs. Semple!
6   **CUSTOMER:** Hello, Logan. Come on in.
7   **SALESPERSON:** Thank you for letting me do this demo. It
8       really helps me out a lot.
9   **CUSTOMER:** I'm glad to hear that, honey. Now, you're sure
10      you'll get paid just for showing me the product? As I
11      told you on the phone, I'm not in the market for
12      cutlery.
13  **SALESPERSON:** Absolutely, Mrs. Semple. Our program
14      rewards sales reps just for getting our company name
15      out there. I'm paid by the demo, unless I make more in
16      commissions. It's as easy as that.
17  **CUSTOMER:** Well, that's good news. Won't you have a seat?
18  **SALESPERSON:** Thank you. *(Sits at table.)*
19  **CUSTOMER:** *(Sits opposite SALESPERSON.)* How's your
20      mother?
21  **SALESPERSON:** She's doing well. She and my dad are on
22      vacation this week.
23  **CUSTOMER:** That sounds wonderful.
24  **SALESPERSON:** Shall we get started?

1 CUSTOMER: Yes, I'm ready. Do you need anything from
2     me?
3 SALESPERSON: Nope! Nothing at all, except for you to
4     make yourself comfortable.
5 CUSTOMER: I'm ready when you are. What is it that you're
6     showing me?
7 SALESPERSON: *(Stands and begins unrolling cloth. Sets*
8     *cutlery out carefully in a row and begins to polish each*
9     *piece with the cloth in turn.)* Mrs. Semple, you're in for
10     a treat. Today I'm going to show you the finest cutlery
11     in the world.
12 CUSTOMER: Really? I didn't know the brand of cutlery
13     made much of a difference. I've never used a fork or
14     spoon that didn't do the same basic job.
15 SALESPERSON: In that case, you've been missing out.
16 CUSTOMER: I have?
17 SALESPERSON: Don't tell me you've never heard of
18     Cutler's Cutlery!
19 CUSTOMER: I'm afraid I haven't.
20 SALESPERSON: I'm surprised! Cutler's is internationally
21     recognized as the world's best.
22 CUSTOMER: What makes it so much better than other
23     brands? My forks have tines. My spoons hold oatmeal
24     and yogurt. What more do I need from them?
25 SALESPERSON: If that's all you're asking of your spoons
26     and forks, you've been living a deprived life. Let me
27     start you off with our soup spoon.
28 CUSTOMER: I'm afraid I don't need soup spoons. I've
29     simply never liked soup.
30 SALESPERSON: Never liked soup? But Mrs. Semple, have
31     you ever stopped to ask yourself why you don't like
32     soup?
33 CUSTOMER: It's because of the flavor, I suppose.
34 SALESPERSON: Not at all! The secret to perfect soup is in
35     the spoon.

1   CUSTOMER: It is? How so?

2   SALESPERSON: Would you drink wine from an egg cup?

3   CUSTOMER: No, I wouldn't.

4   SALESPERSON: And why not? Because it's the wrong
5       shape, of course! The perfect spherical shape of this
6       soup spoon ensures that not a single nuance of flavor
7       will escape your senses.

8   CUSTOMER: But what if they're nuances of a flavor I
9       don't like in the first place?

10  SALESPERSON: I assure you that you don't enjoy soup
11      because you haven't tasted it as it's meant to be
12      enjoyed – from a perfectly shaped spoon.

13  CUSTOMER: Let's table the soup discussion. What other
14      spoons do you have?

15  SALESPERSON: I'm glad you asked. Next up is our cereal
16      spoon. What sets our cereal spoon apart is its unique
17      temperature-regulating technology that keeps your
18      hot cereal hot and cold cereal cold the entire way
19      from the bowl to your mouth.

20  CUSTOMER: Can temperature really change much in that
21      transition?

22  SALESPERSON: Of course it can! Do you know the
23      temperature range considered by the Food and Drug
24      Administration to be the food danger zone?

25  CUSTOMER: I used to know this.

26  SALESPERSON: It's between forty-one and one-thirty-five
27      degrees Fahrenheit. And what separates the safe
28      food temperature of forty point nine nine nine
29      degrees from the unsafe food temperature of forty-
30      one? An infinitesimal fraction of a degree
31      Fahrenheit!

32  CUSTOMER: All right, I see where you're going.

33  SALESPERSON: Cutler's Cutlery makes your safety our
34      number-one priority. No one wants to eat unsafe
35      cereal.

1  CUSTOMER: Is that a third spoon?

2  SALESPERSON: It certainly is. Intrigued?

3  CUSTOMER: Yes, I'm intrigued as to why I need three

4      spoons in one table setting.

5  SALESPERSON: This third spoon is my personal favorite

6      because it's for the dessert course. It's a multitalented

7      spoon. It's designed with a fine edge and streamlined

8      shape for cutting through the crisp crust of crème

9      brûlée as easily as it slices into a scoop of hard-packed

10     ice cream. Yes ma'am, this spoon is made for

11     everything from sundaes to burnt cream to custard!

12 CUSTOMER: I hate to say it, but I'm on a diet. A dessert-

13     specific spoon is the last temptation I need lying

14     around the house. And just out of curiosity, my cereal

15     spoon won't work for dessert because ...

16 SALESPERSON: *(Holds two spoons up.)* Look more closely.

17     See the razor-fine edge on the dessert spoon as

18     compared with the cereal spoon? A cereal spoon just

19     won't slice into all your favorite creamy confections

20     with the same finesse.

21  CUSTOMER: I'm feeling overwhelmed by the spoons, and

22     you're making me hungry for ice cream. Let's skip

23     ahead to the forks. I see you have three of those too.

24 SALESPERSON: Of course we do! We wouldn't want to let

25     the spoons have all the fun!

26 CUSTOMER: There's a salad fork, I presume?

27 SALESPERSON: Definitely. That's this one right here. See

28     its toothpick-sharp points and the fishhook shape of

29     the middle tines? No vitamin-packed spinach leaf is

30     ever going to escape you again. Over the course of a

31     lifetime, the average American is eluded by four to

32     five hundred leaves of spinach on any number of

33     dinner plates. You know, the leaves that become

34     glued to the plate by salad dressing and you just can't

35     get them in a civilized manner? Each one of those

1     leaves contains cancer-combating antioxidants. Over

2     the course of a lifetime, by letting you get every last

3     spinach leaf, this fork can be the difference between

4     lifelong good health and cancer.

5  CUSTOMER: Are those statistics accurate? I had no idea

6     the effect of a lost spinach leaf here and there could

7     add up to such disastrous consequences. I have a

8     family history of cancer, you know.

9  SALESPERSON: I had no idea! Are you taking the proper

10    precautions?

11  CUSTOMER: Well, I do regular screenings, and I do my

12    very best to eat healthy. But —

13  SALESPERSON: But you never thought twice about the

14    role your fork could play in protecting you from

15    disease. When you get right down to it, this fork

16    could be the difference between life and death.

17  CUSTOMER: May I? *(Reaches for fork.)*

18  SALESPERSON: Of course! And see how nicely it pairs

19    with our other forks? Here we have our steak fork

20    with adjustable tines. This is a Cutler's specialty.

21    Everyone prefers different-sized bites of steak. You

22    wouldn't expect a three-hundred pound dad to share

23    a steak fork with his five-year-old daughter, would

24    you?

25  CUSTOMER: Of course not. That's just insensitive.

26  SALESPERSON: Exactly! But here you have the solution to

27    that problem: a fork that adjusts to fit the needs of

28    everyone around the table.

29  CUSTOMER: And this fork? It's miniscule! What can it

30    possibly do?

31  SALESPERSON: The better question would be, what can't

32    it do? This little sucker is ready and willing to stab

33    anything that comes in your path at a cocktail bar:

34    olives, mini-onions, peanuts or pretzels. No one likes

35    to touch those snacks with their hands. Am I right?

1   CUSTOMER: Now that you mention it, that sounds terribly
2      germy. Maybe I need one of these little guys.
3   SALESPERSON: Now, don't jump the gun, Mrs. Semple.
4      You still haven't seen the knives. You'll get the best
5      deal by far on our cutlery if you buy our complete
6      cutlery set.
7   CUSTOMER: Is that right? And just how much would the
8      full shebang set me back?
9   SALESPERSON: I'll get there in a minute. First, behold the
10   finest butter knife in America: the Electric Butter Eel!
11  CUSTOMER: I've never heard of any brand name that
12     sounds more unappetizing! Why would anyone name
13     their knife an Electric Butter Eel?
14  SALESPERSON: Because it really is electric! Riddle me
15     this, Mrs. Semple: What's the most frustrating
16     kitchen hitch you run into on a regular basis?
17  CUSTOMER: When my husband leaves his dirty dishes in
18     the sink.
19  SALESPERSON: What about when you forget to set the
20     butter out to thaw before you need it? You're groggy
21     on Monday morning, you go to have a nice waffle
22     with a pat of melty butter and drizzle of maple syrup,
23     and instead you get a fat buttery ice cube in the
24     middle of your toasted waffle. It cools the whole
25     thing down instantly!
26  CUSTOMER: It is annoying when that happens. I get tired
27     of having to let butter thaw before I bake, too. Maybe
28     that *is* my biggest kitchen pet peeve.
29  SALESPERSON: Of course it is! It's universal. Check this
30     out: *(Holding up a knife)* flip this convenient,
31     ergonomic switch hidden discreetly at the base of the
32     knife, and the Electric Butter Eel slides straight
33     through even the most Antarctic butter.
34  CUSTOMER: All right, Logan. I have to admit you caught
35     me. That butter knife is truly remarkable. How much

1     does it cost?

2     SALESPERSON: Mrs. Semple, I couldn't let you buy just

3     one lonely knife. What a rip-off! The price point

4     drops breathtakingly when you buy the full set of

5     Cutler's Cutlery.

6     CUSTOMER: Fine, just go ahead and tell me. What does

7     the set run for?

8     SALESPERSON: Because you're one of my oldest

9     neighbors and family friends, I can offer you a price

10    you can't find anywhere on store shelves.

11    CUSTOMER: How much?

12    SALESPERSON: Five hundred.

13    CUSTOMER: Five hundred ... dollars?

14    SALESPERSON: Yes, ma'am.

15    CUSTOMER: For a set of how many place settings?

16    SALESPERSON: One place setting.

17    CUSTOMER: You must be joking!

18    SALESPERSON: Think about it, Mrs. Semple. I'm offering

19    you a set of silverware that has the power to open you

20    up to a whole new food group, *(Holding up soup*

21    *spoon)* protect your family from food poisoning,

22    *(Holding up cereal spoon)* make eating dessert easy on

23    your arm, *(Holding up dessert spoon)* let you declare

24    victory once and for all over modern humans' age-

25    old kitchen nemesis, frozen butter, *(Holding up*

26    *butter knife)* and very probably keep your family out

27    of the deathly jaws of that hideous monster, cancer,

28    *(Holding up salad fork)* and so much more that we

29    haven't even discussed! Now, tell me that isn't worth

30    five hundred dollars of the money that's sitting in

31    your bank account collecting cobwebs and dust right

32    this moment.

33    CUSTOMER: I would need four sets! For Darby and the

34    kids and me.

35    SALESPERSON: I can do that for you. Have I mentioned

1      our layaway plan or told you about our lifetime

2      guarantee?

3 CUSTOMER: Darby would kill me with his own two hands

4      if he found out I spent two thousand dollars on forks

5      and knives.

6 SALESPERSON: The finest forks and knives money can

7      buy. What he ought to do is thank you on bended

8      knee. What do you say? Shall I fill out your order form

9      for you?

10 CUSTOMER: *(Long pause as CUSTOMER looks longingly*

11      *over the cutlery spread out before her.)* **Oh, all right. Do**

12      **it quickly! Darby will be up from his nap any minute.**

13 SALESPERSON: Of course! I've got the form pre-drawn up

14      for just these sorts of sales. *(Sets paper and a pen in*

15      *front of CUSTOMER.)* If you would, check the box that

16      best matches your preferred payment plan, and let

17      me get your credit card here and your John Hancock

18      right down here. I'll leave you with my cutlery set

19      right now and pick another three up for you from the

20      office when I go in tomorrow morning.

21 CUSTOMER: *(Filling out form)* That's all there is to it?

22 SALESPERSON: That's all! Pretty easy, no?

23 CUSTOMER: That was almost too easy!

24 SALESPERSON: I really appreciate your business, Mrs.

25      Semple. You've been a great customer. I'll send the

26      rest of the cutlery over tomorrow. Give me a call if

27      you ever want to see our specialty catalogue, OK?

28      There's so much more to be had from Cutler's!

29 CUSTOMER: I'll do that! But first I'm going to show Darby

30      what I just got!

31 SALESPERSON: *(Shifts uncomfortably at this thought and*

32      *pushes cutlery set on its cloth toward CUSTOMER.)* I'll

33      let you get back to your afternoon. Thank you so

34      much for having me here! *(Stands and begins to leave.)*

35 CUSTOMER: *(Stands to walk SALESPERSON to the door.)*

1    OK, honey. Thank you for the cutlery! Be sure to tell
2    your mother hello, and best of luck with the job!
3    SALESPERSON: I'll see you later, Mrs. Semple. Enjoy the
4    world's finest cutlery!
5    CUSTOMER: Thank you, Logan! Buh-bye! *(Pantomimes*
6    *shutting door. Returns to table and admires cutlery*
7    *delightedly for a moment. Then she walks past table*
8    *toward opposite site of stage, yelling)* Darby, honey!
9    Wake up and come downstairs! I want to show you
10   what I just got us!

# 30. Forced to Go to Camp

**Cast:** SAM and MAX. Players should be of the same sex.

**Setting:** No special set required.

**Props:** None

1  SAM: I am *so* excited about going to camp. I wish we were
2      leaving today!
3  MAX: Not me. I'm only going because my parents won't let
4      me stay home. They think I need a role model and the
5      camp counselor will be it.
6  SAM: Seriously? A role model?
7  MAX: A role model. They also say I need to make friends.
8  SAM: They may be right about that.
9  MAX: I already have all the friends I want.
10 SAM: You do?
11 MAX: I do.
12 SAM: But do you have a close friend? A best friend?
13 MAX: I have two extremely close friends.
14 SAM: I never see you hanging out with anyone at school.
15 MAX: They don't go to this school.
16 SAM: What are their names?
17 MAX: Beanie and Grumpypants.
18 SAM: Beanie is your dog, and Grumpypants is your cat.
19 MAX: I know who they are! They're my best friends, and I'd
20     have lots more friends if the stupid Homeowner's
21     Association rules didn't limit each household to no
22     more than two animals.
23 SAM: Four-legged friends don't count.
24 MAX: Why not? They're better than most of the two-legged
25     variety.
26 SAM: Be serious.
27 MAX: I am perfectly serious. Has your dog ever spread
28     rumors about you behind your back?

1 SAM: Of course not.

2 MAX: Has your cat ever been nice to you only while she
3      runs for class secretary and then quits being nice as
4      soon as the election is over?

5 SAM: Well, no, but —

6 MAX: Does your dog ask to copy your homework because
7      he was too busy playing computer games to do it
8      himself?

9 SAM: Be reasonable.

10 MAX: Four-legged friends are just as important as the two-
11      legged kind. Maybe more important. They are
12      definitely less annoying.

13 SAM: Beanie and Grumpypants are great pets, but friends
14      are supposed to be human.

15 MAX: Says who? I don't need more humans mucking up
16      my life. I just want to be left alone, and instead I am
17      forced against my will to go to camp, and what's
18      more, I am expected to participate in all the
19      ridiculous camp activities. I have strict orders to
20      *enjoy myself.* As if!

21 SAM: The camp activities sound cool. We're going to learn
22      how to row boats. We'll put on skits. There'll be two
23      volleyball teams.

24 MAX: Bleh! I'd rather lie on my bunk and read or walk
25      along the lakeshore by myself. Better yet, I'd read
26      with Grumpypants beside me on my bunk and go for
27      a walk with Beanie.

28 SAM: You really are a loner.

29 MAX: What's wrong with that? I'm not hurting anyone.
30      I'm happy this way.

31 SAM: What you need is a Gregarious Pill to make you
32      outgoing and eager to meet the other campers. You
33      might even lead a sing-along around the campfire.

34 MAX: That would be my nightmare.

35 SAM: Alas, Gregarious Pills do not yet have FDA approval.

1 MAX: The leaders of Camp Jovial are stuck with me the
2       way I am.
3 SAM: Actually, I like you the way you are.
4 MAX: You do?
5 SAM: With most kids, I feel like I have to be all bubbly and
6       enthusiastic. I pretend to like everything they like.
7       With you, I can relax and be myself. You're
8       nonjudgmental. You accept me the way I am and
9       don't criticize.
10 MAX: Just like Beanie and Grumpypants.
11 SAM: So you really don't want to go to camp?
12 MAX: I really don't want to go. But I'm going whether I
13       want to or not.
14 SAM: I was hoping we could be camp roommates. There's
15       a place on the form where we can request who we
16       bunk with.
17 MAX: Are your parents making you do this? Did my mom
18       call your mom?
19 SAM: No.
20 MAX: Then why are you suggesting it?
21 SAM: I thought it would be fun to room together.
22 MAX: You honestly want to room with me?
23 SAM: Yes, if you want to room with me.
24 MAX: Well, sure. I'd like to room with you. Thanks! Camp
25       might not be so bad if you were my roommate.
26 SAM: Good. Then that's settled.
27 MAX: I thought one reason you want to go to camp is to
28       make new friends.
29 SAM: It is. I'll still meet new people, but it will be nice to
30       have someone I already know as my roommate. This
31       way there's no chance either of us will get stuck with
32       some kid who smuggles in cigarettes or who tells
33       endless bad jokes.
34 MAX: I still wish they allowed animals at Camp Jovial. It'd
35       be even more fun if Beanie were there with us.

1   SAM: What about Grumpypants? Don't you want to take
2      him along?
3   MAX: No way. He would hate going to camp even more
4      than I do. He's a loner. Like me.
5   SAM: Beanie would love all the people, though. He's
6      social. Like me.
7   MAX: Actually, Beanie is like both of us. He enjoys it when
8      people give him attention, but he's also content to
9      stay home and do nothing. He's happy no matter
10     what.
11  SAM: Which seems like a good way to live.
12  MAX: My dog can be my role model!
13  SAM: I think your parents are right. You *do* need to go to
14     camp.

# 31. Mourning a Noun Cements

**Cast:** HAYDEN and BLAKE

**Setting:** A high school newsroom. A desk and two chairs face the audience.

**Props:** Hayden and Blake each have a piece of paper from which they read.

1　*(As scene opens, HAYDEN and BLAKE sit side by side at*
2　*the desk, facing the audience. Their papers are on the*
3　*desk in front of them.)*
4　**HAYDEN: Good morning, and welcome to Pretown High**
5　**School's morning video announcements. I'm Hayden**
6　**Jorgensen ...**
7　**BLAKE: And I'm Blake Bendix, and we're here to make**
8　**Pretown High sound less boring than it actually is.**
9　**Take it away, Hayden.**
10　**HAYDEN: A lot's happened since last Monday, Blake.** *(Reads*
11　*from paper.)* **This week's feature story centers around**
12　**one very concerning statistic. According to a school-**
13　**wide study conducted by the Academic Resource**
14　**Center, student spelling scores have decreased by ten**
15　**percent since last year. That's statistically significant,**
16　**folks.**
17　**BLAKE: The sudden drop in spelling competence concerns**
18　**our administration because spelling ability has been**
19　**linked directly with success on state-administered**
20　**reading and writing exams. A student-teacher task**
21　**force has been assembled to further investigate the**
22　**issue and recommend a course of action.**
23　**HAYDEN: Serious stuff, Blake. Moving on to a report on**
24　**school health:** *(Reads)* **Our school nurse, Ms. Hasson,**
25　**says she's seen a record amount of patience with the**
26　**flu this season.** *(Looks at audience.)* **Now hold on a**

1     minute. You're not supposed to be patient with the
2     flu. You're supposed to drink tons of fluids and take
3     vitamin C.
4  BLAKE: That's what I do too. Thanks for bringing our
5     attention to the issue, Ms. Hasson. Don't let your flu
6     get the best of you. Take control and put the kibosh
7     on it.
8  HAYDEN: *(Reads.)* Speaking of the flu, I have an update on
9     everyone's favorite calculus teacher, Mr. Severson.
10    Mr. Severson has been recovering from the flu
11    himself, and the math department would like
12    everyone to know that "Get Well" carbs can be
13    dropped off at the door of Mr. Griffin's classroom
14    any time before the end of the school day tomorrow.
15  BLAKE: What kinds of carbs? Breads? Pasta? That's the
16    last thing I would want after a bad bout of the flu. My
17    mom always makes me a hearty beef stew.
18  HAYDEN: That sounds better to me too, but we're not the
19    ones recovering, Blake. Anyway, whatever baguettes
20    or rolls you've got lying around, Mr. Griffin will be
21    collecting them tomorrow afternoon and taking
22    them to Mr. Severson at his home. He is expected to
23    make a full recovery and be back to teaching sines
24    and cosines in no time.
25  BLAKE: *(Reads.)* In fact, we have a message here to pass
26    along from Severson himself: "You still have to turn
27    in your homework on time."
28  HAYDEN: Dang. Really?
29  BLAKE: Focus, Hayden.
30  HAYDEN: Right you are, Blake. *(Reads.)* On to sports. The
31    golf team is sponsoring an amateur golf tournament
32    to raise money for their trip to 3A regionals. Pars of
33    two should sign up with Coach Ruben by November
34    15th.
35  BLAKE: Pars of two! No one's going to sign up for that! I'm

1    like a par ten.

2    HAYDEN: Me too. Easily. Maybe Coach Ruben can do it. I

3    heard he was pro in his day.

4    BLAKE: Unreal. Anyway, thanks Hayden. *(Reads.)* Now,

5    we'll take a break for a massage from our dearly

6    beloved principal, Mr. Veith. *(Looks at HAYDEN.)* Wait,

7    Mr. Veith is going to give us a massage? That's weird.

8    I would think he would have more important things

9    to take care of. I could use a massage, but preferably

10    not from him.

11   HAYDEN: *(Stage whisper)* Blake, pay attention. It's

12    supposed to say "message."

13   BLAKE: Oh. *(To camera)* And now we'll take a break for a

14    message from our dearly beloved principal, Mr.

15    Veith. He has a public service announcement for us:

16    "No testing while driving."

17   HAYDEN: *(To BLAKE)* What kind of tests does he think

18    we're taking behind the wheel?

19   BLAKE: I don't know. Maybe he means he wants us to

20    boycott the driver's test.

21   HAYDEN: That'd be fine. I've failed my driver's test three

22    times already.

23   BLAKE: Or maybe he means people are finishing take-

24    home tests on their way to school in the mornings.

25    *(To camera)* That's cutting it a little close, people.

26    Please don't test and drive. It can wait.

27   HAYDEN: Have we got anything from the counselor's

28    office today, Blake?

29   BLAKE: *(Reads.)* Looks like we do! Ms. Michelle says to tell

30    you all that her collage essay contest is now open for

31    submissions. Please submit your collage essay in the

32    drop box outside her door.

33   HAYDEN: Wait, I'm confused on behalf of our viewers. Do

34    they need to submit a collage or an essay?

35   BLAKE: Maybe both. Or either. It's nice to have a little

1      room for creativity on a contest like this. Maybe I'll
2      do a photo essay. Sounds pretty quick and easy.
3  HAYDEN: I guess a picture really is worth a thousand
4      words these days. I wonder if I could submit a collage
5      for my college essay.
6  BLAKE: Ask Ms. Michelle. She's here as a resource on
7      these sorts of things. How about a weather report,
8      Hayden?
9  HAYDEN: Sure thing. *(Reads.)* Tomorrow through Friday
10     it's going to be windy with an eighty percent chance
11     of crowds.
12  BLAKE: Eighty percent chance we'll see crowds? For what
13     event?
14  HAYDEN: I'm not positive. Maybe for the football game on
15     Friday?
16  BLAKE: That's a good guess. Don't forget to come out and
17     cheer the team, guys. Just because our record is two
18     and twenty-one doesn't mean we can't make a
19     comeback.
20  HAYDEN: *(Stage whisper)* Blake. It totally does mean that.
21  BLAKE: *(To camera)* And either way, the homecoming
22     dance is Friday night after the game! *(Reads.)* This
23     year's theme will be topical.
24  HAYDEN: Oh, good. What's the topic?
25  BLAKE: It doesn't say. Usually homecoming is "Hawaiian
26     Paradise" or "Margaritaville" or something island-y.
27     I'm not sure why they didn't specify it this year.
28  HAYDEN: What matters is that we'll get to have a great
29     time with our classmates.
30  BLAKE: That's right. Speaking of classmates, are there
31     any updates on the class election campaign?
32  HAYDEN: It's going to be a blowout victory. Kate
33     Wallingford is the only one running for precedent.
34  BLAKE: OK, I understand that student health goals are an
35     important aspect of each candidate's platform, but

1     setting a precedent for running isn't the solution to
2     all of our problems. We need to eat healthy and
3     exercise. Besides, how does running show that
4     someone's going to be a good leader?
5  HAYDEN: *(To camera)* In short, Blake would like to
6     encourage everyone to do their research before
7     casting a hasty vote. This is an important election.
8     Make your voice heard.
9  BLAKE: Thank you, Hayden. *(Reads.)* One last thing I've
10    been asked to mention ... Mrs. Latona, the art teacher,
11    is collecting cats for her students' final art projects.
12    She's planning to hang them up on the wall, but she
13    doesn't have enough.
14  HAYDEN: Excuse me? That's animal cruelty.
15  BLAKE: That's what it says. I didn't want to mention it at
16    all, either. I'm an active member of PETA, and —
17  HAYDEN: *(Looking over BLAKE's shoulder)* Wait a second,
18    Blake. That's supposed to say tacks. Not cats. Mrs.
19    Latona wants to hang the art projects up on the wall
20    using tacks.
21  BLAKE: That's even worse! Poor things. What kind of
22    multi-media projects count as art these days? I'm all
23    about creativity, but hanging up cats is taking things
24    too far.
25  HAYDEN: Blake. No cats are going to be harmed during
26    the making of these art projects. I bet they're doing
27    paintings or papiér-mâché.
28  BLAKE: Either that or they're all working on their collage
29    essays.
30  HAYDEN: I guess we'll find out soon enough. *(To camera)*
31    You can drop off tacks in Mrs. Latona's room today
32    during tutorial. Anything else, Blake?
33  BLAKE: I think that sums it up, Hayden. We want to thank
34    you for watching Pretown High School's morning
35    announcements, remind you to check your spelling ...

1    HAYDEN: And wish you a happy Monday!

2    BLAKE and HAYDEN: Blake and Hayden, over and out.

# 32. Paul Revere's Publicist

**Cast:** WILLIAM and SAMUEL

**Setting:** No special set required.

**Props:** None

1 WILLIAM: There they go again, reciting that pack of lies.
2     The words drift out of the classroom windows, and I
3     can't escape hearing them.
4     "Listen, my children, and you shall hear
5     Of the midnight ride of Paul Revere."
6 SAMUEL: I can't stand it! I think every school in the country
7     has assigned that poem to their students.
8 WILLIAM: The worst part is that they all think it's true. They
9     believe Henry Wadsworth Longfellow's poem told what
10     really happened.
11 SAMUEL: Ha! We rode that night too, but does anyone ever
12     mention William Dawes or Samuel Prescott? No way!
13     Paul Revere gets all the glory.
14 WILLIAM: We should write down the factual account. We
15     could start with how Joseph Warren heard through the
16     revolutionary underground that the British were
17     planning to surprise the Patriot leaders, John Hancock
18     and Samuel Adams, in Lexington and arrest them.
19 SAMUEL: The underground? I heard he got his information
20     from the wife of a British general.
21 WILLIAM: However he found out, he knew he had to
22     prevent the attack. The British not only planned to
23     arrest the leaders, they intended to go on to Concord
24     and destroy all the supplies that were stored there.
25 SAMUEL: So Dr. Warren cooked up this great plan to send
26     two messengers to Lexington to alert Adams and
27     Hancock.
28 WILLIAM: First, he sent for me, William Dawes. Then he

1     sent for Paul Revere. I was not as well known as
2     Revere, and therefore less likely to be stopped, so he
3     gave me the more difficult land route. I was also a
4     fine actor, if I do say so myself. I could don a floppy
5     hat and pretend to be a drunkard. One way or
6     another, I knew that I could get past the British
7     sentinels.
8     SAMUEL: Half an hour after you set off, Dr. Warren sent
9     for Paul Revere and told him to cross the Charles
10    River and then continue on horseback to Lexington.
11    First, though, Revere needed to contact the church
12    sexton and have him hold up two lanterns, the
13    prearranged signal that the British were traveling by
14    water.
15    WILLIAM: In the poem, Paul Revere sees the lantern
16    signal.
17    SAMUEL: In reality, he gave the signal.
18    WILLIAM: Two friends rowed Paul across the river, where
19    he borrowed a horse and began his ride. It was a good
20    plan. By using two messengers and two different
21    routes, chances were good that one of us would make
22    it to Lexington.
23    SAMUEL: As it turned out, you both did.
24    WILLIAM: Yes. We arrived in time to warn Samuel Adams
25    and John Hancock, who then sought safety in
26    Philadelphia. After a half hour's rest, Paul and I
27    mounted our weary horses and headed for Concord
28    to warn the people there.
29    SAMUEL: That's where I, Samuel Prescott, enter the story.
30    I had been visiting my fiancée and was on my way
31    home when the two of you rode up and passed along
32    the warning. I decided to help spread the word.
33    WILLIAM: We were mighty glad to have your help, but it
34    wasn't long before the British patrols found us. Paul
35    Revere had ridden ahead, and he got captured.

1  SAMUEL: I made a break for it. My horse jumped a wall,
2      and I escaped. Because I was familiar with the area, I
3      was able to find my way back to the main road. I
4      found other riders to join the cause, and I made it to
5      Concord to save the supplies.
6  WILLIAM: I got away from the patrols, but in all the
7      shouting and excitement, my horse threw me and
8      then galloped off. I had to walk back to Lexington.
9  SAMUEL: So if you and Paul Revere both made the trip
10     from Boston to Lexington to warn the leaders that the
11     British were coming, why is it that Paul gets all the
12     credit?
13 WILLIAM: For one thing, he was a well-known silversmith
14     at the time. I was an unknown tanner of hides. You
15     know how the press is, always impressed by a
16     celebrity. Also, I was focused on my goal of saving our
17     leaders, so I rode hard and went straight through all
18     the villages and towns. Paul Revere hollered and
19     carried on, woke up the town leaders and military
20     commanders, and told all of them the news. He got
21     everyone fired up, and later, of course, they
22     remembered that he had warned them. Nobody
23     remembered me.
24 SAMUEL: No one remembers me, either, and I'm the only
25     one of the three riders who made it all the way to
26     Concord.
27 WILLIAM: Dang horse. I would have got there too if he
28     hadn't bucked me off.
29 SAMUEL: Why should Paul Revere get a famous poem
30     written about him when you and I did as much or
31     more than he did? It isn't fair.
32 WILLIAM: My theory is that Longfellow may have received
33     a fine silver bowl not long after he penned those
34     words.
35 SAMUEL: You don't know that. You can't accuse a famous

1    poet of accepting a bribe when you have no proof.

2    Maybe Longfellow only wrote about one rider

3    because the poem worked better that way.

4    "Listen, my children, and you shall hear

5    Of the midnight ride of William Dawes, Samuel

6    Prescott, and Paul Revere" doesn't have much of a

7    ring to it.

8    WILLIAM: He could have said, "Listen my children,

9    without a pause

10    To the stirring tale of William Dawes."

11    SAMUEL: That eliminates Paul Revere, which really isn't

12    fair, either. Nothing much rhymes with Prescott, so

13    I'm out of luck.

14    WILLIAM: What really bothers me is that a poet of such

15    renown would be inaccurate, and nobody cares.

16    SAMUEL: Maybe Longfellow intended the piece to be

17    fiction. Does it really matter? It isn't as if Paul Revere

18    got any royalties from what Longfellow wrote.

19    WILLIAM: He got fame. He went from being a silversmith

20    to owning a huge company that makes copper-

21    bottomed cookware. He made a pile of money while

22    you and I slid into obscurity.

23    SAMUEL: I served as a surgeon in the Continental Army.

24    WILLIAM: I fought at the Battle of Bunker Hill.

25    SAMUEL: Paul Revere had a disastrous military career.

26    WILLIAM: After the war, I set up a store.

27    SAMUEL: I never got to marry the sweetheart I was

28    visiting that April night.

29    WILLIAM: Paul Revere married and had sixteen children!

30    SAMUEL: " 'Twas the eighteenth of April in seventy-five.

31    Hardly a man is now alive who remembers that

32    famous day and year."

33    WILLIAM: I remember!

34    SAMUEL: And I remember!

35    WILLIAM: It's high time we set the story straight.

1    SAMUEL: I'll bet some of Paul Revere's kids hired a
2          publicist. They probably sent a copy of Longfellow's
3          poem to every school district in the country. Why else
4          would everyone read it when it's full of errors?
5    WILLIAM: I say we organize a protest.
6    SAMUEL: We'll demand our just due!
7    WILLIAM: "Listen, my children, and you'll agree ... "
8    SAMUEL: "That the midnight ride was done by three."

# 33. The Worst Day Ever

**Cast:** KELSEY and DEVON. Each plays multiple roles.

**Setting:** A high school auditorium. A small table is Center Stage.

**Props:** Eight hats. These are used as a way to designate change of character. Kelsey and Devon each wear a hat as scene opens. The rest are on the table.

1 **KELSEY: Welcome to Hapless High School's annual "Worst**
2 **Day Ever" contest. This year, our contestants will**
3 **compete to see who had the worst day during this**
4 **school year. Events didn't have to take place at the**
5 **school building but must have happened between**
6 **August 28, when school started, and today.**
7 **DEVON: You will each have two minutes to tell us why your**
8 **day was the most awful experience of your school**
9 **career. After all the contestants have spoken, our**
10 **audience will vote to decide the winner. First**
11 **contestant, please.** *(Both remove their hats and place*
12 *them on the table.)*
13 **KELSEY:** *(Puts on a different hat.)* **I was so excited when I got**
14 **a part-time job with a company that prepares income**
15 **tax forms. Starting March first, I was supposed to stand**
16 **in front of their office every afternoon wearing a long**
17 **blue dress and a crown like the Statue of Liberty.**
18 **Instead of holding a torch, I held a sign that advertised**
19 **the company's income tax services. I was supposed to**
20 **wave the sign back and forth at every car that drove by.**
21 **This wasn't the greatest job in the world, but I needed**
22 **the money. I showed up a few minutes early on March**
23 **first and donned my Miss Liberty costume. Then I went**
24 **outside and stood on the corner. On March first we**
25 **broke the all-time record for regional rainfall. It was a**
26 **record low temperature too, so the rain turned to hail.**

1　Then it sleeted. The wind gusts were clocked at
2　seventy miles an hour. My crown blew off, and I had
3　to run into traffic to get it back. My arms ached from
4　the heavy sign, and I caught a cold that turned into
5　pneumonia. The doctor's bill came to way more than
6　I earned, because I quit at the end of that first day.
7　March first was definitely my worst day ever.
8　*(Removes hat.)*
9　**DEVON:** *(Puts on a different hat.)* **My worst day was the day**
10　of the cross-country team's final race. I knew I had a
11　good chance at winning, but when we left the paved
12　road and started across the field, I saw a crow up
13　ahead. I thought, "Cool, there's a big crow in the sky."
14　Then it started circling, and all of a sudden, it
15　swooped down a few yards ahead of me and caught a
16　snake! As it flew back up, I could see the huge nasty
17　thing dangling out of its beak. I hate snakes. I was
18　grossed out, but at least the crow got it out of my path.
19　The crow flew up and out of my sight, and I kept
20　running my hardest. But suddenly, I felt something
21　in my hair. I thought maybe it was a leaf, so I reached
22　up to brush it off, and it was moving! The crow had
23　dropped the snake on my head! I totally freaked out
24　and shook my head like a crazy person and whacked
25　at my hair with my hands until the snake fell back
26　onto the grass and slithered away. Getting the snake
27　off my head only took a few seconds, but checking my
28　hair again and again slowed my race time a lot. All the
29　other runners stared at me brushing at my hair and
30　shaking my head as they ran past. I lost the race, and
31　I still get the heebie-jeebies when I think about the
32　snake. *(DEVON shudders and removes hat.)*
33　**KELSEY:** *(Puts on a different hat.)* **On my worst day, my**
34　English teacher, Mr. Withycombe, made an awful
35　announcement. We were expected to turn in a ten-

1    page paper by the very next morning! I had never
2    written a ten-page paper, and I was so nervous I
3    could hardly focus through the rest of my classes. I
4    skipped lunch with my friends to do research at the
5    library and almost got a speeding ticket rushing
6    home from school. I spent the whole beautiful sunny
7    afternoon writing frantically, even when my friend
8    Hayley called and offered me an extra ticket to the
9    season opener against the Red Sox. I fell into bed at
10   four a.m. and slept through my alarm. At the seven-
11   thirty bell, I came running into Mr. Withycombe's
12   class still wearing my pajama shirt with my hair
13   unwashed. When Mr. Withycombe asked us to turn in
14   our ten-page papers, everyone chuckled. I started to
15   stand up to bring mine to the front of the class, and
16   everyone stared at me in disbelief. That's when I
17   noticed the date on the board ... April second. The
18   assignment had been Mr. Withycombe's idea of an
19   April Fool's joke, and I was the only one who had
20   fallen for it. Mr. Withycombe didn't even offer to give
21   me extra credit. He just laughed with everyone else.
22   *(Removes hat.)*
23  **DEVON:** *(Puts on a different hat.)* The morning of my worst
24    day, I was so excited: a big-name talent scout was
25    having open auditions at the mall. My entire life,
26    there's nothing I've wanted more than to be on TV.
27    I'd spent months preparing a song and dance routine
28    and practicing my smile in the mirror. Even when
29    Mom asked me to babysit my obnoxious little sister
30    on audition day, I was undeterred. I'd just got my
31    driver's license, and I could take Anna along with
32    me. We waited in line for two hours, Anna whining
33    the whole time, until finally it was my turn. I told her
34    to sit still for sixty seconds while I went into the
35    audition room. Sixty seconds! When I came back out,

1        **know what she was doing? She was mimicking my**
2        **choreographed routine in front of the entire line!**
3        **Everyone was staring, including the talent scout's**
4        **assistant. He said, "Ma'am, I think we've found what**
5        **we're looking for." Sure enough, a month later,**
6        **Anna's the star of a cereal commercial and a local**
7        **celebrity. Mom and Dad threw her a big barbeque,**
8        **she got her picture in the school paper, and her**
9        **smarmy little face is on TV eating Trix every night. I**
10       **can't even watch my favorite shows anymore. Oh**
11       **yeah, and guess who got to drive her into the city for**
12       **filming?** *(Points at self.)* **This girl.** *(Removes hat.)*
13 **KELSEY:** *(Puts on a different hat.)* **Last October I got the flu**
14       **and missed two days of school. On the third day, I felt**
15       **better but I planned to stay home again because there**
16       **was a movie on TV that I wanted to see. I didn't take a**
17       **shower or wash my hair because I wanted to look as**
18       **wretched as possible so Mom would let me stay in**
19       **bed. I even wore my worst old clothes, but Mom**
20       **didn't buy it. She just said, "I'll drive you to school.**
21       **Let's go," and handed me my excuse. When I took the**
22       **excuse into the office, the office aide said I was**
23       **supposed to go to the gym instead of to class. I**
24       **thought we were having a special program, but when**
25       **I got there, they were taking our senior class pictures!**
26       **Mrs. Strictly saw me trying to sneak away and made**
27       **me come back. Now my picture's in the yearbook for**
28       **all to see ... me with my greasy uncombed hair and**
29       **puffy eyes and ratty old T-shirt. Definitely my worst**
30       **day ever.** *(Removes hat.)*
31 **DEVON:** *(Puts on a different hat.)* **My worst day was a blind**
32       **date. The guy was a friend of my neighbor, and he**
33       **called and asked if I'd like to go out to dinner and**
34       **then to a car show. I'd never had a real date, so I was**
35       **excited. I bought a new dress and borrowed my**

1     mom's pearls and wore heels. Well, guess where he
2     took me for dinner? A gas station! I had my choice of
3     a corn dog or a stale ham sandwich. We had to eat
4     standing up, and all I could smell was gasoline. The
5     car show was in a field behind the gas station. It had
6     rained, so the field was muddy and I ruined my
7     shoes. Dinner was the worst part, though. When you
8     invite a girl to dinner, is it too much to expect a nice
9     seafood restaurant or one of the Italian or Mexican
10     places? I would have settled for pizza. But a gas
11     station? *(Removes hat. Both KELSEY and DEVON put*
12     *their original hats back on.)*
13   KELSEY: This concludes Hapless High School's "Worst
14     Day Ever" contest, so it's time for the audience to
15     vote.
16   DEVON: All those in favor of cross-country snake, talent
17     scout, and class pictures, say aye.
18   KELSEY: All those in favor of Miss Liberty, April fool, and
19     gas station dinner, say aye.
20   DEVON: It's too close to call. In recognition of all six
21     contestants' truly terrible days, you're all winners!

# 34. Mall Survey

**Cast:** JAMIE and DREW

**Setting:** A shopping mall. No special set required.

**Props:** Clipboard and pen for Jamie.

1    *(As scene opens, JAMIE stands Center Stage holding a*
2    *clipboard and pen. DREW enters, walking briskly. As*
3    *DREW approaches, JAMIE speaks.)*
4    **JAMIE: Excuse me. I'm taking a survey. Could you answer a**
5    **few questions?**
6    **DREW: Are you selling something?**
7    **JAMIE: No.**
8    **DREW: If this is going to turn into a sales pitch, you can save**
9    **your breath.**
10  **JAMIE: It's a survey. We're trying to learn about the**
11    **shopping preferences of our customers.**
12  **DREW: I don't have much time. I need to catch a bus.**
13  **JAMIE: I'll be quick. First question: How often do you shop**
14    **here at Mismatched Mall?**
15  **DREW: Never.**
16  **JAMIE: You're here now.**
17  **DREW: True, but I'm not shopping.** *(Holds up empty hands.)*
18    **See? No purchases.**
19  **JAMIE: Oh, I get it. You're window shopping. You're making**
20    **a mental wish list of all the things you'll buy as soon as**
21    **you have money.**
22  **DREW: I have money now.**
23  **JAMIE: You do?**
24  **DREW: Yep. I just got paid.**
25  **JAMIE: You just got paid, and you're at the mall, but you**
26    **aren't shopping?**
27  **DREW: That's right.**
28  **JAMIE: Let's move on to question two. On average, how**
29    **much do you spend each time you come to Mismatched**

1       Mall? A, Five dollars. B, Twenty dollars. C, One
2       hundred dollars or more.
3   DREW: None of the above. I already told you, I don't shop
4       here.
5   JAMIE: *(Reading next question)* If you could win a fifty
6       dollar gift certificate from any store in Mismatched
7       Mall, which one would you choose?
8   DREW: That's a sneaky question.
9   JAMIE: It is?
10  DREW: You're really trying to find out which store people
11      like best.
12  JAMIE: Just answer the question, please. If you could have
13      a gift certificate from any of the stores in
14      Mismatched Mall, which one would you choose?
15  DREW: Favorite Foods.
16  JAMIE: And why would you prefer Favorite Foods?
17  DREW: They sell food, which I can use. The other stores
18      don't sell anything I need.
19  JAMIE: There are lots of clothing stores in Mismatched
20      Mall. You wear clothes. Everyone needs clothes.
21  DREW: I don't need designer jeans for two hundred and
22      fifty dollars a pair.
23  JAMIE: The jeans you're wearing seem nice. That's a cool
24      shirt, too.
25  DREW: Thanks.
26  JAMIE: Do you mind telling me where you bought them?
27  DREW: Value Village.
28  JAMIE: That's a thrift shop. Do you always buy
29      secondhand clothes?
30  DREW: Always. I paid four dollars for the jeans and one-
31      fifty for the shirt.
32  JAMIE: Wow! Good finds.
33  DREW: Look, it's been nice chatting with you, but I really
34      need to catch my bus.
35  JAMIE: I'm almost finished. What time do you usually

1      arrive when you come to Mismatched Mall?

2    DREW: Five a.m.

3    JAMIE: The mall doesn't open until ten.

4    DREW: Well, I come at five.

5    JAMIE: Are you one of the mall walkers? Those people who

6      come before the shops open and walk around to get

7      their exercise?

8    DREW: Nope.

9    JAMIE: What do you do here at five o'clock in the

10    morning?

11   DREW: Is that question on your survey?

12   JAMIE: No, I'm just curious.

13   DREW: I wash windows. I also clean the bathrooms. Lucky

14    me.

15   JAMIE: Oh! You *work* at Mismatched Mall.

16   DREW: You got it.

17   JAMIE: But you don't shop here? That doesn't seem very

18    loyal.

19   DREW: By the time I get off work, I can't wait to get out of

20    here.

21   JAMIE: Well, thanks for taking the survey.

22   DREW: I have one question for you.

23   JAMIE: OK.

24   DREW: Do you shop at Mismatched Mall?

25   JAMIE: Never. I'm only here because they hired me to ask

26    people to take this survey. *(DREW nods, then starts to*

27    *walk away.)*

28   JAMIE: Wait! I need to know one more thing.

29   DREW: *(Pauses.)* What now?

30   JAMIE: Where's that Value Village? I need some new jeans.

# 35. Pick Me Up at Eight

**Cast:** JOEL and ELENORE

**Setting:** A French restaurant. A table with two chairs placed across from each other is Center Stage.

**Props:** Two papers to serve as menus. A flower for Joel. A purse for Elenore.

**Costume:** Both players should dress in date attire.

1 *(As scene opens, JOEL is standing to one side of the stage*
2 *holding the flower. ELENORE enters holding purse and*
3 *looking around uncertainly. JOEL watches her, looks*
4 *away, looks back, begins to approach her, and stops a few*
5 *steps away.)*
6 **JOEL: Are you ... Elenore?**
7 **ELENORE: Yes! Joel?**
8 **JOEL: Yes. Nice to meet you.**
9 **ELENORE: Nice to meet you too.**
10 **JOEL:** *(Handing ELENORE the flower)* **I brought you this**
11 **flower.**
12 **ELENORE: Oh. Thank you! It's lovely.** *(They stand quietly for*
13 *a second. ELENORE smells the flower.)*
14 **JOEL: Do you want to sit down?**
15 **ELENORE: Yes! Definitely.**
16 **JOEL: Great. The sign said to take a seat anywhere.**
17 **ELENORE: Perfect.**
18 **JOEL: Where do you want to sit?**
19 **ELENORE: I don't care.**
20 **JOEL: By the window? By the wall?**
21 **ELENORE: How about by the window?**
22 **JOEL: Good choice!** *(They walk to the table. JOEL follows*
23 *ELENORE around the table to pull her seat out for her,*
24 *but ELENORE has already sat down and scooted in before*
25 *JOEL gets there. JOEL returns to his own seat and sits.)*
26 **ELENORE: There's a nice breeze here by the window.**

1   JOEL: There certainly is.
2   ELENORE: The view is good too.
3   JOEL: I agree. *(They stare at each other for a second before*
4       *picking up the menus from the table.)*
5   ELENORE: Have you been to this restaurant before?
6   JOEL: No. Never. It got good reviews online, and I
7       remembered you said you liked French food.
8   ELENORE: Mmmmm.
9   JOEL: The vichyssoise is supposed to be very good.
10  ELENORE: Is it? Maybe I'll have that.
11  JOEL: Would you like something to drink?
12  ELENORE: Just water is great.
13  JOEL: That sounds good to me too. I'll flag down the
14      waiter. *(JOEL looks around for a waiter.)*
15  ELENORE: *(Studying menu)* The quiche looks delicious.
16      I've always liked quiche.
17  JOEL: *(Looking at menu)* Sounds amazing. With ham and
18      Gruyère and fresh herbs.
19  ELENORE: What kind of food do you like?
20  JOEL: I'll eat anything. But French is one of my favorites,
21      so I'm glad you like it too.
22  ELENORE: Yes, that's lucky.
23  JOEL: So Elenore. Tell me a little bit about yourself.
24  ELENORE: What do you want to know?
25  JOEL: How did you start online dating?
26  ELENORE: Some of my friends were doing it. I thought I
27      might as well give it a try.
28  JOEL: Has it been working out for you?
29  ELENORE: This is the first date I've been on.
30  JOEL: Really?
31  ELENORE: Yes. How's it working out for you?
32  JOEL: I've been on the site for a couple months now. I
33      haven't really met anyone special yet.
34  ELENORE: I'm sure you will.
35  JOEL: Do you have any brothers or sisters?

1  ELENORE: I have one little sister. How about you?

2  JOEL: I'm one of three boys.

3  ELENORE: Wow. Oldest or youngest?

4  JOEL: Middle child.

5  ELENORE: That must be fun.

6  JOEL: It is most of the time. Do you have any hobbies?

7  ELENORE: I like to dance. And knit.

8  JOEL: Who do you knit for?

9  ELENORE: My family and friends, mostly. Sometimes I

10     knit hats and donate them or sell them at craft fairs.

11  JOEL: That sounds like it takes talent.

12  ELENORE: It's not so hard.

13  JOEL: I'm terrible with crafts.

14  ELENORE: What do you like to do?

15  JOEL: I enjoy waterskiing and hiking.

16  ELENORE: Is that right?

17  JOEL: Yep. I picked up waterskiing a few years ago, and

18     I've always loved to hike.

19  ELENORE: Very cool.

20  JOEL: I wonder where the waiter is.

21  ELENORE: Maybe we should have waited for someone to

22     seat us.

23  JOEL: The sign definitely says to seat yourself.

24  ELENORE: Maybe they forgot to change it when they got

25     busy.

26  JOEL: Maybe. *(Looks around for waiter.)* Excuse me!

27     *("Waiter" passes them by.)* So what kind of French

28     food do you like?

29  ELENORE: I like quiche.

30  JOEL: That's right. You said that. *(ELENORE and JOEL look*

31     *awkwardly at each other for a long moment.)* OK, can

32     we just admit that this is awkward?

33  ELENORE: So awkward!

34  JOEL: Why did we decide to go on a date? We've only

35     messaged like three times.

1   ELENORE: I don't know! This was your idea.

2   JOEL: You looked cute! I thought I'd give it a shot.

3   ELENORE: I *looked* cute? As in only in my profile photos?

4   JOEL: No! You *are* cute. But I'm so nervous I can't think of

5       anything clever to say.

6   ELENORE: Better than me. I can't think of anything to say

7       at all.

8   JOEL: And to top it off, the waiter won't even come over to

9       distract us.

10   ELENORE: I really think you read the sign wrong. They're

11       probably ignoring us because we weren't supposed to

12       seat ourselves. French restaurants are so snooty.

13   JOEL: But you like French restaurants! That's pretty much

14       the only thing I remember from our messages.

15   ELENORE: I don't, actually.

16   JOEL: You don't? But you said —

17   ELENORE: I couldn't think of anything that sounded

18       better in the message.

19   JOEL: Elenore! Why didn't you just say what you actually

20       like to eat?

21   ELENORE: I wanted to seem sophisticated.

22   JOEL: What do you really like?

23   ELENORE: Pizza. Burgers. Chinese take-out.

24   JOEL: Well, I hate French food. Pizza would have been way

25       better. Do you actually dance and knit hats?

26   ELENORE: Yeah, I do dance. And I've knit like four hats,

27       but it's not my favorite thing to do.

28   JOEL: What is?

29   ELENORE: I play cribbage.

30   JOEL: No way!

31   ELENORE: You know the game?

32   JOEL: I love cribbage! I didn't say that in my profile,

33       because everyone always calls it a grandma game.

34       That would have been a way better date.

35   ELENORE: Joel. I have a cribbage board in my purse.

1     Should we play?

2     JOEL: Will they care if we start playing cribbage on the

3         table? This place is kind of fancy.

4     ELENORE: Forget this place. Let's go get pizza.

5     JOEL: What, just get up and leave?

6     ELENORE: Yes! The waiter hasn't even brought us water.

7         It might be another hour.

8     JOEL: I don't want to seem rude.

9     ELENORE: Do you want pizza or not?

10    JOEL: Yes, I want pizza.

11    ELENORE: And cribbage?

12    JOEL: Yes to cribbage.

13    ELENORE: We'll sneak out. They'll never notice. *(She*

14       *stands up.)* And if they notice, who cares?

15    JOEL: You're right. Not me.

16    ELENORE: That's the spirit. Come on.

17    JOEL: *(Standing up and looking around)* But do try to look

18       incognito.

19    ELENORE: *(Laughs.)* Joel! Didn't we just establish that we

20       didn't care?

21    JOEL: Quick! They're not looking! Let's go! *(ELENORE and*

22       *JOEL hurry off the stage.)*

# 36. Clever Cat, Devoted Dog

**Cast:** DOG and CAT
**Setting:** No special set required.
**Props:** None
**Costumes:** Dog and cat attire optional.

1  CAT: I am Cat! I rule my domain.

2  DOG: I am Dog. Everyone tells me what to do.

3  CAT: Nobody bosses me.

4  DOG: They tell me, "Sit! Stay!"

5  CAT: I am independent.

6  DOG: "Shake hands! Heel!" I understand all their
7  commands.

8  CAT: I am king (*Or queen*) of the world. My ancestors were
9  royalty. The Egyptian goddess of love had the head of a
10  cat.

11  DOG: I am a descendent of the grey wolf. That's why I turn
12  in circles before I lie down. Wolves in the wild trample
13  tall vegetation to use for their beds. Circling also helps
14  determine which direction the wind is blowing. A wolf-
15  descendant prefers to sleep with his nose to the wind.

16  CAT: Is that why you like to hang your head out the car
17  window?

18  DOG: Yes! Nose to the wind! Ears flapping! I love car rides.

19  CAT: I hate car rides. If I could, I would bite the driver and
20  claw the upholstery and jump out the window. I can't
21  because they stuff me in a carrier. The only place the
22  car ever goes is to the vet.

23  DOG: Sometimes we go to the dog park.

24  CAT: Oh, how awful! A dog park would be even worse than
25  the vet.

26  DOG: Don't you ever go to a cat park?

27  CAT: There are no cat parks. No self-respecting cat would

1      want to play at a cat park.

2    DOG: At the dog park, my person throws a ball for me. I

3        run to get it and carry it back to him.

4    CAT: How demeaning. If my person wants a ball, he can go

5        get it himself.

6    DOG: Are you always this cranky?

7    CAT: I'm not cranky. I am Boss of the Universe. Nobody

8        tells me what to do.

9    DOG: When I bring back the ball, I get praised. I am

10      ecstatic when they say, "Good dog." Sometimes I get

11      treats. I like being with my people.

12  CAT: Cats have lived with people for more than ten

13      thousand years. Scientists found an ancient cat

14      cemetery in Tunisia with more than three hundred

15      thousand cat mummies.

16  DOG: Archeologists in Peru found an ancient cemetery

17      where dog skeletons were lovingly wrapped in llama-

18      wool blankets with fish bones next to their noses.

19  CAT: Fish bones?

20  DOG: The Peruvians loved their dogs so much that they

21      made sure the dogs would have food in the afterlife.

22  CAT: If I need to, I can catch my own food.

23  DOG: I know how to point at birds and deer to help my

24      person see them. I can retrieve a duck or a pheasant.

25  CAT: Point? Retrieve? Bah! I do the whole business by

26      myself. I am a mighty hunter, stalking my prey alone.

27  DOG: Well-trained dogs like me make perfect pets.

28  CAT: Cats are the most popular house pet of all. There are

29      ninety million pet cats.

30  DOG: Maybe cats are popular because they catch their

31      own food. Pet food is expensive, but mice are free.

32  CAT: Or maybe it's because humans admire our

33      independent spirit. Dogs are too subservient.

34  DOG: I am not subservient.

35  CAT: Sit! *(DOG sits on the floor.)*

1  CAT: **Shake hands!** *(DOG and CAT shake hands.)*
2  CAT: *(Walks a couple of steps to one side.)* **Heel!** *(DOG jumps*
3  *up and walks right behind CAT.)*
4  CAT: **Not subservient, huh?**
5  DOG: **I'm not subservient. I'm loyal. I obey because I want**
6  **to please.**
7  CAT: **I want to please too. I want to please myself. I do let**
8  **them feed me, though.**
9  DOG: **When it's supper time, I let them know. I sit by my**
10  **bowl and stare at my people. I plead with my eyes.**
11  CAT: **I complain loudly if my bowl is empty. If they don't**
12  **listen, I scratch the furniture.**
13  DOG: **I eat whatever is in my bowl. Also anything that's**
14  **dropped on the floor. Also anything I find in the yard.**
15  **If you leave a sandwich where I can reach it, don't**
16  **expect it to be there when you come back.**
17  CAT: **My people know which brand of cat food I like. The**
18  **expensive kind. And it needs to be fresh. If I don't**
19  **happen to be hungry when it's put in my bowl I will**
20  **ignore it. Two hours later, when it's dried up, I**
21  **complain until it's thrown out and fresh food is**
22  **offered. My people are well trained.**
23  DOG: **When my people come home, I wiggle and wag. I do**
24  **my happy hops, even if they've only been gone for five**
25  **minutes.**
26  CAT: **When my people have been out, I pretend not to**
27  **notice when they return.**
28  DOG: **If someone calls my name, I run to them. I am a**
29  **good dog. Good, good dog.**
30  CAT: **If they call me, I pretend not to hear. I've been known**
31  **to sit on a closet shelf for more than an hour while**
32  **everyone searches for me. "Here, kitty," they say.**
33  **"Here, kitty kitty." They look under the beds. They**
34  **look in the clothes hamper. They panic that I might**
35  **have slipped unnoticed out the door, so they walk all**

1     around the neighborhood, calling my name. They
2     don't find me until I decide to emerge. I am a clever
3     cat. Clever, clever cat.
4 DOG: My people take me for walks. I prance in circles
5     when I see my leash. I know the words "walk" and
6     "out" and "let's go."
7 CAT: Try to put a harness on me, and you will have
8     shredded arms.
9 DOG: I would never fight with my family. I am loved. I get
10     petted and hugged. I even get kissed, unless I've just
11     eaten something gross that I found outside. I show
12     my pleasure by wagging my tail and dancing.
13 CAT: When I am full and sleepy, if someone offers me
14     their lap, I will jump up. I curl my tail around my
15     chin and purr my pleasure.
16 DOG: Everyone smiles at my doggie dance.
17 CAT: Everyone smiles at my kitty lullaby.
18 DOG: *(Together with CAT)* I like being a dog.
19 CAT: *(Together with DOG)* I like being a cat.

# 37. That's How Rumors Start

**Cast:** ONE and TWO. Both players play multiple roles. One plays Molly, Lena, Steph, Ruby, Libby, and then Molly again. Two plays Amy, Katie, Kristie, Sunni, and then Amy again.

**Setting:** A school hallway. A curtain, screen, or some other divider is mid-stage: players will walk behind this divider to indicate a change in character.

**Props:** Cell phone for One and pen, paper, and cell phone for Two, all kept in pockets.

1  ONE: Hey, Amy. Can I tell you a secret?
2  TWO: Hey, Molly! Of course. What's up?
3  ONE: I'm trying out for the school play!
4  TWO: No way! What play?
5  ONE: *Chicago!* I'm so nervous. I've never tried out for
6      anything. But when I saw that we were putting on
7      *Chicago,* I knew I had to go for it. It's my favorite
8      musical in the world. I'm only trying out for a tiny role,
9      so it's not a big deal. You're the only person I've even
10      said anything to.
11  TWO: You're going to do so great! When are the auditions?
12  ONE: Right now! I've got to hurry. I don't want to be late.
13      Wish me luck!
14  TWO: Not luck, remember? Break a leg! *(ONE waves at TWO,*
15      *walks behind divider to the right, and re-emerges from*
16      *the left.)*
17  ONE: Was that Molly? What's she running off for?
18  TWO: Oh, hey Lena. She's headed to auditions for the school
19      play, *Chicago.* I think she was kind of keeping it a
20      secret, but it's probably fine for you to know. You're
21      going to find out soon enough anyway. She's trying out
22      right now, and I'm sure she'll get the part.

1  ONE: We're putting on *Chicago?* I wish I'd known ahead of
2      time, I would have auditioned myself. I'd love to star
3      in *Chicago*. But I'm sure Molly will be great. *(TWO*
4      *walks behind divider to the right and re-emerges from*
5      *the left.)* Katie! Did you know the school was putting
6      on *Chicago?*
7  TWO: No. Why?
8  ONE: Just curious. I didn't hear about it. But I think
9      Molly's trying out.
10  TWO: I didn't know she acted.
11  ONE: I didn't either, but I can totally see her being the
12      star.
13  TWO: Yeah, I could see that. Cool! *(ONE walks behind*
14      *divider to the right and re-emerges from the left.)*
15      Steph! Guess what? Apparently Molly is going to be
16      the star of *Chicago!*
17  ONE: Chicago?
18  TWO: Yeah! Crazy, right?
19  ONE: That's intense! Does Kristie know?
20  TWO: I don't know. I just heard it from Lena. *(TWO walks*
21      *behind divider to the right and re-emerges from the left.)*
22  ONE: Kristie! Have you heard yet?
23  TWO: Heard what?
24  ONE: Molly's going to Chicago to be a big star!
25  TWO: What?! Since when?
26  ONE: I think it just happened! Someone must have
27      discovered her as an amazing untapped talent or
28      something.
29  TWO: Awesome! I've always wanted a friend who's
30      famous.
31  ONE: Me too. Maybe she can introduce us to Brad Pitt!
32      *(ONE walks behind divider to the right and re-emerges*
33      *from the left.)*
34  TWO: Ruby! Molly's gonna be a movie star!
35  ONE: Excuse me? Our friend Molly?

1   TWO: Yeah! She just got discovered and she's going to
2        Chicago. Steph said something about Brad Pitt.
3   ONE: You're kidding. Can she get us tickets to her movie
4        premiere?
5   TWO: Probably. Anything's possible when you're friends
6        with Brad Pitt. *(TWO walks behind divider to the right*
7        *and re-emerges from the left.)*
8   ONE: Sunni! Are you coming to Molly's movie premiere?
9   TWO: What?
10  ONE: She's starring in something with Brad Pitt! The
11       premiere's in Chicago, and I think he can get us all
12       tickets!
13  TWO: I hope I'm invited! When is it?
14  ONE: I don't know, but I'm going to save every weekend in
15       the near future.
16  TWO: Me too! Has anyone told Libby? I'm supposed to go
17       camping with her family next weekend, but I think
18       she'd agree this takes precedence. Especially if Brad
19       Pitt's buying the tickets! *(ONE walks behind divider to*
20       *the right and re-emerges from the left.)*
21  TWO: Libby! Have you told your mom we might have to
22       postpone the camping trip?
23  ONE: Why would we do that?
24  TWO: We don't want to risk missing Molly's movie
25       premiere! Brad Pitt's getting us all VIP tickets!
26  ONE: Sunni, what are you saying?
27  TWO: Molly's in a movie! With Brad Pitt! She's like his
28       protégé. And he can get everyone tickets! I just heard
29       all this from Ruby.
30  ONE: Who did Ruby hear it from?
31  TWO: I have no idea, but I'm glad she told us in time to
32       reschedule camping. This is a once in a lifetime
33       opportunity!
34  ONE: This definitely takes precedence over camping. I'll
35       call my mom right now.

1  **TWO: I'll go pack! Just in case!** *(TWO walks behind divider*
2     *to the right.)*
3  **ONE:** *(Takes out her phone and pretends to dial.)* **Hey, Mom!**
4     **We can't do camping this weekend! Molly invited me**
5     **and Sunni to her movie premiere with Brad Pitt! All**
6     **expenses paid!** *(Pauses.)* **Mom. We definitely don't**
7     **have to pay Brad Pitt back. He's like a bazillionaire. I**
8     **bet he's just happy to do this for his protégé's**
9     **friends, you know?** *(Pauses.)* **No, Sunni didn't say the**
10    **name of the movie, but just bump camping back**
11    **until I hear the final details from Molly. OK? OK,**
12    **thanks. Love you. Bye!** *(ONE walks behind divider to*
13    *the right.)*
14 **TWO:** *(Re-emerges from behind divider from the right, takes*
15    *phone out of pocket Center Stage.)* **Hello, this is Amy.**
16    **Mom? Slow down, I can't understand a word you're**
17    **saying. Wait, Libby's mom said that? Are you sure?**
18    *(Pauses.)* **Wait, Brad Pitt discovered her? But I just**
19    **saw her twenty minutes ago! Is he at our school?!**
20    *(Pauses.)* **I don't know if the whole school's going!**
21    **This is the first I've heard about this! Mom, I've got to**
22    **call you back. Maybe I can catch Brad Pitt and Molly**
23    **in the auditorium!** *(Hangs up phone and starts toward*
24    *divider, right.)*
25 **ONE:** *(Re-enters from behind divider from the right.)* **Amy! I**
26    **think I got the —**
27 **TWO: Molly! I can't believe this! Is Brad Pitt in the**
28    **auditorium now? How did you ever score a movie**
29    **deal that fast? You told me you were trying out for a**
30    **tiny role! I can come to the premiere, can't I?**
31    *(Yanking pen and paper from her pocket)* **Can I have**
32    **Brad's autograph? Wait ... can I have *your* autograph?**
33    *(Holds pen and paper out to ONE. ONE stares at TWO*
34    *and the pen and paper, and then turns slowly to look at*
35    *the audience in disbelief.)*

# 38. Teen Reading Club

**Cast:** AMARI and QUINN

**Setting:** Quinn's house. One chair is Center Stage.

**Props:** A chair and a book

| | |
|---|---|
| 1 | *(As scene opens, QUINN is seated, reading the book.* |
| 2 | *AMARI enters.)* |
| 3 | **AMARI: What are you doing?** |
| 4 | **QUINN: What does it look like I'm doing? I'm reading.** |
| 5 | **AMARI: Do you want to play tennis? Or go get milkshakes?** |
| 6 | **QUINN: No thanks.** |
| 7 | **AMARI: I have the car.** |
| 8 | **QUINN: Shhhh. Don't bother me.** |
| 9 | **AMARI: It's sunny and warm outside. We could take inner** |
| 10 | **tubes to the creek and float downstream.** |
| 11 | **QUINN: Not today. This is a really good book. I want to keep** |
| 12 | **reading.** |
| 13 | **AMARI: It's a perfect day for being on the water. I have a** |
| 14 | **cooler with soft drinks and a new tube of sunscreen.** |
| 15 | **All you have to do is put on your swimsuit.** *(QUINN* |
| 16 | *continues to read.)* **Hello? Anybody home? I'm talking to** |
| 17 | **you.** |
| 18 | **QUINN: I've noticed, and I wish you would stop.** |
| 19 | **AMARI: What are you reading that's so interesting?** |
| 20 | **QUINN: It's a novel set in ancient Egypt.** |
| 21 | **AMARI: Come on! If you don't want to go inner tubing, we** |
| 22 | **can go out to the state park and play Frisbee or** |
| 23 | **badminton.** |
| 24 | **QUINN: The main character is a modern-day girl who** |
| 25 | **accidentally traveled back in time. Now she's living in** |
| 26 | **the Pharaoh's palace and trying to get back to her own** |
| 27 | **century.** |
| 28 | **AMARI: You can read when we get home. We won't be late,** |
| 29 | **because I need to have the car back home by six-thirty.** |

1     You'll have all evening to finish your book.

2     QUINN: Would you please go away? I'll go to the park with

3         you another time.

4     AMARI: How many pages does your book have?

5     QUINN: I don't know. What difference does it make?

6     AMARI: I signed up for the Teen Reading Club this

7         summer. I have to read ten books to qualify for a

8         prize, but the books don't count unless they have at

9         least fifty pages.

10   QUINN: Fifty isn't very many pages. *(Flips to end of book.)*

11       This one has two hundred fourteen pages.

12   AMARI: No kidding? Why would you choose such a long

13       book? I can read four books in the time it will take

14       you to read that one.

15   QUINN: This is a good story. I wish it would last forever.

16   AMARI: I already have six titles on the list of books I've

17       read for the Teen Reading Club.

18   QUINN: Be quiet. I only have three more chapters, and I

19       want to find out what happens. The protagonist has

20       to taste the food before it gets served to the Pharaoh,

21       and I'm afraid she might get poisoned. It's exciting.

22   AMARI: I want to read ten because the second prize is a

23       pizza party.

24   QUINN: You don't want the first prize?

25   AMARI: First prize is an e-reader.

26   QUINN: I know.

27   AMARI: The books I've read so far were all boring, and I

28       figure they'll be just as boring on an e-reader.

29   QUINN: They're probably boring because you choose

30       babyish books with hardly any pages just so you can

31       read them quickly and write them on your list. The

32       best book I read last summer was *War and Peace,*

33       which has about six zillion pages.

34   AMARI: I may drop out of the Teen Reading Club.

35   QUINN: Good. More prizes for the rest of us.

1  AMARI: You're in the Teen Reading Club too?
2  QUINN: Yes. I do it every summer.
3  AMARI:  Is that why you're reading instead of having fun?
4  QUINN: I am having fun, or I would be if you would leave
5      me alone and let me finish my book.
6  AMARI: So when you're done reading that book, you'll add
7      it to your list?
8  QUINN: Sure. Although I would read it anyway, even if I
9      hadn't signed up for Teen Reading Club.
10  AMARI: How many books are on your list so far? Are you
11      getting close to ten?
12  QUINN: I've already read way more than ten. I think this
13      one is number twenty-eight.
14  AMARI: If you already have ten books on your list, why are
15      you still reading?
16  QUINN: I *like* to read! Last summer I read forty-two books,
17      and I want to beat my own record this year.
18  AMARI: Forty-two? You actually read forty-two books in
19      one summer?
20  QUINN: Yep. It would have been forty-three, but my
21      parents made me leave my book at home while we
22      went to my aunt's birthday party.
23  AMARI: But you only have to read ten to qualify for the
24      prize drawing.
25  QUINN: I am aware of the rules.
26  AMARI: You read thirty-two books that you would not have
27      had to read! You could have stopped at ten and still
28      won a prize because the prizes are given randomly.
29      All the names of people who read at least ten books
30      get put in a bowl and names are drawn to see who
31      wins. I have just as good a chance with ten books as
32      you had with forty-two.
33  QUINN: The purpose of the Teen Reading Club is not to
34      win prizes.
35  AMARI: It is for me.

1  QUINN: Fine. I hope you win something.
2  AMARI: Did you win a prize last year?
3  QUINN: Yes. I won a really cool blank book.
4  AMARI: Blank? No words at all?
5  QUINN: That's right.
6  AMARI: Does it have more than fifty pages? I could read
7     that in a hurry.
8  QUINN: It isn't a book to read. It's a journal.
9  AMARI: Oh. I hope I don't win one of those. I don't like to
10    write. Writing is even harder than reading.
11 QUINN: I hope you don't win one, either. It would be a
12    waste of a perfectly good journal. I'd like another
13    one, though. Mine from last year is already full.
14 AMARI: Full of what?
15 QUINN: Mostly poems that I wrote and quotations that I
16    liked so much that I copied them into the journal.
17 AMARI: I don't want a journal, but a pizza party would be
18    cool. Do you want to win that?
19 QUINN: I'd rather win the e-reader, although I still prefer
20    real books with pages. *(Starts reading again.)*
21 AMARI: I guess you don't want to go to the park. *(QUINN*
22    *continues reading.)* I guess you're going to keep your
23    nose in that book. *(QUINN continues reading.)* You are
24    really going to waste a beautiful day by reading.
25 QUINN: And you are really going to waste a beautiful life
26    by *not* reading. *(AMARI exits. QUINN continues to*
27    *read.)*

# 39. Hair Salon Gossip

**Cast:** STYLIST and CUSTOMER

**Setting:** A hair salon. A chair is Center Stage facing the audience. A small table is set to one side of the chair.

**Props:** A cloth or towel to wrap around Customer is draped over the back of the chair. A hand mirror, comb, hair dryer, and two hair clips are on table. The authors recommend that scissors be pantomimed.

**Costume:** Customer should have long hair (a wig may be used).

1     *(As scene opens, STYLIST enters followed by*
2     *CUSTOMER.)*
3   **STYLIST: Come on back, honey. Have a seat.** *(Removes cloth*
4     *from back of chair and waits for CUSTOMER to be*
5     *seated.)*
6   **CUSTOMER:** *(Sits.)* **Thanks.**
7   **STYLIST:** *(Drapes cloth around CUSTOMER's shoulders and*
8     *clips it in place using a hair clip.)* **It's been a long time**
9     **since you were in.**
10 **CUSTOMER: Almost a year.**
11 **STYLIST: A whole year!**
12 **CUSTOMER: I know. I have tons of split ends. I've been**
13     **meaning to come in forever.**
14 **STYLIST:** *(Stands behind CUSTOMER and looks forward as if*
15     *both are facing a mirror.)* **Well, we'll fix that. What are**
16     **we doing today? Cut? Color? Style?**
17 **CUSTOMER: Just a trim, please.**
18 **STYLIST:** *(Arranging CUSTOMER's hair.)* **You would look**
19     **great with a little brown in your hair. Just a few shades**
20     **darker.**
21 **CUSTOMER: That's OK. I just want a couple inches off, and**
22     **some layers.**
23 **STYLIST: How about bangs?** *(Folds a lock of hair over*

1    *CUSTOMER's forehead to look like bangs.)*

2    **CUSTOMER: I don't know. I've had bangs before. They**

3        **drive me crazy, and then I have to wait months for**

4        **them to grow out.**

5    **STYLIST: Well, you can think about it while I get started.**

6        *(Begins to comb hair.)* **Tell me what's new with you,**

7        **honey.**

8    **CUSTOMER: Nothing much. Just going to school.**

9        **Working. Hanging out with friends.**

10   **STYLIST: Did you get that job you told me about last time?**

11   **CUSTOMER: Which one?**

12   **STYLIST: You were applying to work at some restaurant.**

13   **CUSTOMER: Oh, that was ages ago. I'm a barista now.**

14   **STYLIST: Ah. Good for you! And how's school?**

15   **CUSTOMER: Good. I like my classes this semester.**

16   **STYLIST: That's wonderful!** *(Begins parting CUSTOMER's*

17       *hair.)*

18   **CUSTOMER: How's your family?**

19   **STYLIST: They're doing very well. Mia's almost three.**

20       **There she is, right there.** *(Points forward as if*

21       *indicating a photo by the mirror.)* **That picture was**

22       **taken on the first day of gymnastics class. Isn't she**

23       **darling?**

24   **CUSTOMER: She's beautiful.**

25   **STYLIST: Thank you! Yes, family life is good.** *(Pauses and*

26       *narrows eyes suddenly.)* **My sister's family, on the**

27       **other hand —**

28   **CUSTOMER:** *(As if comb has caught a knot)* **Ow!**

29   **STYLIST: Sorry, honey. I just get so mad when I think of**

30       **my brother-in-law right now.** *(Sets down comb and*

31       *picks up clip.)*

32   **CUSTOMER: What do you mean? What happened?**

33   **STYLIST: Well, did I tell you the last time you were in that**

34       **my sister was engaged?** *(Clips left side of hair at an odd*

35       *angle.)*

1   CUSTOMER: Yeah, I think I remember you saying
2       something about that. You didn't like the guy, right?
3   STYLIST: No one did! My whole family was against it from
4       the start.
5   CUSTOMER: But she married him anyway?
6   STYLIST: Six months ago. They eloped to Las Vegas.
7       *(Draws hair out as far as it extends above CUSTOMER's*
8       *head and considers it. Pretends to pick up scissors from*
9       *side table.)*
10   CUSTOMER: What?!
11   STYLIST: That's right. They'd barely known each other
12       three months. And they'd set a date for next June. But
13       they decided they couldn't wait. We all thought she
14       was pregnant. *(Pretends to snip hair. Begins to repeat*
15       *this process.)*
16   CUSTOMER: I thought your sister already had kids. Aren't
17       you an aunt?
18   STYLIST: She has two kids from her first marriage.
19       Doesn't make the best choices, my sister.
20   CUSTOMER: So what happened?
21   STYLIST: Well, they moved in together. Her kids plus the
22       two of them in a two-bedroom townhouse. He didn't
23       make a very steady income, this guy. He called
24       himself a professional online gambler.
25   CUSTOMER: Can you make those layers a little shorter?
26   STYLIST: Sure thing, honey. *(Holds chunk of hair out and*
27       *makes as if to cut it a few inches from CUSTOMER's*
28       *head.)* Anyway, like I was saying —
29   CUSTOMER: Wait, not that short!
30   STYLIST: *(Repositions scissors.)* How about here?
31   CUSTOMER: That's good.
32   STYLIST: *(Snips and continues to repeat the process.)*
33       Anyway, like I was saying, they moved in together. But
34       he was always glued to his computer. He wasn't
35       making any money, so she had to pick up extra hours

1    at work. She thought he would at least be able to take
2    care of the kids while she was away, but he said he
3    couldn't have his attention diverted. So she hired a
4    nanny too. It was all very costly for my sister.
5    CUSTOMER: I can imagine. Why didn't she make her
6        husband find a real job?
7    STYLIST: Well, she should have. But she was way too easy
8        on him. There she was working all those extra hours,
9        and he was at home gambling away her money
10       online. *(Removes clip from left side of hair and clips*
11       *right side. Begins to cut.)*
12   CUSTOMER: That's terrible.
13   STYLIST: Oh, that's not all. About a month ago, my sister
14       started to get weird vibes from the nanny. The
15       woman was suddenly offering to work on the
16       weekends too, so my sister could go to the gym, or
17       spa, or grocery store. My sister had always taken the
18       kids along on errands so she wouldn't have to pay the
19       nanny for more hours, and suddenly the woman was
20       all eager to work overtime.
21   CUSTOMER: Maybe she just needed the money. Nannies
22       don't make very much, right?
23   STYLIST: Well, that's what my sister told herself. Still, she
24       was uneasy. After two weeks of suspicion, my sister
25       made up her mind to fire the nanny. Did you decide
26       about the bangs?
27   CUSTOMER: Oh. Uh, what do you think?
28   STYLIST: They'll frame your face beautifully.
29   CUSTOMER: OK, I guess. If you really think they'll look
30       good. *(STYLIST pretends to cut bangs, and then picks*
31       *up hairdryer.)*
32   CUSTOMER: So, what happened with your sister and the
33       nanny?
34   STYLIST: Oh, yes! *(Pauses with the hairdryer.)* Oh, there
35       was so much drama. So I told you my sister was going

1      to fire the nanny? Well, she made the mistake of
2      talking to her husband about it the night before she
3      was going to do it.
4      CUSTOMER: And what did he say?
5      STYLIST: *(Pantomimes turning the dryer on and begins*
6      *drying hair.)* **Nothing! But the next morning –**
7      CUSTOMER: *(Loudly)* ***What? I can't hear you over the***
8      ***hairdryer!***
9      STYLIST: *(Loudly)* ***The next morning my sister woke up to***
10      ***find my brother-in-law gone and a note saying he'd***
11      ***run away with the nanny!*** *(Turns dryer off.)*
12      CUSTOMER: What was that last part?
13      STYLIST: Her husband ran away with the nanny!
14      CUSTOMER: You're joking! They'd been having an affair
15      all along?
16      STYLIST: *(Shrugs.)* **Guess so. Serves her right for eloping**
17      **with an online gambler, I suppose. Now she's right**
18      **back where she started, except she lost all her money.**
19      *(Sets dryer down and looks hair over.)* **What do you**
20      **think?**
21      CUSTOMER: I think that's despicable.
22      STYLIST: *(Picking up hand mirror)* **It certainly is. But what**
23      **do you think of your hair?** *(Holds mirror behind*
24      *CUSTOMER's head.)*
25      CUSTOMER: Oh! Looks good to me. Thanks.
26      STYLIST: *(Sets hand mirror down and takes cloth from*
27      *around CUSTOMER's shoulders.)* **I'm glad you like it.**
28      CUSTOMER: *(Stands and runs fingers through hair, taking*
29      *one more look toward audience/mirror.)* **What do I owe**
30      **you?**
31      STYLIST: Come on. I'll ring you up at the front desk.
32      *(Starts walking toward exit.)*
33      CUSTOMER: *(Follows STYLIST toward exit.)* **So what's going**
34      **to happen to your sister now?** *(They exit.)*

# 40. Adoption Day

**Cast:** SANDY and TEAGAN
**Setting:** No special set required.
**Props:** None

1 TEAGAN: Sandy! Congratulations! I just heard the news.

2 SANDY: What news is that?

3 TEAGAN: I saw your sister at the mini-mart, and she told me
4      about the new addition to your family. That is so
5      exciting. I'm thrilled for you!

6 SANDY: Oh. Yeah, it's great. We're picking him up tomorrow.

7 TEAGAN: I had no idea your parents were considering such
8      a thing. Why didn't you ever mention it?

9 SANDY: I thought they were never actually going to say yes,
10      but they finally changed their minds. Julie and I have
11      begged them to do this for years, and they always had
12      some excuse not to.

13 TEAGAN: Whatever happened that changed their minds,
14      I'm really glad for all of you. I was in a hurry when I
15      saw Julie, so I didn't get any details. How old is he?

16 SANDY: About six months.

17 TEAGAN: About? Don't you know his birthday for sure?

18 SANDY: No. He came from an abusive situation, and we
19      don't have a whole lot of information on his
20      background.

21 TEAGAN: That is the most unselfish thing I've ever heard of.
22      I really admire you and your parents. Imagine!
23      Adopting him when you don't even know his birthday.

24 SANDY: I don't think it's all that uncommon, actually. When
25      my cousin's family adopted Susie, they didn't have a
26      clue how old she was.

27 TEAGAN: How long ago was that?

28 SANDY: Let's see. I was seven then, so it's been ten years. I
29      remember being really jealous when they brought

1     Susie home.

2  TEAGAN: And it's worked out OK?

3  SANDY: Sure. Susie's great. Everyone adores her.

4  TEAGAN: Have you chosen his name? Or do you have to

5      keep the name he had?

6  SANDY: We get to choose. We decided to call him Rufus.

7  TEAGAN: Rufus? You're kidding, aren't you? You didn't

8      really name him Rufus.

9  SANDY: That's the name he had, and we thought it would

10     be easier for him if we kept it. As it is, he has to get

11     used to a new home and new people. We thought a

12     new name might be too much.

13  TEAGAN: At age six months, I don't think it would matter.

14     Being called Rufus would take some getting used to at

15     any age.

16  SANDY: I like Rufus, and we can always change it in a

17     couple of weeks if we decide Rufus doesn't seem to fit

18     him.

19  TEAGAN: But by then you'll have told everyone his name.

20     Are you going to send out announcements?

21  SANDY: Uh, no. No announcements.

22  TEAGAN: Did you adopt him privately – from an

23     individual? Or did your parents go through some

24     kind of an agency?

25  SANDY: An agency. They said that was the only way they'd

26     consider doing it.

27  TEAGAN: So you didn't meet Rufus's mother or father.

28  SANDY: Nope.

29  TEAGAN: Did you see pictures of them?

30  SANDY: Why would we do that?

31  TEAGAN: I would think you'd want to know what they look

32     like, so you'd have some idea of what Rufus will look

33     like when he's older.

34  SANDY: He's adorable. I only saw him for about half an

35     hour, but I love him already, and I'm sure we'll all

1      love him even more after he's lived with us for a
2      while. I can't wait to bring him home tomorrow.
3   TEAGAN: Was it terribly expensive?
4   SANDY: Not too bad. I think it was about one hundred and
5      fifty dollars, and that included all his vaccinations
6      and the surgery.
7   TEAGAN: Surgery! What surgery? Does he have some kind
8      of deformity? Is Rufus going to be handicapped all
9      his life? Is that why he was available for adoption?
10  SANDY: No! He's perfectly healthy. He had to be neutered,
11      and the adoption fee covered that charge. That's why
12      we didn't take him home yesterday as soon as we
13      chose him. He's getting neutered today and can go
14      home tomorrow.
15  TEAGAN: Neutered? As in, making sure he can never be a
16      father?
17  SANDY: Right.
18  TEAGAN: That is shocking! Why in the world would you
19      do that?
20  SANDY: Because there are too many unwanted dogs in the
21      world, and we don't want Rufus to be responsible for
22      producing more of them. You should have seen that
23      place! Cage after cage of dogs who need homes. Good
24      dogs, nice dogs. All of them sad-eyed and hopeful. It
25      was heartbreaking.
26  TEAGAN: Rufus is a dog?
27  SANDY: What did you think he was?
28  TEAGAN: A baby! I've been all excited because I thought
29      you were getting a little brother.
30  SANDY: Is that what Julie told you?
31  TEAGAN: No. Now that I think back, I overheard her
32      telling someone else that he had dark, curly hair. I
33      asked who she was talking about, and she said the
34      new little sweetie that you guys were adopting. I
35      guess I sort of jumped to the wrong conclusion.

1   SANDY: That's for sure! A baby!
2   TEAGAN: I think we need to start this conversation over.
3         Where did you get him?
4   SANDY: From the county Humane Society.
5   TEAGAN: What kind of dog is he?
6   SANDY: A mixed breed.
7   TEAGAN: That's the best kind. They have fewer health
8         problems than purebreds.
9   SANDY: We think he's part toy poodle, part cairn terrier,
10        and part who-knows-what. He's cute and very
11        friendly. You'll have to come over to meet him.
12  TEAGAN: I'd like that. You're really lucky, you know that?
13        I've begged my parents for a dog since I was four
14        years old, and I still don't have one.
15  SANDY: Don't give up. Sometimes if you keep asking, you
16        wear them down. You might catch your parents in a
17        weak moment, and they'll surprise you by saying yes.
18  TEAGAN: I'll keep trying.
19  SANDY: Tell them that every day in the United States,
20        thousands of healthy dogs get euthanized for no
21        reason except that they have no home. That statistic
22        is what convinced my mom and dad to adopt a shelter
23        dog. Maybe it will work for your family too.
24  TEAGAN: I hope so. Lucky Rufus.
25  SANDY: Lucky me.
26  TEAGAN: Rufus. What a great name for a dog!

# 41. National Threat

**Cast:** TSA OFFICER and VACATIONER

**Setting:** An airport security checkpoint. A long table or row of desks stands between characters and audience.

**Props:** A plastic bin sits at one end of the table. Vacationer carries a suitcase with a small bottle of shampoo and various clothes. Six pennies are in one of Vacationer's smallest shorts pockets. A wand and a walkie-talkie for TSA Officer. (Drumstick, toy light saber, or similar will work for wand; cell phone may replace walkie-talkie.)

**Costume:** Vacationer wears cargo shorts, flip-flops, and a watch. TSA Officer wears some sort of uniform.

*(As scene opens, TSA OFFICER stands Center Stage angled toward where VACATIONER waits, presumably at the front of a security line. TSA OFFICER has wand in his pocket/belt loop. VACATIONER checks his watch.)*

1  **TSA OFFICER: Next.**

2  **VACATIONER: Through here?**

3  **TSA OFFICER: Hold it, sir. You need to remove your shoes**
4  **and place them in the plastic bin.**

5  **VACATIONER: Flip-flops aren't OK?**

6  **TSA OFFICER: Sir, I'm going to need your cooperation on**
7  **this. There's a long line of folks behind you.**

8  **VACATIONER: I'm sorry. I just thought they'd be fine.**
9  *(Removes shoes and places them in bin.)* **There we go.**
10  *(Begins to walk forward.)*

11  **TSA OFFICER:** *(Holds up hand to stop VACATIONER.)* **And the**
12  **contents of your pockets.**

13  **VACATIONER: I don't have anything in them.**

14  **TSA OFFICER: Sir, I'm going to need you to empty your**
15  **pockets, please.**

16  **VACATIONER: I already did. My phone and wallet are going**
17  **through.** *(Points at table, then sighs. Sets suitcase down*

1    *and turns out pockets.)* **There. See?**
2    **TSA OFFICER: And the other ones.**
3    **VACATIONER: I never use the other ones.**
4    **TSA OFFICER: Then why did I hear jingling coming from**
5        **one of your pockets? Let's see them all, please.**
6    **VACATIONER:** *(Begins going through cargo pockets.)* **Look —**
7        **nothing, nothing, nothing** — *(Finds pennies.)* **Oh.**
8    *(Removes pennies.)*
9    **TSA OFFICER: That's what I thought.**
10   **VACATIONER: I'm sorry. I didn't know those were there.**
11   **TSA OFFICER: Next time I'd like you to comply more**
12       **directly.**
13   **VACATIONER: Look, it's six pennies. I have no idea what**
14       **they're from. Here they go. In the bin.** *(Puts pennies in*
15       *bin and slides bin forward across the table.)* **Can I go**
16       **now?**
17   **TSA OFFICER: Put your suitcase through the scanner**
18       **first.**
19   **VACATIONER:** *(Setting suitcase on table)* **That's what I'm**
20       **doing.**
21   **TSA OFFICER: Sir, I'm not sure I like your attitude. My job**
22       **is to keep this airport and everybody in it safe, and I**
23       **intend to do my job correctly. Put your suitcase**
24       **through the scanner.**
25   **VACATIONER:** *(Pushes suitcase to slide forward along*
26       *tabletop behind bin.)* **It's already going! Look!**
27       **Through the scanner! Can I come through now?**
28   **TSA OFFICER: Sir, I'm going to have to ask you to calm**
29       **down.**
30   **VACATIONER: Excuse me? What part of me is not calm?**
31   **TSA OFFICER:** *(Holds out hand.)* **Wait right there.**
32   **VACATIONER: I'm waiting.**
33   **TSA OFFICER: All right. Walk straight ahead with your**
34       **arms by your sides.**
35   **VACATIONER: Since when is that a rule?**

1  TSA OFFICER: That has been a rule as long as I've worked
2      here. Walk straight ahead.
3  VACATIONER: *(Begins to walk forward.)* **Why have I never**
4      had anyone else ask me to walk with my arms held by
5      my sides? This is getting a little ridiculous. You're
6      already scanning my whole body and everything I
7      own, including the six pennies I found in a remote
8      pocket of my cargo shorts. What do you care where
9      my arms are if you can already see through them?
10  TSA OFFICER: Stop right there. What are you carrying
11      that set off the scanner?
12  VACATIONER: You tell me! Isn't that your job?
13  TSA OFFICER: Sir, I'm going to need you to step aside with
14      me.
15  VACATIONER: You've got to be kidding.
16  TSA OFFICER: Security is not a matter we kid about here.
17      Follow me. *(VACATIONER follows TSA OFFICER a*
18      *short distance away, past end of table and forward*
19      *toward audience. VACATIONER stands facing*
20      *audience. TSA OFFICER takes wand from pocket.)*
21      Stand with your feet in the mat prints. Arms out.
22  VACATIONER: *(Complies.)* So this is what my tax dollars
23      are being wasted on.
24  TSA OFFICER: What was that?
25  VACATIONER: Nothing.
26  TSA OFFICER: Do I need to bring someone else over here?
27  VACATIONER: No. You don't. Just hurry.
28  TSA OFFICER: I'm not sure you understand. National
29      security is not something we're willing to hurry.
30      Stand still. *(Begins to run wand up side of*
31      *VACATIONER.)*
32  VACATIONER: Are you trying to make me miss my flight?
33      Let me guess. United is paying you to hold me up so I
34      have to buy another of their exorbitant tickets.
35  TSA OFFICER: Why are you in such a rush, sir?

1 VACATIONER: Like I just said, I'm going to miss my flight,
2     sir.
3 TSA OFFICER: *(Stops at VACATIONER's hip.)* **Right there.**
4     **What's that beeping?**
5 VACATIONER: **The button on the pocket of my shorts?**
6 TSA OFFICER: **Show me.**
7 VACATIONER: *(Lifts hem of shirt to show top of pants*
8     *pocket.)* **There it is. I can't take that off to go through**
9     **security. How often do you stop people because of the**
10     **button on their shorts? Real efficient system you're**
11     **running here. Now can I go?**
12 TSA OFFICER: **I'm going to have to take a look at your bag.**
13 VACATIONER: **Why? What's wrong with my bag? My bag**
14     **didn't set off the scanner; I did.**
15 TSA OFFICER: **Stay right where you are.** *(Points.)* **Is that**
16     **your bag there?**
17 VACATIONER: **Yes, that's my bag. The one full of stuff for**
18     **Cancun that I won't get to use at the rate we're going.**
19 TSA OFFICER: **I'm going to ask you again. What's your**
20     **rush?**
21 VACATIONER: **I've already told you. You're making me**
22     **miss my flight. You took a disliking to me as soon as I**
23     **forgot to take my shoes off, and here you are still**
24     **trying to prove to me who's boss. That's not the level**
25     **of maturity I'd expect from someone who's supposed**
26     **to be serving the public.**
27 TSA OFFICER: *(Walks to bag and begins feeling the outside.)*
28     **Airport guidelines posted on our website clearly**
29     **indicate to would-be travelers that they must allow**
30     **three hours from the time of arrival at the airport to**
31     **boarding time. Even so, we make no guarantees that**
32     **passengers will reach their gate on time. That's your**
33     **responsibility, not ours.**
34 VACATIONER: **If everyone followed those guidelines, we'd**
35     **all end up sitting around the terminal for two and a**

1    half hours every time we fly. Which I'm sure the
2    airport would love since we'd be forced to buy more
3    bland ten-dollar sandwiches. I left more than enough
4    time to make my flight.
5  TSA OFFICER: Our guidelines are designed to account for
6    situations like this.
7  VACATIONER: Since when did this become a "situation"?
8  TSA OFFICER: Come over here and open your bag for me.
9  VACATIONER: Wait a second. Are you making me open it
10    because you aren't allowed to do it yourself? Because
11    if so, I'm going to politely refuse. You have no reason
12    to go through my bag, and I barely got it closed after
13    three hours of packing last night. There's no way I'll
14    get it repacked if I take it all out here.
15 TSA OFFICER: Either you open your bag, or I call my
16    manager over and have her do it. I guarantee that the
17    latter will take longer. My manager and I deal with
18    mouth-offs like you every day, and she's got a long
19    line of people to get through before she'd be able to
20    check your bag.
21 VACATIONER: Or you could just not check my bag.
22 TSA OFFICER: Your refusal to show me the bag's contents
23    tells me you think you have a reason to hide
24    something. It gives me good cause to search your
25    luggage.
26 VACATIONER: That's what counts as good cause these
27    days? Asking to do something you don't have reason
28    for, and then using my refusal as reason enough? I
29    may not be a lawyer, but that doesn't seem like it
30    would hold up in court. Regardless, you're giving me
31    no choice, because if I don't give you what you want,
32    you're going to do everything in your power to hold
33    me up until I miss my flight. Here you go. *(Unzips*
34    *bag.)* Go ahead, throw everything out of it. That's not
35    inconvenient at all.

1  TSA OFFICER: *(Begins digging through suitcase. Holds up*
2    *small bottle.)* **Shampoo?**
3  VACATIONER: **Yes. And you'll notice it's less than three**
4    **ounces. I expect it to last me for about one shower.**
5  TSA OFFICER: *(Tosses a bundle on table and indicates it*
6    *with his hand.)* **What's this? Your underwear?**
7  VACATIONER: **What are you, the Spanish Inquisition? Yes,**
8    **that's obviously what that is. Are you done? Find what**
9    **you needed?**
10 TSA OFFICER: **You can pack that back up now.**
11 VACATIONER: **Gee, thanks for allowing it.**
12 TSA OFFICER: **You're welcome.** *(Begins to walk back to*
13    *original position.)*
14 VACATIONER: *(Shaking head, begins stuffing things in*
15    *suitcase. Sarcastically, to self.)* **Glad we got those ten**
16    **bombs taken care of.**
17 TSA OFFICER: *(Spins around.)* **What did you just say?**
18 VACATIONER: **Oh, for Pete's sake. I'm being sarcastic. I'm**
19    **sorry I said anything.**
20 TSA OFFICER: **I'll bet you are.** *(To walkie-talkie)* **Lisa! I**
21    **need backup at checkpoint six. We have a situation.**
22    **I'm detaining a suspicious person now.**
23 VACATIONER: *(Spreads arms wide in disbelief.)* **Who do you**
24    **think you're detaining? What is this? I give up my**
25    **freedom of speech because I tried to walk through**
26    **the scanner with flip-flops on? You may not**
27    **appreciate a heated comment, but to suspend my**
28    **rights over it? What's next? You get to lock me up on**
29    **suspicions of terrorism because I muttered the word**
30    **"bomb" in an airport?**
31 TSA OFFICER: **Get your arms behind your back. You're**
32    **coming with me.**
33 VACATIONER: **Get away from me. Where are you taking**
34    **me?**
35 TSA OFFICER: **A temporary detention facility. We'll decide**

1       if we need to pursue further action from there.
2       **VACATIONER:** *(Taking a step back from TSA OFFICER)* **And**
3       **if you decide that you do? Will every word I say – no**
4       **matter what its obvious intention – be used against**
5       **me in court? Or don't we do trials in this country**
6       **anymore?**
7       **TSA OFFICER:** *(Roughly grabs VACATIONER's arms and*
8       *forces them behind his back as if putting him in*
9       *handcuffs.)* **Come quietly. We don't need a scene.**
10      *(Begins pushing VACATIONER ahead of him toward*
11      *exit.)*
12      **VACATIONER:** *(Being pushed ahead, trying to resist)* **You**
13      **bet you don't! Someone might notice what abuses of**
14      **power we've come to accept in the name of national**
15      **security. Help! Somebody help me!** *(They exit.)*

# 42. Nummy's Fudge Shop Diet

**Cast:** MICKEY and BOBBY

**Setting:** No special set required.

**Props:** None

1    MICKEY: Do you want to go to Nummy's Fudge Shop?

2    BOBBY: No, thanks. I'm on a diet. Starting today, I will eat

3      only small portions of healthy food. No sweets. No

4      potato chips. And absolutely no chocolate.

5    MICKEY: Chocolate's good for you. Especially dark

6      chocolate.

7    BOBBY: Not if you're addicted, which I am. One bite of

8      chocolate, and I'm done for. I eat the whole candy bar

9      or every piece in the box. Once I consumed an entire

10    bag of Hershey's Kisses in one sitting. The jumbo size

11    bag.

12    MICKEY: Whoa. Didn't you get sick?

13    BOBBY: No, but I got fat.

14    MICKEY: You are not fat. You're an average size.

15    BOBBY: I don't want to be average. I want to be skinny. I

16      figure six hundred calories per day should be about

17      right.

18    MICKEY: Six hundred? That isn't nearly enough. You'll feel

19      starved all day long, and then you won't be able to stick

20      with your eating plan. You'll end up scarfing down

21      more than you would have if you had eaten regular

22      meals.

23    BOBBY: No way. I am totally psyched for this. I am so ready

24      to diet that I may even fast for a few days.

25    MICKEY: I don't think that's a good idea.

26    BOBBY: Why not? The less I eat, the sooner I'll get rid of my

27      fat stomach.

28    MIKEY: Malnutrition causes big potbellies. Haven't you ever

1        seen photos of starving children in Africa?

2   BOBBY: Those are kids who don't get enough to eat for

3        months and months. I'm only going to diet until I've

4        lost ten pounds. Then I'll eat normally again.

5   MICKEY: And gain it all back.

6   BOBBY: No! I'll still be really careful about what I eat. If

7        I'm going to suffer through six hundred calories a

8        day, I sure don't plan to gain it back.

9   MICKEY: Have you talked to your doctor about this?

10   BOBBY: I don't need to talk to a doctor.

11   MICKEY: Yes, you do. All the diet books and websites say

12        to consult with your physician before embarking on

13        any weight loss plan.

14   BOBBY: They just say that in case somebody with a

15        serious health problem decides to go on a crazy diet

16        and it ends up causing a seizure or a heart attack.

17        They're trying to prevent dieters from suing them.

18   MICKEY: That alone should tell you to go slow. If people

19        sometimes have heart attacks or other serious

20        problems when they don't eat properly, then you

21        need to be careful about how you diet.

22   BOBBY: I'm not going to starve myself until I keel over. I

23        only want to lose ten pounds so I can fit into the black

24        skirt I bought last year. I never wore it because by the

25        time I had an occasion to, I had gained ten pounds

26        and it no longer fit me. So now I am changing my

27        piggish ways. I am giving up all junk food.

28   MICKEY: That's a good idea, but you'd better give up

29        watching television too. If you're bombarded with

30        ads for burgers and pizza and sugary cereals, you'll

31        never be able to resist.

32   BOBBY: Ha! My willpower is mightier than a piece of

33        pizza. Bye-bye, brownies! Farewell, French fries! So

34        long, super-size sodas!

35   MICKEY: Yeah, right. I give this diet three days. Then

1     you'll be so hungry, you'll be gobbling everything in
2     sight.
3     BOBBY: Not me. I am starting a new love affair. I am now
4     in a relationship with salads and steamed vegetables.
5     I click "like" every time I see a piece of asparagus.
6     MICKEY: That's a good thing. Eat lots of veggies, but get
7     some protein too and some whole grains.
8     BOBBY: Next month I'll eat protein and grains. After I've
9     lost ten pounds.
10    MICKEY: You can eat a balanced diet and still lose weight.
11    Hard-boiled eggs are not high in calories. Neither is a
12    piece of broiled salmon. You could sprinkle some
13    garbanzo beans on your salad.
14    BOBBY: You're just jealous.
15    MICKEY: What? Why would I be jealous?
16    BOBBY: You're jealous because if I get skinny, it will make
17    you feel fat.
18    MICKEY: I do not feel fat. My clothes fit just fine.
19    BOBBY: What size are those pants?
20    MICKEY: None of your business.
21    BOBBY: Ha! That proves my point. If you were wearing
22    size two pants, you would be more than happy to say
23    so.
24    MICKEY: If I was wearing size two pants, I would still be
25    eight years old.
26    BOBBY: It's all right. You don't need to feel guilty about
27    being jealous. I used to envy people who were skinny
28    too.
29    MICKEY: And now you don't?
30    BOBBY: Now I don't because I have not eaten a single
31    thing so far today. Zero calories! Soon I'll be the
32    thinnest person in our school.
33    MICKEY: I'd rather be smart or happy. Or both.
34    BOBBY: You don't get it. It's smart to be skinny.
35    MICKEY: It's smart to care more about your health than

1      about some silly fashion trend. I'm happy with how I
2      look. Life is too short not to enjoy it. A good dessert
3      now and then makes me happy.
4   **BOBBY:** It makes me happy to be skinny.
5   **MICKEY:** OK. If that's how you feel, then good luck with
6      your diet. I hope the pounds disappear quickly.
7   **BOBBY:** Thanks.
8   **MICKEY:** I need to get going. I'm meeting the gang at
9      Nummy's. We're going to try the new Freaked-out-on-
10   Fudge Milkshakes.
11   **BOBBY:** Freaked-out-on-Fudge Milkshakes?
12   **MICKEY:** They're made with peppermint ice cream and
13      fudge sauce. I hear they are fabulous. *(Starts to exit.)*
14   **BOBBY:** Stop! Those sound unreal.
15   **MICKEY:** They're served with whipped cream on top, and
16      you get enough in the shake container to refill your
17      glass a second time.
18   **BOBBY:** *(Holds stomach.)* **Peppermint ice cream has**
19      **protein ... whipped cream has calcium ...**
20   **MICKEY:** See you later. I'm off to get freaked out on fudge.
21      *(Exits.)*
22   **BOBBY:** I think I'll start my diet tomorrow. *(Rushes after*
23      *MICKEY.)* **Hey! Wait up!**

# 43. Between Hipsters

**Cast:** SIDNEY and ROBIN
**Setting:** Two chairs are Center Stage, facing the audience.
**Props:** Phone with headphones for Robin. Phone for Sidney.

1     *(As scene opens, ROBIN sits listening to his headphones*
2     *and paying no attention to SIDNEY sitting next to him.*
3     *SIDNEY, pretending to text on his phone, glances at*
4     *ROBIN.)*
5     **SIDNEY: What are you listening to?**
6     **ROBIN:** *(Takes one headphone out.)* **What?**
7     **SIDNEY: I was just wondering what you were listening to.**
8     **ROBIN: Oh. It's a pretty niche band. They haven't made it**
9     **big yet, so you've probably never heard of them.**
10    **SIDNEY: I've heard of a lot of bands.**
11    **ROBIN: I'm pretty sure you won't know this one.**
12    **SIDNEY: Try me.**
13    **ROBIN:** *(Sighs.)* **They're called The Dosages. They're from**
14    **Australia, which is probably why you don't know them.**
15    **SIDNEY: Not know The Dosages? I'd have to have been living**
16    **under a rock to not know the Dosages. I used to like**
17    **them way back before they sold out. But I find all their**
18    **new albums to be complete trash.**
19    **ROBIN: This isn't a new album; it's from when they first**
20    **formed the band, before they even called themselves**
21    **The Dosages.**
22    **SIDNEY: You mean when they were Unclean Slate? Those**
23    **albums are OK in a real pinch. But they mooched all**
24    **their best hooks off of Benny McKing. For several years**
25    **I owned an extensive collection of McKing vinyl, and I**
26    **recognized the similarities the first time I heard them.**
27    **Of course most people wouldn't, because McKing was**
28    **very much an unknown in spite of his genius.**
29    **ROBIN: McKing a genius? He never wrote a single song. His**

1    brother Billy was the unsung hero behind all of his
2    hits. I would feel dirty owning a McKing record that
3    wasn't one of Billy's.
4  SIDNEY: You're still listening to records, huh?
5  ROBIN: *(Holds up phone.)* Apart from this, it's all I own.
6    Tapes and CDs became mainstream so quickly.
7  SIDNEY: Of course they did, but the same is true of
8    modern vinyl. I used to buy those sorts of records
9    back when I was young and trying to be cool. I broke
10   them all up to use in an installation art project a few
11   years back. I won't listen to music nowadays unless
12   it's on my Victrola.
13 ROBIN: What's that?
14 SIDNEY: It's a pre-1929 acoustic phonograph. It only plays
15   laterally-cut 78 RPMs.
16 ROBIN: Where did you find it?
17 SIDNEY: At Goodwill, of course. It's the only place I shop.
18   The last time I went to a mall was when I was about
19   twelve.
20 ROBIN: I can't say I've ever been to a mall. I make all my
21   clothes myself.
22 SIDNEY: The only thing malls are good for is to watch all
23   the people playing slaves to capitalism. I used to sit in
24   the corner and read Marx just to see if anyone would
25   notice the irony. But I'm guessing they didn't
26   because I was reading the original version, and the
27   title was in German. Marx is so much more eloquent
28   in his native tongue.
29 ROBIN: Is that right?
30 SIDNEY: Are you telling me you haven't read *Das Kapital?*
31 ROBIN: I gave up reading in homage to the high illiteracy
32   rates among my native people. I'm part Cherokee.
33 SIDNEY: So am I. What fraction?
34 ROBIN: Well ... I know it's at least one-sixty-fourth. But
35   there's evidence in some recently unearthed family

1     documents suggesting that I could be as much as one-
2     eighth.
3 SIDNEY: Who isn't one-sixty-fourth Cherokee? Stop
4     anyone on the street and they'll tell you they're one-
5     sixty-fourth Cherokee. I'm one-sixteenth, but I don't
6     self-identify as Native American, even though I could.
7     I don't need to be pigeonholed by the historical
8     connotations of ethnic labels.
9 ROBIN: I'm probably one-eighth. Anyway, it's not about a
10    societally imposed number. It's about a connection
11    with the spirit of my people.
12 SIDNEY: How did you read the family documents if you
13    gave up reading?
14 ROBIN: My brother translated them to spoken word
15    poetry for me. We communicate best that way.
16 SIDNEY: You mean he read them aloud for you?
17 ROBIN: *(Shrugs.)* If that's the way you want to see it. I'm
18    planning to walk the Trail of Tears this summer.
19 SIDNEY: That's pretty Ameri-centric. Thousands of
20    indigenous peoples are still being marginalized
21    every day. It's why I'm going to work on a farm in the
22    Peruvian Andes this summer. I actually might not
23    come back. Our national culture of conformism is
24    exhausting to my creativity.
25 ROBIN: Please don't be offended, but I think your desire
26    to volunteer abroad exemplifies a high degree of
27    conformism. Society places value on volunteerism,
28    and you're eating right out of their hands.
29 SIDNEY: I'll be documenting my experiences through
30    Polaroid photography, to juxtapose the way we
31    remember the past with the way we construct a
32    shared humanity in the present.
33 ROBIN: That's a coincidence. I dabble in photography
34    myself. Have you ever heard of Constantinopolis?
35 SIDNEY: No.

1  ROBIN: It's a Turkish café located behind a warehouse
2      deep in the industrial district. The entire area has yet
3      to be gentrified, but I prefer it to any of the so-called
4      "hip" neighborhoods these days. Anyway, I have a
5      show up there at the moment.
6  SIDNEY: Wait, I think I have heard of that place. As I
7      recall, my friend invited me to a very small concert
8      there, but I was busy bottling my home-brewed
9      kombucha.
10 ROBIN: What kind of kombucha did you make? I just
11     finished a batch of juniper-hawthorne. I'm making a
12     dandelion one next.
13 SIDNEY: I find predetermined flavors to be oppressive.
14     You can't fully understand the taste of something
15     unless you don't know what it is you're drinking. You
16     can sample some of mine sometime if you'd like. I
17     harvested the ingredients in the wilds of British
18     Columbia — you can't get most of them around here
19     at all.
20 ROBIN: No thanks. I don't eat anything not grown within
21     a mile of my house. Would you like to see a picture of
22     my latest meal? *(Pulls up a screen on his phone to show*
23     *SIDNEY.)*
24 SIDNEY: *(Looks and shrugs.)* Yeah, I'd say that's about
25     what my meals look like every day. I tend not to use
26     silverware, though. It's even more oppressive than
27     predetermined flavors. Would you like to see a
28     picture of my Victrola? *(Already pulling up a screen to*
29     *show ROBIN.)*
30 ROBIN: *(Looks and shrugs.)* I think I would have framed
31     that photograph a little differently.
32 SIDNEY: Don't feel bad. Most people don't understand my
33     art. Anyway, I do my best work with my Polaroid.
34 ROBIN: I'll take your word for it. How would you like to
35     see a picture of my kombucha setup?

1   **SIDNEY: How would you like to see a picture of mine?**

2   *(Both pay no attention to the other and continue*

3   *scrolling through their phones.)*

# 44. Shopping for Bargains

**Cast:** ELLEN and KAILEY

**Setting:** No special set required.

**Props:** None

1 KAILEY: The sale starts at seven a.m. tomorrow, but we'll
2     need to be in line by five-thirty to be sure we get first
3     choice on the specials.
4 ELLEN: You are crazy. Tomorrow is the only morning all
5     week that we can sleep in, and you plan to get up at five-
6     thirty to go shopping? It will still be dark out.
7 KAILEY: It won't be dark inside the mall. If we set our
8     alarms for four-fifteen, we'll have time to shower and
9     still get there by five-thirty.
10 ELLEN: I am not getting up at four-fifteen. At four-fifteen, I
11     will be sleeping soundly in my snug little bed.
12 KAILEY: The early bird gets the worm.
13 ELLEN: I don't want any worms. What do you plan to buy
14     that's so important you'd get up that early?
15 KAILEY: Shoes! All shoes are buy one pair, get the second
16     pair at half price. That's an amazing bargain — fifty
17     percent off the regular price on shoes!
18 ELLEN: Actually, that wouldn't be fifty percent off the
19     regular price. It would be twenty-five percent off.
20 KAILEY: No, the ad says half price. "Buy one pair and get the
21     second pair at half price." Half is fifty percent.
22 ELLEN: If you pay full price for the first pair and half price
23     for the second pair, then your total discount for both
24     pairs is twenty-five percent.
25 KAILEY: Oh. Well, that's still a good bargain.
26 ELLEN: It's only a bargain if you need shoes. You got new
27     shoes for your birthday. Your closet overflows with
28     shoes. Why do you need more shoes?

1   KAILEY: Need, schmeed. You can never have too many
2       shoes. You should come with me. It'll be fun.
3   ELLEN: I don't want more shoes. I want more sleep.
4   KAILEY: Shoes aren't the only specials. There's lots of
5       other stuff on sale too. All toys and games are marked
6       down. Drills and screwdrivers are half price until
7       eight. You can get an electric egg cooker for only ten
8       dollars.
9   ELLEN: Why would I want an electric egg cooker? Or a
10      screwdriver?
11   KAILEY: You're missing the point, and if you stay home,
12      you'll miss the bargains, too. Not to mention the thrill
13      of the hunt! Where's your sense of adventure? Who
14      knows what fabulous deals we might find if we're the
15      first shoppers to rush inside the door?
16   ELLEN: Even bargains cost money. How do you plan to pay
17      for all this?
18   KAILEY: I'll use the fifty dollars that Grandma gave me for
19      Christmas. She gave you fifty dollars too, so there's no
20      reason you can't go shopping.
21   ELLEN: Yes there is.
22   KAILEY: What's the reason?
23   ELLEN: I no longer have my fifty dollars.
24   KAILEY: You only got it two days ago. How could you have
25      spent it so soon? What did you buy?
26   ELLEN: Well, I —
27   KAILEY: Wait! I know. You put the money in your savings
28      account, didn't you? Grandma's always telling us how
29      quickly compound interest adds up, and that if we
30      save our money now we'll be really glad in the future,
31      so you stuck your fifty bucks in the bank and now
32      Grandma's all proud of you for being smart and
33      thrifty, and I'm going to look like a brainless dodo
34      bird for spending mine at the mall instead of saving
35      it.

1   ELLEN: Nobody thinks you're a brainless dodo bird.
2   KAILEY: Oh, no? I'll come home tomorrow with my two
3       pairs of shoes that I don't really need and a game that
4       nobody wants to play and maybe even a screwdriver
5       — a screwdriver! — that I'll give to Dad on his
6       birthday, even though he already has plenty of
7       screwdrivers, and you'll look smug because you
8       know that ten years from now when I'm destitute
9       and begging on the street corner, you'll be living in
10      your own house that you bought with all the money
11      from your savings account.
12  ELLEN: You are seriously jumping to conclusions.
13  KAILEY: Why can't you be a normal person? Why do you
14      have to be so perfect? Now I can't even enjoy going to
15      the sale because I'll feel like I'm blowing my money
16      on something worthless instead of saving it for my
17      future.
18  ELLEN: I never said you shouldn't go to the sale. I only
19      said I'm not going.
20  KAILEY: You're not going because your fifty dollars is in a
21      savings account compounding like crazy and making
22      you rich.
23  ELLEN: My money is not compounding. I didn't put it in
24      my savings account.
25  KAILEY: Oh, great! You bought a mutual fund! That's even
26      worse! You learned all about investments and now
27      you own shares of Starbucks and Microsoft and your
28      fifty dollars are already worth fifty-one dollars and
29      thirteen cents.
30  ELLEN: If you think I own shares of Starbucks and
31      Microsoft, maybe you are a brainless dodo bird.
32  KAILEY: You didn't buy a mutual fund?
33  ELLEN: I don't know the first thing about mutual funds.
34      Even if I wanted to invest in the stock market, which
35      I don't because I don't have any money left to invest,

1    I wouldn't have a clue how to go about it.
2    KAILEY: If you didn't buy stocks and you didn't put the
3        money in your savings account, what did you do with
4        it?
5    ELLEN: I spent it.
6    KAILEY: Already? All of it?
7    ELLEN: All of it.
8    KAILEY: On what?
9    ELLEN: Chocolate-covered caramels.
10   KAILEY: You spent the whole fifty dollars on chocolate-
11       covered caramels?
12   ELLEN: I like chocolate-covered caramels.
13   KAILEY: It's amazing you didn't get sick.
14   ELLEN: I didn't eat them all yet. I still have most of them.
15       Chocolate-covered caramels are my favorite treat in
16       the whole world, and I love having a big box of them
17       in my drawer. Sometimes I open the box just to smell
18       them. Nothing smells better than chocolate-covered
19       caramels.
20   KAILEY: Grandma might not be disappointed in me after
21       all. Six months from now you won't have anything to
22       show for your Christmas money except maybe a
23       cavity. At least I'll have shoes to wear.
24   ELLEN: I'll have good memories. I'll remember how great
25       it was to have all these chocolate-covered caramels
26       and to know I could eat one any time I got a craving,
27       which is pretty much every day.
28   KAILEY: You're right. You'll have fun memories, and so
29       will I. The shoes aren't really why I want to go to the
30       sale. It's the fun of getting up early and being there
31       when the stores open and racing around like a
32       NASCAR driver, searching for fantastic prices. That's
33       the part I like. That's what I'll remember.
34   ELLEN: I hope you find lots of amazing bargains
35       tomorrow morning. Just don't buy me an electric egg

1           cooker for my birthday – and don't wake me up when

2           you leave.

3    KAILEY: I won't on one condition.

4    ELLEN: What's that?

5    KAILEY: Can I have a chocolate-covered caramel?

# 45. The Tooth Fairy Conspiracy

**Cast:** KID and MOM

**Setting:** No special set required.

**Props:** A dollar bill for Mom, kept in her pocket. A small object to represent Kid's tooth.

1   KID: Mom! I lost a tooth!

2   MOM: Honey! That's great! It's about time; that tooth was

3         hanging on by a thread.

4   KID: My first one! Look at it! *(Holds out tooth.)*

5   MOM: Looks like a healthy tooth. You're doing a good job of

6         brushing. Let's see your smile. *(KID grins widely.)* Very

7         nice.

8   KID: My class is gonna be so jealous! Can I take it to school

9         in the morning?

10  MOM: Aren't you going to put it under your pillow?

11  KID: What for?

12  MOM: For the tooth fairy, of course.

13  KID: The what?

14  MOM: Haven't I ever told you about the tooth fairy?

15  KID: No. I don't like the sound of that. Does it bite?

16  MOM: She's not called the tooth fairy because of her own

17        teeth. She takes away your baby teeth when they fall

18        out.

19  KID: And gives you big kid teeth?

20  MOM: No, you're going to grow your adult teeth yourself.

21  KID: Then how come the tooth fairy gets my baby teeth?

22  MOM: The tooth fairy will give you a quarter in exchange for

23        every tooth you lose.

24  KID: Actually, I heard Eric talking about this tooth fairy

25        thing once at school. But why does she need baby teeth?

26  MOM: Baby teeth have sentimental value.

27  KID: To the tooth fairy? I don't even know the tooth fairy.

1   MOM: The tooth fairy knows you.

2   KID: That's a little weird.

3   MOM: It's not weird. The tooth fairy knows everyone.

4   KID: Does the tooth fairy know Grandpa? Grandpa

5      doesn't have any teeth.

6   MOM: Grandpa used to have teeth. He just lost them a

7      long time ago.

8   KID: He lost them? Or the tooth fairy took them?

9   MOM: The tooth fairy won't come and steal your teeth.

10     You have to offer them to her. That's why you should

11     put your tooth under your pillow tonight. When the

12     tooth fairy makes her rounds, she'll see that you lost

13     a tooth and she'll take it away and replace it with a

14     quarter.

15   KID: How does she know who lost a tooth? Does she have

16     to check every pillow every night?

17   MOM: She has her ways of knowing.

18   KID: Well, what are they? Cameras? Spies? I don't like the

19     idea of being watched all the time. And how does she

20     get around to everyone?

21   MOM: I suppose she flies.

22   KID: She must fly pretty fast.

23   MOM: Santa flies around the world in one night.

24   KID: Santa has nine reindeer to help him.

25   MOM: The tooth fairy's had a lot of practice. She's been

26     around since I was a little girl.

27   KID: Really? She must be ancient.

28   MOM: Excuse me?

29   KID: Just sayin'. Hey, how does the tooth fairy get the tooth

30     from under the pillow?

31   MOM: You sure have a lot of questions about this. I'm

32     guessing she just reaches under the pillow for it.

33     Why?

34   KID: I'll be sleeping on my pillow! I don't want the tooth

35     fairy sneaking around my bed while I'm trying to

1  sleep. I have a soccer game against the second
2  graders tomorrow at recess, and I need my rest.
3  MOM: I'm sure the tooth fairy will be very careful not to
4      wake you up. She's a professional.
5  KID: What if she sees something she likes better than my
6      tooth and takes that instead?
7  MOM: The tooth fairy is not going to rob you.
8  KID: How do you know? If she has honest business to do
9      with me, she can come during the day when I'm
10     awake. Why isn't she here now? *(Yells.)* Hey, tooth
11     fairy! Come out and we'll talk about how much I'm
12     willing to part with this tooth for.
13 MOM: This isn't a business transaction! The tooth fairy
14     comes to everyone. It's tradition. And prices are non-
15     negotiable.
16 KID: I heard one of the second graders say she got a dollar
17     from the tooth fairy one time. Besides, this is a good
18     tooth! No cavities, nice white color. I bet Eric would
19     buy this tooth from me for more than a quarter.
20 MOM: Eric doesn't want your tooth. It's all germy.
21 KID: Doesn't it seem suspicious that the tooth fairy wants
22     it, then? You think she's not going to touch my video
23     games or slingshot but is going to leave money for my
24     germy little tooth? What does she do with all the teeth
25     she collects, anyway? It makes me think they might
26     actually be more valuable than you're letting on.
27 MOM: Why would I lie to you about the value of your
28     tooth?
29 KID: You might be in cahoots with the tooth fairy.
30 MOM: That's the most ridiculous thing I've ever heard.
31 KID: Are you?
32 MOM: None of my friends' kids made this much of a fuss.
33     They all cooperated with the tooth fairy.
34 KID: You're not answering the question.
35 MOM: What do you think the tooth fairy and I have to be

1   in cahoots about?
2   KID: Who can say? Maybe you're afraid that if I get a fair
3        price for this tooth, I'll spend it all on candy. All I
4        know is that the tooth fairy has the tooth market
5        cornered, because she refuses to come out and
6        negotiate a fair price while anyone is awake.
7   MOM: The tooth fairy gives you a quarter. She doesn't
8        have to give you anything at all.
9   KID: Sure she does, because if she didn't, I wouldn't leave
10       my tooth under the pillow. I'd lock it up in my safe
11       and wait for it to become a valuable antique. Anyway,
12       she buys my tooth wholesale, and then she sells it at
13       a mark-up and takes a cut of the profits –
14  MOM: Who do you think is out there buying up teeth for a
15       higher price than the tooth fairy?
16  KID: Moms! Now that I think about it, I bet you'd really
17       like to have this tooth. Only moms like things with
18       "sentimental value." But if the tooth fairy has a
19       monopoly on buying and selling teeth, you would
20       have no choice but to pay any price she asks. You're
21       perpetuating the cycle! I bet she would re-sell you
22       this little tooth for four times what she paid.
23  MOM: Where did you learn so much about economics?
24  KID: Look Mom, let's cut out the middle man. I'll offer you
25       a fair price for this tooth, and we can bust up the
26       tooth fairy monopoly once and for all. It's the free
27       market economy at its best.
28  MOM: And just what are you asking for your tooth?
29  KID: For this fine incisor? I'd be willing to accept two
30       dollars. Only because you're my mom.
31  MOM: I'll give you a dollar.
32  KID: One dollar! That's highway robbery!
33  MOM: Welcome to the free market. That's my final offer.
34  KID: I still think Eric would pay more. But I'll take a
35       dollar if you throw a few extra Oreos in my lunch this

1     week.

2     **MOM: You've got yourself a deal.** *(KID and MOM shake*

3     *hands, MOM hands KID the dollar from her pocket, and*

4     *KID drops tooth into MOM's hand.)*

5     **KID: Pleasure doing business with you.** *(They nod at each*

6     *other, and KID and MOM turn and exit in opposite*

7     *directions.)*

# 46. Yellowstone National Yawn

**Characters:** GUIDE and TEXTER

**Setting:** A tour bus in Yellowstone National Park. A plain chair serves as a bus seat.

**Props:** Cell phone for Texter

1　*(As scene opens, TEXTER is seated in the chair with the*
2　*cell phone. He continues to look at phone throughout*
3　*duologue. TEXTER's lines are what he's typing. GUIDE*
4　*stands beside TEXTER, looking out the window.)*
5　**GUIDE: Welcome to Yellowstone National Park. My name is**
6　**_____ *(Giving real name)* and I'll be your guide for**
7　**today's bus tour.**
8　**TEXTER: Hey, yoooo! What's up?**
9　**GUIDE: Yellowstone was established in 1872 and is**
10　**America's first national park.**
11　**TEXTER: We're in some park. Parents insisted we take a**
12　**tour. I'm crammed on a bus with thirty other people. At**
13　**least there's cell service.**
14　**GUIDE: Be sure to watch for wildlife as we go. Yellowstone is**
15　**home to grizzly bears, wolves, elk, bison, and bighorn**
16　**sheep. Feeding the animals is not allowed. If you leave**
17　**the bus, you must stay one hundred yards from wolves**
18　**and bears, and twenty-five yards from all other**
19　**animals. If you cause an animal to move, you are too**
20　**close.**
21　**TEXTER: Had to get up at six today. Not my idea of vacation.**
22　**GUIDE: On your left you can see the Norris Geyser Basin,**
23　**the hottest of Yellowstone's thermal areas. Norris has**
24　**had thermal activity for at least one hundred and**
25　**fifteen thousand years.**
26　**TEXTER: Our guide is babbling about history. If I wanted a**
27　**history lesson, I would have gone to summer school.**

| | |
|---|---|
| 1 | GUIDE: Most of the water in the Norris area is acidic, |
| 2 | including some rare acidic geysers. Right over there |
| 3 | *(Pointing)* is Steamboat Geyser, the tallest geyser in |
| 4 | the world. It measures between three hundred and |
| 5 | four hundred feet. |
| 6 | TEXTER: What are you doing tonight? |
| 7 | GUIDE: Yellowstone has almost sixty percent of the |
| 8 | world's geysers, one hundred and fifty of them in one |
| 9 | square mile! Of these, only five erupt regularly |
| 10 | enough for the park staff to predict their eruptions. |
| 11 | Old Faithful is the best known of these. |
| 12 | TEXTER: I heart baseball games! Wish I could go with you, |
| 13 | but no, stuck on worst road trip ever. |
| 14 | GUIDE: The time between eruptions of Old Faithful varies |
| 15 | from thirty-five minutes to two hours. Each eruption |
| 16 | lasts from one and a half to five minutes, and the |
| 17 | length of each eruption determines how long before |
| 18 | the next eruption. |
| 19 | TEXTER: I suppose you're going to Pizza Palace |
| 20 | afterwards. |
| 21 | GUIDE: We are now crossing the Firehole River, which is |
| 22 | world famous for its beauty and its challenging fly |
| 23 | fishing. The river has an abundance of brown, brook, |
| 24 | and rainbow trout. |
| 25 | TEXTER: Try their Sausage Delight with extra cheese. Best |
| 26 | pizza I've ever had. Meh! Now I'm hungry. |
| 27 | GUIDE: The Excelsior Geyser, with a crater that measures |
| 28 | two hundred by three hundred feet, discharges four |
| 29 | hundred gallons of water per minute into the |
| 30 | Firehole River. |
| 31 | TEXTER: Parents are oohing and aahing 'cause somebody |
| 32 | spotted an eagle. Like, seriously? We can see birds at |
| 33 | home. |
| 34 | GUIDE: The bus has stopped because we are now on the |
| 35 | forty-fifth parallel, an imaginary line that circles the |

1      globe exactly half way between the equator and the

2      North Pole. This same line goes through

3      Minneapolis-St. Paul, Ottawa, Venice, Belgrade, and

4      the northern tip of the Japanese islands.

5      TEXTER: We've stopped. I hope we don't have a flat tire or

6      something because there definitely isn't anything to

7      see or do here.

8      GUIDE: Isa Lake sits on the Continental Divide, and when

9      the snow melts in the spring, Isa Lake drains into the

10    Atlantic and the Pacific Oceans at the same time!

11    TEXTER: Wanna hang out when I get back? There're a

12    million shows on Netflix. *Game of Thrones*

13    marathon, maybe?

14    GUIDE: Just ahead you'll see beautiful Yellowstone Lake.

15    It covers thirty-two square miles and is the largest

16    lake in the park. Many arrowheads, spearheads, and

17    other Native American artifacts have been found on

18    its shores. You won't want to go swimming, though.

19    The average temperature of the water is forty-one

20    degrees.

21    TEXTER: I hope we get home Saturday afternoon, but if

22    we keep wasting time on tours, we might not make it

23    until Sunday. I swear we've stopped the car at every

24    historic marker in the last five hundred miles and

25    not a single one was worth reading. Right now we're

26    stopped at some lake. Maybe we get to go swimming.

27    GUIDE: In 1988, fire burned Yellowstone's lodgepole pine

28    forest. The North Fork Fire started from a discarded

29    cigarette and burned for weeks. In one day, the winds

30    increased to sixty miles per hour and the fire raced

31    out of control across the Lewis River Canyon. In that

32    one day, now known as Black Saturday, more acres

33    burned than in the entire previous history of

34    Yellowstone.

35    TEXTER: No swimming apparently, we're bumbling along

1       again. Have you seen Mark or Chelsea? They both
2       promised to text me, but they're M.I.A.
3   GUIDE: Look off to the left in those trees! There's a wolf.
4   TEXTER: What movie are you going to?
5   GUIDE: Two wolves! The wolves had vanished from
6       Yellowstone, but they were reintroduced in 1995 and
7       1996.
8   TEXTER: I'm so jeals! Wait 'til I get home, and I'll go with
9       you. I love nature documentaries. I saw a sweet
10      National Geographic special once about wolves. I'd
11      watch that again if you're interested.
12   GUIDE: Having natural predators keeps the park's
13      ecosystem balanced. The wolves have thrived, and
14      there are currently more than three hundred of them
15      in the greater Yellowstone area.
16   TEXTER: What else have you done since I left?
17   GUIDE: Yellowstone has more than ten thousand
18      brilliantly colored hot springs, bubbling mudpots,
19      and steam vents.
20   TEXTER: You're so lucky. I wish my parents would let me
21      sleep in every day and play computer games. But no,
22      I have to be dragged across the country so I can listen
23      to some guide yammer on about mud and steam. Next
24      summer I'm getting a job so I have an excuse to stay
25      home.
26   GUIDE: In the peak summer months, thirty-five hundred
27      people are employed by Yellowstone National Park
28      concessioners. Eight hundred more work for the
29      National Park Service.
30   TEXTER: I suppose I'll apply at Pizza Palace. Not many
31      other choices. It'll be boring, but not as bad as a road
32      trip with the 'rents.
33   GUIDE: I hope you have enjoyed this brief tour of
34      Yellowstone National Park and will explore it further
35      on foot or horseback.

1  TEXTER: Finally! Tour is finished. I can get off this
2      abysmal bus. Text me later!

# 47. My Rotten Roommate

**Cast:** GEORGE and NATHAN

**Setting:** A college dorm. Two small desks if available, but two chairs will work.

**Props:** A laptop for each player.

1  *(As scene opens, GEORGE and NATHAN are both writing*
2  *letters on their laptops, angled slightly away from each*
3  *other.)*
4  **GEORGE: Dear Mom and Pop, You left just in time. If you**
5  **had stayed another fifteen minutes, you might have**
6  **met my roommate.**
7  **NATHAN: Hey, sibs, Here it is, your first letter from the**
8  **family's official college student. And the verdict is ...**
9  **dorm life is not all it's cracked up to be. The problem is**
10  **my roommate.**
11  **GEORGE: I was alphabetizing my books on the shelf when**
12  **Nathan arrived. He rushed in, said, "Yo, roomie,"**
13  **dropped a backpack on the floor, and left. He came**
14  **back ten minutes later with two black garbage bags full**
15  **of stuff. That was his luggage!**
16  **NATHAN: George had finished unpacking when I got there**
17  **and was trying to find a place to store his three-piece**
18  **set of matched monogrammed luggage. I told him**
19  **that's why I packed my stuff in plastic bags. He raised**
20  **an eyebrow at me and promptly took up half the closet**
21  **space with his suitcases.**
22  **GEORGE: Nathan lost his key to our room on the first day.**
23  **Please don't ask me where he could have put it that**
24  **fast, because I don't know. It costs fifty dollars to**
25  **replace a key, so rather than buy a new one, he has**
26  **taken to using our dorm room window as a door.**
27  **NATHAN: The second night of school, George called campus**

1     security on me. He had locked the window earlier in
2     the day, so when I got home late from the library, I
3     had to try to jimmy the latch. He thought I was a
4     burglar breaking in, so he hid in the closet and called
5     security on his cell phone. Next thing I know, I've got
6     flashlights shining in my face and a disapproving
7     security guard asking me if I'm a student here.
8 GEORGE: Nathan and I are both musically inclined,
9     which is the only reason I can imagine why the
10     misguided housing office decided to put us together.
11     Nathan plays the saxophone. Constantly. He drowns
12     out the chords on my guitar.
13 NATHAN: George thinks he's musical too. He can play one
14     song on the guitar, and it's "Banana Pancakes" by
15     Jack Johnson. Sometimes I pick up my sax and start
16     playing just so I don't have to listen to "Banana
17     Pancakes" for the five hundredth time.
18 GEORGE: We've been here a week now, and Nathan has
19     yet to make his bed. I made it for him the first two
20     days, but then I found a candy wrapper between the
21     sheets. It's like a personalized invitation for ants.
22     Now I try to ignore it and tell myself that *my* side of
23     the room is tidy and sanitary, and that's what
24     matters. But his side of the room is too close for my
25     liking, especially when he leaves his dirty underwear
26     on the floor.
27 NATHAN: George and I share a closet, which is fine, but
28     would you believe that his clothes are hung by color?
29     Shirts first, from dark to light, and then his pants. He
30     has some weird things called shoe trees that he sticks
31     in his loafers when he isn't wearing them. Every
32     night before bed, he chooses what he's going to wear
33     the next day and hangs it on a special hook he put on
34     the back of our door. His favorite outfits include
35     sweater vests.

1   GEORGE: I've begun kicking Nathan's boxers under his
2        bed so I don't have to look at them. The first time he
3        ran out of clean underwear, he got confused until he
4        figured out where it had all gone. Then he fished
5        everything out and, surprisingly, did laundry.
6        Unsurprisingly, he threw everything in the machine
7        at the same time. No wonder his shirts came out as
8        dingy as they went in.
9   NATHAN: This dude irons his socks! No, I'm not kidding.
10      He brought his own personal iron from home, and he
11      irons his socks, his sheets, and his T-shirts. I actually
12      saw him iron his tighty-whities! I think he would iron
13      my backpack if I left it on his side of the room. I've
14      started keeping it under my desk just in case he tries.
15  GEORGE: I think Nathan might be a hoarder. He hides his
16      backpack and all his jeans under his desk like he's
17      afraid I'll do something to them. He also sneaks food
18      from the dining hall like every meal is his last supper.
19      Pizza, cookies, toast ... you name it. Where does he put
20      it all? In our shared mini-fridge. I've had to throw out
21      six stale grilled-cheese sandwiches. I don't know why
22      he bothers bringing food back. He keeps a colossal
23      box of Pop-Tarts in there that should last him a
24      month at least.
25  NATHAN: There's this mini-fridge in our room. I thought
26      we'd share the space, and maybe share some food.
27      Instead, George has decided that I have the top two
28      shelves and he has the bottom two. The dining hall
29      grilled-cheese sandwiches are the best, so I tried
30      keeping extras in the fridge a few times. George
31      threw every one of them away. I've started hiding the
32      sandwiches in a cardboard box that used to hold Pop-
33      Tarts, which so far has kept them safe from him.
34  GEORGE: I wouldn't be surprised if Nathan's deplorable
35      eating habits lead directly to diabetes. At first I really

1     encouraged him to have more organic produce. I

2     thought I was making progress when I came home to

3     find that my fruits and veggies had been moved.

4     Maybe, I thought, he was looking at the stickers to

5     see where he could buy some of the same. But then I

6     watched him eat three king-sized Snickers bars for

7     lunch, so now I save my breath.

8  NATHAN: George is a health food junkie. His shelves hold

9     apples, broccoli, carrots, and yogurt. Please note that

10     these foods are arranged alphabetically. That's not a

11     coincidence. I know because yesterday I switched the

12     broccoli and the apples while George was at class, just

13     to see what happened. They were back in their proper

14     places in a matter of hours, and now they're labeled

15     with his initials. I used to keep Snickers bars cold in

16     the fridge, but every time George opened the fridge to

17     get a baby carrot, he started groaning about how I was

18     going to get diabetes and he was going to have to give

19     me insulin shots. I moved my Snickers into my desk

20     drawer, but sometimes I like to eat three or four of

21     them at once just to see his face get pale.

22  GEORGE: Yesterday I went to the Student Housing Office

23     and practically begged for a single. The housing

24     officer said every one of them is taken this semester

25     and told me he thought things would work out. I told

26     him the chances were a million to one.

27  NATHAN: Yesterday I went to the Student Housing Office

28     and asked to switch roommates. The housing guy

29     said if I can find someone else to room with, we can

30     apply for a different room and move out in the next

31     few weeks. But to be honest, I haven't really met

32     anyone here besides George.

33  GEORGE: Right now Nathan's hunched over his

34     computer, probably figuring out how to order

35     Snickers bars in bulk. He definitely doesn't want

1      anything to do with me.

2  NATHAN: I know I should try a little harder, but I can't

3      imagine anything that George and I could have in

4      common. He's at his desk across the room right now,

5      probably ordering more closet organizers on

6      Amazon. I miss you guys and the days where we

7      would all go hang out and play Frisbee in the park or

8      do whatever. I wish I had a roommate who'd be down

9      for that.

10 GEORGE: OK, fine. I can practically hear you saying I

11     should give him a second chance. I will turn around

12     and ask him right now if he wants to hang out. But I

13     can guarantee he'll say no. *(GEORGE turns to look*

14     *over at NATHAN.)* Do you want to go play Frisbee or

15     something?

16 NATHAN: *(Looks up at GEORGE. They pause.)* Sure. *(He and*

17     *GEORGE turn slowly back to their computers.)* Um,

18     actually, you'll never believe what just happened.

19     George wants to play Frisbee right now.

20 GEORGE: OK, fine. Scratch that last part. Now I actually

21     have to go play Frisbee with Nathan. This doesn't

22     necessarily mean we're going to be friends. But I

23     guess I'll let you know.

24 NATHAN: I've gotta go. Frisbee might be disastrous, but

25     I'll write you guys more soon. *(He and GEORGE shut*

26     *their laptops and stand up together.)* How did you

27     know I like Frisbee?

28 GEORGE: I didn't. I was just hoping you did. I used to play

29     Ultimate Frisbee in high school.

30 NATHAN: *(They start walking together.)* You're joking. So

31     did I!

32 GEORGE: No way! What position?

33 NATHAN: Handler. Are you gonna try out for the school

34     team?

35 GEORGE: I think so! Are you? *(They exit.)*

# 48. Coyote Passage

**Cast:** PILAR and ANTONIO

**Setting:** A Mexican border town. A chair is Center Stage.

**Props:** A pencil and piece of paper for Antonio

1    *(As scene opens, ANTONIO is seated, poring over the*
2    *piece of paper. He has a pencil in his pocket. PILAR*
3    *enters, walks to where ANTONIO sits, and stands before*
4    *him. ANTONIO looks up in slight surprise.)*
5    **ANTONIO: Your face looks familiar, girl.**
6    **PILAR: I've been here before. Six months ago.**
7    **ANTONIO: You came with your family.**
8    **PILAR: Yes.**
9    **ANTONIO: Mother, father, and little brother. Where are they**
10   **now?**
11   **PILAR: My parents are in prison.**
12   **ANTONIO: How unfortunate.**
13   **PILAR: How dare you call it unfortunate. It's your fault.**
14   **ANTONIO: My fault? Check yourself, girl. Who sent them**
15   **there? Not Antonio.**
16   **PILAR: No. Not Antonio. You disappeared and left us**
17   **sinking into the strait.**
18   **ANTONIO: You knew there would be danger when you came**
19   **to me six months ago.**
20   **PILAR: You led us to believe that you knew what you were**
21   **doing.**
22   **ANTONIO: I know very well what I'm doing. I know the**
23   **risks, and I communicated them to you.**
24   **PILAR: You put our chances of reaching the United States at**
25   **ninety percent.**
26   **ANTONIO: And you fell into the unlucky ten.**
27   **PILAR: I've talked to other migrants since returning to**
28   **Mexico. That wasn't the first time your ring was**
29   **caught.**

1 ANTONIO: Of course it wasn't. There's not a coyote along
2     the Mexican border who hasn't been caught.
3 PILAR: You sped away awfully easily in that little boat of
4     yours.
5 ANTONIO: Who runs this operation? I do. Hundreds of
6     migrants a year owe their escape from Mexico to me.
7     I know the route and I know the officials. The border
8     agents and I have an understanding – I don't give
9     them reason to arrest me, and I can try the crossing
10     again the next week. That's why I lead the crossings
11     in my own separate boat. If I were taken into custody,
12     the knowledge of this route would be lost.
13 PILAR: You left your accomplice to the authorities, right
14     along with the rest of us.
15 ANTONIO: Óscar? He is only sixteen years old. The U.S.
16     government can't try him under their federal laws
17     because he is a minor.
18 PILAR: And the other forty people you were supposed to
19     be transporting? If the American agents hadn't found
20     the boat, everyone would have drowned.
21 ANTONIO: Better back here than dead at the bottom of the
22     Caribbean.
23 PILAR: Maybe.
24 ANTONIO: How is it that you are out of prison, anyway?
25 PILAR: I didn't go to prison. I hid under the capsized boat
26     while the border agents hauled the rest of them into
27     the cutter. Then I swam for shore. I was almost a mile
28     away from the boat when I saw the agents come back
29     for it in their helicopter. They lifted it out of the
30     middle of the strait on four long ropes. I swam
31     underwater and held my breath for as long as I
32     possibly could while the helicopter rose up and flew
33     away with the boat.
34 ANTONIO: You were the only one?
35 PILAR: A man I didn't know hid with me. We were the only

1      two who knew how to swim. I made my way back to
2      my home, desperate to find my family. Then I
3      learned that my parents were locked up by our own
4      government for leaving without papers. My
5      grandmother is caring for my brother, but she has no
6      job and can barely support herself through the
7      charity of our neighbors.
8  ANTONIO: So what is it that you want from me? To berate
9      me? You have no case against me. What you tried to
10     do is just as illegal as how I make my living.
11  PILAR: I have to try the crossing again.
12  ANTONIO: Try again? *(Shakes his head.)* I have a boat
13     leaving tomorrow night, but I'm not sure you will be
14     able to afford it. Immigration reform has made
15     crossing the border even riskier. My prices have
16     risen.
17  PILAR: You owe me a passage.
18  ANTONIO: I don't owe you anything. The cash your father
19     paid up front is nonrefundable. He knew that.
20  PILAR: How much will it take now?
21  ANTONIO: Twenty-five hundred dollars a head. Half up
22     front and half when we arrive.
23  PILAR: Twenty-five hundred!
24  ANTONIO: Plenty of people charge more. Especially for
25     girls. Girls are more likely to die on the journey. You
26     die, and the coyotes don't get paid. It's why I charge
27     half up front.
28  PILAR: But everything we paid you the first time got us
29     nowhere!
30  ANTONIO: Just because you didn't make it across the
31     border doesn't mean there weren't costs. The boat,
32     the rations, the officials — none of it comes cheap. I
33     run a business here, missy. Not a charity.
34  PILAR: I have nothing. We spent our entire savings on the
35     first attempted passage. I'm here to cross the border

1     so I can work for the money to care for my
2     grandmother and little brother. There are no living
3     wages where I come from.
4  ANTONIO: Look, girl. I'm sorry I can't help, but I'm not
5     the end of the line. I have people I have to pay too. It
6     may not seem fair to you, but nothing's fair on the
7     U.S. border.
8  PILAR: There must be something you can do. You know
9     the people here. I know no one. Is there anybody who
10    will take me across for cheaper?
11  ANTONIO: *(Sighs.)* I know a man who runs a much riskier
12     smuggling ring than the one I operate. He will let you
13     cross for free, but you will have to carry certain illicit
14     substances with you that could land you in prison for
15     the rest of your life if you were to be caught.
16  PILAR: Where can I find him?
17  ANTONIO: You should not take this risk lightly, girl. The
18     conditions are much worse than mine were. You will
19     walk across the border through some of the harshest
20     parts of the desert. You may not see food or water for
21     days. If you get across without being found, you will
22     travel north through other checkpoints packed into
23     compartments in the floor of a truck. It may be
24     difficult to breathe.
25  PILAR: I have no other option.
26  ANTONIO: *(Tears a corner from his paper, takes pencil from*
27     *his pocket, and scrawls something on the paper.)* This is
28     how you get in contact with him. You may be able to
29     leave tonight.
30  PILAR: Thank you, for lack of better words.
31  ANTONIO: Good luck. That's all you can wish for.

# 49. Where There's a Will

**Cast:** LANE and KENDALL
**Setting:** No special set required.
**Props:** Pencil and notebook

1     *(As scene opens, KENDALL is writing in the notebook.)*
2   **LANE:** What are you writing?
3   **KENDALL:** I'm filling out my will.
4   **LANE:** Will? As in, when you die, who gets your money?
5   **KENDALL:** Yep.
6   **LANE:** Are you sick?
7   **KENDALL:** I'm fine now, but what if I got hit by a truck on
8       my way to school tomorrow? If I didn't have a will, you
9       wouldn't know my wishes.
10 **LANE:** Do you have a hidden fortune that I haven't heard
11      about? Because the last I knew, you were broke and
12      trying to borrow five bucks from me so you could go to
13      a movie.
14 **KENDALL:** I'm still broke.
15 **LANE:** Then why are you bothering to write a will?
16 **KENDALL:** Everyone should have a will. Wills are not just
17      for designating who gets your money. You can also
18      decide who gets all your possessions. That's what I'm
19      doing.
20 **LANE:** I've seen your room. If you get hit by a truck, Mom
21      and Dad will rent a Dumpster and toss all your junk in
22      it and have it hauled to the dump.
23 **KENDALL:** Junk, ha! If they tossed everything in my room,
24      they'd be throwing away a lot of valuable stuff.
25 **LANE:** Like what?
26 **KENDALL:** Like my autograph collection.
27 **LANE:** You have an autograph collection? I didn't know that.
28      Whose autographs do you have?
29 **KENDALL:** Tweetmore Birdsong, for one.

1　LANE: Who?
2　KENDALL: Don't tell me you've never heard of Tweetmore
3　　　Birdsong!
4　LANE: Is he a singer?
5　KENDALL: Tweetmore Birdsong is only the most famous
6　　　avian impersonator of all time. He can duplicate the
7　　　sounds of forty-nine different birds.
8　LANE: You're making this up, right?
9　KENDALL: No! I saw Tweetmore Birdsong on TV. He did
10　　　an imitation of a robin, a blue jay, a mourning dove,
11　　　and an owl. He can even imitate a hummingbird.
12　LANE: Whoopee. No doubt there's a big demand for
13　　　hummingbird impersonators. Can he fly too?
14　KENDALL: He is a genius at mimicking bird calls. If you
15　　　had a mourning dove on one side of your yard and
16　　　Tweetmore Birdsong on the other side and they were
17　　　both calling, you wouldn't be able to tell which was
18　　　the real bird.
19　LANE: Except the real bird would be sitting in a tree and I
20　　　assume Tweetmore Genius Birdsong would be on the
21　　　ground.
22　KENDALL: Tweetmore Birdsong is amazing!
23　LANE: How did you get his autograph?
24　KENDALL: I wrote him a letter and enclosed a self-
25　　　addressed stamped envelope. I told him I thought he
26　　　was the most talented act I'd ever seen and asked if I
27　　　could have his autograph. He signed a picture of a
28　　　crow and sent it to me.
29　LANE: Who gets Tweetmore Birdsong's autographed crow
30　　　when you kick the bucket?
31　KENDALL: The Smithsonian Museum in Washington, D.C.
32　　　They'll appreciate it, and lots of people will see it
33　　　when it's displayed there.
34　LANE: I'm sure the Smithsonian will be thrilled. What
35　　　other autographs do you have?

1 KENDALL: So far I only have Tweetmore Birdsong.

2 LANE: You said you had a collection. You need a

3     minimum of three items in order for it to be

4     considered a collection.

5 KENDALL: Says who?

6 LANE: Everyone knows you need at least three items to

7     make a collection.

8 KENDALL: *(Tears a page out of the notebook and hands it*

9     *and the pencil to LANE.)* **Here. Sign this, please.**

10 LANE: What for?

11 KENDALL: I want your autograph to add to my collection.

12 LANE: Oh, please.

13 KENDALL: Come on. It won't hurt you to sign your name.

14 LANE: *(Sighs, rolls eyes, and signs name. Hands paper back*

15     *to KENDALL.)* **There. Are you happy now?**

16 KENDALL: You're the one who should be happy. Imagine

17     being in the same collection as Tweetmore Birdsong!

18 LANE: That's still only two signatures.

19 KENDALL: Wrong. *(Signs name.)* I'm number three. I now

20     have an official autograph collection.

21 LANE: What else is in your will?

22 KENDALL: My game day football. It's the ball that made

23     the touchdown that won the game that clinched the

24     championship.

25 LANE: What championship? You're not on a football team.

26 KENDALL: I used to be. I made the game-winning

27     touchdown in the toddler league championship.

28 LANE: Toddler league? How old were you?

29 KENDALL: Three.

30 LANE: There are no football leagues for three-year-olds.

31 KENDALL: It wasn't exactly an official league. It was my

32     play group, and we made up our own rules.

33 LANE: Is that the highlight of your life? A touchdown

34     when you were three years old?

35 KENDALL: No, but it was important at the time.

1   LANE: Who is the lucky recipient of this treasured
2      football?
3   KENDALL: I don't know. The only people who would
4      remember that game are the kids I played it with, and
5      that was when we still lived in Pittsburgh. I don't
6      know where any of them live now. I don't even
7      remember their last names.
8   LANE: Moving right along ...
9   KENDALL: OK, maybe I shouldn't put the football in my
10    will.
11   LANE: The football is definitely Dumpster material.
12   KENDALL: No! You can donate it to one of the thrift stores.
13      Some little kid will be glad to have that football.
14   LANE: What other bequests are you making?
15   KENDALL: I'm trying to decide what to do with my jars of
16      toenail clippings.
17   LANE: Ew! Please tell me you have not saved your toenail
18      clippings.
19   KENDALL: I've saved them for two years, and if you were
20      smart, you'd save yours too.
21   LANE: What possible use would I have for toenail
22      clippings?
23   KENDALL: They're for drug tests. Toenails contain the bio-
24      material keratin, which means tests on them can
25      show deposits of drugs and drug metabolites. Toenail
26      clippings can confirm the presence of cocaine,
27      amphetamines, opiates, oxycondone, and other
28      drugs.
29   LANE: I don't use drugs and neither do you. Do you?
30   KENDALL: Of course not.
31   LANE: Then what makes you think you'll be asked to take
32      a drug test?
33   KENDALL: If I decide to go out for a sport, a drug test
34      might be required. To absolutely prove the absence of
35      drugs, more than one test is necessary and, since

1   toenails grow so slowly, the clippings need to be
2   taken several weeks apart. By being prepared, I'll
3   save lots of time.
4 LANE: I thought the sports teams tested your urine. You
5   pee in a jar, and two days later, you're either on the
6   team or eliminated.
7 KENDALL: Toenail clippings avoid the embarrassment.
8   Some employers demand a drug test too, before
9   they'll hire you. If you have your toenail clippings on
10   hand, you can speed up the process.
11 LANE: Somehow I can't picture myself going on a job
12   interview and handing the interviewer a jar of my
13   toenail clippings.
14 KENDALL: My motto is "Think Ahead." That's why I'm
15   writing my will.
16 LANE: Once you're dead, you won't be trying out for a
17   sports team or applying for a job, so it's probably safe
18   to leave the toenail clippings out of your will.
19 KENDALL: Oh. Then I suppose they're destined for the
20   Dumpster.
21 LANE: Forget the toenails. What about your good stuff?
22   Who gets your Mickey Mouse watch?
23 KENDALL: I hadn't thought about that. Do you want it?
24 LANE: Yes. I love that watch.
25 KENDALL: I thought you said all of my stuff belonged in
26   the Dumpster.
27 LANE: Everything except your Mickey Mouse watch.
28 KENDALL: What's it worth to you?
29 LANE: You want to sell me your Mickey Mouse watch?
30   Grandma and Grandpa gave that to you.
31 KENDALL: I'd never sell it. I just want to know what you'll
32   give me if I leave the watch to you in my will.
33 LANE: Much as I might hope otherwise, you are probably
34   going to live for at least another sixty years. By then I
35   won't care about a Mickey Mouse watch.

1  KENDALL: By then a genuine Mickey Mouse watch will
2      probably be worth a fortune. I'll leave it to you in my
3      will if you mow the lawn for me all this month.
4  LANE: Forget it. This whole conversation is ridiculous.
5  KENDALL: I'll make you a deal. I'll leave you my Mickey
6      Mouse watch in my will if you make a will and leave
7      me your Miss Piggy T-shirt.
8  LANE: I'll think about it.
9  KENDALL: You never wear that Miss Piggy T-shirt.
10  LANE: You never wear your Mickey Mouse watch.
11  KENDALL: You want to trade?
12  LANE: You mean now?
13  KENDALL: My watch for your T-shirt. Neither of us has to
14      wait sixty years.
15  LANE: It's a deal. *(They shake hands, and exit.)*

# 50. Focus

**Cast:** REESE and JORDAN
**Setting:** A library study room. A table is Center Stage. Two chairs are positioned across the table from one another.
**Props:** Small pill bottle for Reese. Textbooks and laptops for both players.

1   *(As scene opens, REESE and JORDAN are seated across*
2   *from each other with textbooks and laptops open. REESE*
3   *has the pill bottle in his pocket. He jiggles his leg and*
4   *types intently on his computer. JORDAN stares*
5   *contemplatively at his computer. REESE suddenly looks*
6   *up at JORDAN.)*
7   REESE: Hey, Jordan. You *are* coming camping with us
8       tomorrow, aren't you?
9   JORDAN: *(Heaves a sigh.)* I can't, dude. I wish. I'm going to be
10      right here in this study room all weekend. It's my final
11      push on this awful senior project.
12  REESE: You're that far behind?
13  JORDAN: Yeah. I put it off way too long.
14  REESE: But camping! We've done it every year!
15  JORDAN: I know it. I'm going to be so jealous of you guys.
16      Especially because this project is straight-up busy
17      work. You know administration only assigned it to
18      keep us from pulling senior pranks. It's not hard ... I
19      just can't concentrate.
20  REESE: How many more pages do you have left to write?
21  JORDAN: Ten. Plus the bibliography.
22  REESE: Dang. You *are* behind. Why'd you leave it so long?
23  JORDAN: Because there's been so much stuff to do!
24      Everyone is finishing up with their senior stuff and
25      barbecuing on the beach and having softball games
26      and going to shows. I can't resist the peer pressure.
27      Every time someone invites me anywhere, I end up

1        saying yes. I keep telling myself that I've gotta take

2        every opportunity and live it up while we're all

3        together for a few more weeks.

4   REESE: That's not a bad thing, is it?

5   JORDAN: No! It's been the best semester of my life. Until

6        right now. Now I'm going to have to miss out on the

7        one thing I care about most because I couldn't say no

8        to the other stuff.

9   REESE: I know a way you can get it all done.

10  JORDAN: Oh, yeah? Time travel?

11  REESE: Nope. Here. *(Removes pill bottle from his pocket*

12      *and rolls it across the table to JORDAN.)* It's on me.

13  JORDAN: *(Picks up the bottle and examines it.)* What's this?

14      ADD meds?

15  REESE: Yeah.

16  JORDAN: I'm not gonna take these, man.

17  REESE: Jordan, it's fine. I've had all I need. I've got about

18      an hour 'til I'm done with my work. Why do you think

19      I've been so productive tonight?

20  JORDAN: You're on these right now? I can't even tell.

21  REESE: It doesn't make a big difference. All it does is let

22      you focus all your attention on the task at hand.

23  JORDAN: Then how come you're not typing a mile a

24      minute?

25  REESE: I'll get there in a sec. Right now the task at hand is

26      convincing you that you've got to leave with us on

27      that camping trip in the morning.

28  JORDAN: Do you always take these?

29  REESE: Only when I'm really pressed for time. I try not to

30      overuse 'em. They're probably not good for me.

31  JORDAN: Yeah, probably not. Don't you think this is kind

32      of sketchy?

33  REESE: Not really. Why?

34  JORDAN: Who do you get these from?

35  REESE: It's my prescription. Look at the bottle.

1   JORDAN: Oh! I thought you were buying them up.

2   REESE: Naw. Do I look like a hoodlum to you?

3   JORDAN: Only when you go around rolling pill bottles

4       across the table!

5   REESE: OK, you've got me there. I didn't mean to weird

6       you out. But like half our classmates have

7       prescriptions for this stuff. It's not hard to get. We're

8       seriously an ADHD generation. Have you never taken

9       it?

10  JORDAN: No. I've never felt like I needed to.

11  REESE: But Jordan, if you were going to take it one time,

12       wouldn't it be the night that you could get ten pages

13       of writing done and go camping with your four best

14       friends in the morning?

15  JORDAN: When you put it like that, yeah. But I also feel

16       like if I take it once, I'll never be able to get anything

17       done of my own accord again. I'll always be like, "I

18       could be so much more productive with those meds."

19  REESE: OK. That's honestly good thinking. I don't think

20       most people who take it actually need it. But for you,

21       this is the last milestone before summer. You won't

22       have another project for months, and the meds will

23       be the last thing on your mind. I mean, I've been

24       taking them since middle school, and I've never felt

25       dependent. It's just a nice push to get my work done

26       on occasion.

27  JORDAN: Maybe you're fine, but I have an addictive

28       personality. Last year I got so hooked on caffeine, I

29       woke up with migraines that only went away around

30       the third cup of coffee. It only took me two months to

31       get that used to it.

32  REESE: Can I suggest that you've been influenced by a

33       slightly closed-minded health curriculum? Try not to

34       think of these as so much of a drug.

35  JORDAN: Maybe health class was one-sided, but they did

1     warn me about peer pressure. Listen to you! You're a
2     bad influence, Reese.
3  REESE: Hey, you're right. I'm sorry, man! I don't mean to
4     pressure you. I just want you to come camping so bad!
5  JORDAN: I know, I know. But here's the way I see it ... if I'm
6     going to sacrifice something in the name of having
7     the weekend of my life with my best friends,
8     shouldn't it be this busy work project the school
9     assigned and not my academic integrity?
10 REESE: I'd buy that. But wait a second ... does this mean
11     you're considering coming camping?
12 JORDAN: *(Sighs again.)* I don't know, man.
13 REESE: OK Jordan, humor me for one more second and
14     then I'll let you work. If we run a cost-benefit analysis
15     of the situation, you've got two options. You either
16     spend a rotten weekend locked away slaving over a
17     project that you said yourself was dumb busy work in
18     the first place, or you cut yourself some slack – just
19     this once – to spend the weekend of your life camping
20     with your best friends one last time before
21     graduation. You've already got a solid GPA, you're
22     accepted at a great school, and they're not going to
23     reject you just because you get a B minus on the final
24     assignment of your high school career.
25 JORDAN: Reese. The peer pressure. You're doing it again.
26 REESE: This is the good side of peer pressure! The one
27     they never talked about in health class. I'm only
28     gonna say one more thing: it's supposed to be eighty-
29     five degrees and spotlessly sunny.
30 JORDAN: You're killing me, man. How many hours 'til you
31     guys were gonna leave?
32 REESE: What time is it now?
33 JORDAN: Nine o'clock.
34 REESE: We've got about ten hours.
35 JORDAN: Ten hours. You know, I haven't pulled an all-

1     nighter in awhile ...
2   REESE: You can sleep in the car!
3   JORDAN: That gives me what, about an hour a page? *(Nods*
4       *to himself, thinking. Then he rolls the pill bottle back*
5       *across the table to REESE.)* **Yo, I don't need this stuff. I**
6       **used to be able to crank pages out like this when I**
7       **was a junior writing college essays. Let's get this**
8       **show on the road!** *(Starts to type.)*
9   REESE: *(Picks up the pill bottle and smiles.)* **I gotta say,**
10      **props, dude. But still — thank goodness for peer**
11      **pressure!**

# 51. Snow White and the Fortune Teller

**Cast:** SNOW WHITE and MADAME SEER
**Setting:** Madame Seer's room. Two chairs face each other.
**Props:** None

1  *(As scene opens, MADAME SEER is Center Stage near the*
2  *chairs. SNOW WHITE enters.)*
3  MADAME SEER: Come in, dearie. I am Madame Seer, teller
4    of fortunes. I can read sadness or joy in your palm and
5    foresee your future. Come, come, my child. I sense your
6    fear, but you need not be afraid of Madame Seer. I will
7    calm you. I will help you.
8  SNOW WHITE: Oh, Madame Seer. I'm so scared I don't know
9    what to do!
10 MADAME SEER: You have come to the right place. I,
11   Madame Seer, will look into the days ahead of you and
12   tell you whom you can trust and what you should do.
13 SNOW WHITE: Thank you!
14 MADAME SEER: You are trembling, my child. What is it that
15   frightens you so?
16 SNOW WHITE: It's Queen Savage. She wants me killed.
17 MADAME SEER: The Queen! Why would Queen Savage, well
18   known to be the wealthiest, most powerful, and most
19   beautiful woman in all the kingdom, want to do away
20   with a sweet girl like you?
21 SNOW WHITE: Because of her mirror. She has a talking
22   mirror, and when she asked it, "Mirror, mirror on the
23   wall, who's the fairest of them all?" she expected the
24   mirror to say it was her. That's what the mirror always
25   said in the past. This time the mirror told her about
26   me. It said I was the fairest in the land.
27 MADAME SEER: So the queen is jealous of your youthful
28   beauty.

1   SNOW WHITE: She hired a woodchopper to hunt me
2         down and kill me and take my heart back to her. I
3         fled through the forest, and when he caught me, he
4         took pity on me and killed a wild boar instead. He cut
5         out its heart and gave it to the Queen.
6   MADAME SEER: Good thinking. Problem solved.
7   SNOW WHITE: The problem was solved until she asked,
8         "Mirror, mirror on the wall, who's the fairest of them
9         all?" and the mirror said again that it was me. The
10        Queen figured out that she had been tricked and that
11        I'm still alive, and now she's coming after me herself!
12  MADAME SEER: Not to brag or anything, but without even
13        looking at your palm, I already know you have
14        serious trouble.
15  SNOW WHITE: You are truly remarkable! Besides being
16        afraid, I feel so guilty! That poor wild pig. All he was
17        doing was rooting around under the trees looking for
18        truffles, and then he got stabbed to death and his
19        heart cut out and carried to the Queen. It wasn't his
20        fault that I have a flawless complexion and naturally
21        curly hair.
22  MADAME SEER: Not to mention an abundance of
23        modesty.
24  SNOW WHITE: I feel bad about the woodchopper, too.
25        He'll never be able to work in these woods again. The
26        Queen put a price on his head, and he had to run
27        away to save his own life. All because of me and my
28        great beauty.
29  MADAME SEER: Please be seated, my dear. I'll take a look
30        at your palm and see what's going to happen next.
31        *(SNOW WHITE sits. MADAME SEER sits opposite her*
32        *and takes SNOW WHITE's hand.)*
33  SNOW WHITE: What do you see? Is there any hope for me?
34  MADAME SEER: I see you living in a cozy cottage with
35        seven men.

1 SNOW WHITE: Seven men! That has to be a mistake. I
2     don't have a boyfriend. I've never even dated. On the
3     night of the junior prom, I stayed home and watched
4     *Cinderella.*
5 MADAME SEER: These men care a great deal for you.
6 SNOW WHITE: They do? All of them?
7 MADAME SEER: All of them. They like having you live
8     with them, and they want to protect you.
9 SNOW WHITE: That's good, I guess. But seven of them?
10     What do they look like? I wonder if I already know
11     any of them.
12 MADAME SEER: They are small men.
13 SNOW WHITE: How small?
14 MADAME SEER: They appear to stand about four feet tall.
15 SNOW WHITE: I'm five foot five. I can't see myself
16     involved with a guy who's only four feet. Are you sure
17     they're full-grown?
18 MADAME SEER: They appear to be dwarfs. Yes, I see that
19     you are living with seven dwarfs.
20 SNOW WHITE: I wonder where I'll meet them. What do
21     they do for a living?
22 MADAME SEER: They're in diamonds.
23 SNOW WHITE: Diamonds! I suppose height isn't the most
24     important consideration when choosing a man.
25 MADAME SEER: They ride deep into a mine each day and
26     dig out the diamonds.
27 SNOW WHITE: Do they get to keep them? I've always
28     wanted a diamond tiara. They're so sparkly. A
29     diamond tiara would be perfect on my naturally curly
30     hair.
31 MADAME SEER: The diamonds belong to the owner of the
32     mine.
33 SNOW WHITE: Oh. Queen Savage must not know about
34     the dwarfs' house.
35 MADAME SEER: She knows. She follows you there and

1     offers you a poisoned apple.

2   SNOW WHITE: I'm glad to know this in advance. I'll

3     refuse her apple and send her away.

4   MADAME SEER: She comes back in disguise. She is a very

5     clever queen, and you are a foolish young girl.

6   SNOW WHITE: Now wait just a minute. What makes you

7     think I'm foolish? I got ninety-eight percent on my

8     last science test.

9   MADAME SEER: I can see the future. The queen will trick

10     you into taking a bite from the poisoned apple, and

11     you will fall into a deep coma.

12   SNOW WHITE: Where are the dwarfs while this is going

13     on? What kind of protectors are they?

14   MADAME SEER: They are at work. When they return from

15     the diamond mine, they find you on the floor.

16   SNOW WHITE: And do CPR, and revive me?

17   MADAME SEER: Alas, the dwarfs do not have first aid

18     skills, only loving and generous hearts.

19   SNOW WHITE: What happens next?

20   MADAME SEER: The dwarfs seal you in a glass coffin and

21     set it outside in their yard, where they can watch over

22     you.

23   SNOW WHITE: Ick! Why would they want to look at a body

24     in a coffin every day? What kind of weirdo dwarfs are

25     they?

26   MADAME SEER: You remain there for ten years.

27   SNOW WHITE: What? I can't lie around in a coffin for ten

28     years! I've applied to cosmetology school. I'm

29     supposed to start in September.

30   MADAME SEER: I can only tell you what I see in your

31     palm, and I have never been wrong.

32   SNOW WHITE: The moral clearly is that I should never

33     bite into another apple as long as I live, no matter

34     who offers it to me. I don't care if Johnny Depp *(Or*

35     *insert name of current movie idol)* shows up and

1    hands me an apple, I'm saying no.

2    MADAME SEER: You can only know the future; you can't

3        change it.

4    SNOW WHITE: What?! I'm paying you twenty dollars to

5        learn that I'll be tricked by the evil Queen and end up

6        lying in a glass coffin? You were supposed to help me!

7        You were supposed to make me feel better. *(SNOW*

8        *WHITE stands.)* I'm leaving!

9    MADAME SEER: Don't you want to know what happens in

10        the end?

11   SNOW WHITE: There's more?

12   MADAME SEER: At the end of ten years, a handsome

13        prince rides up on his stallion, sees you in the coffin,

14        and falls madly in love with you.

15   SNOW WHITE: Is he some kind of pervert? Who falls in

16        love with a dead body?

17   MADAME SEER: The dwarfs allow him to kiss you, and his

18        kiss awakens you.

19   SNOW WHITE: Hallelujah!

20   MADAME SEER: The prince asks you to be his bride.

21   SNOW WHITE: This prince isn't the evil queen's son, is he?

22        Because I sure don't want Queen Savage for my

23        mother-in-law.

24   MADAME SEER: The prince has a kingdom in a faraway

25        land. You ride off with him to his palace.

26   SNOW WHITE: Where he gives me a diamond tiara as a

27        wedding present! Oh, thank you, Madame Seer. You

28        truly have a gift.

# 52. The Brit and the Yank

**Cast:** SHIRLEY, from England, and MARGIE, from the U.S.
**Setting:** No special set required. The year is 1945.
**Props:** None

1   **SHIRLEY:** *(Speaking to audience)* I didn't want to leave. I was
2      ten years old in 1940 when the Nazis began bombing
3      London. The Children's Overseas Reception Board
4      arranged ships to carry thousands of children from
5      targeted British cities to temporary homes in the
6      United States and Canada. My parents sent me to
7      America because it was the only way to ensure that I
8      would be safe, but my mum cried the whole time when
9      she told me that I would be going.
10  **MARGIE:** *(Speaking to audience)* When my folks applied to
11     take in one of the evacuees, I thought it would be fun.
12     I'm an only child, and I had always wanted a sister, so
13     they requested a girl. I anticipated lots of giggling and
14     shared secrets and trading clothes and doing fun
15     things together. I thought we'd get a girl who was much
16     like me. Instead, we got Shirley.
17  **SHIRLEY:** I had never been away from home before. My
18     parents packed one small bag for me, and the
19     government issued me a gas mask. It was in a clumsy
20     metal case that hung around my neck and clunked
21     against my chest when I walked. All of the children
22     who were being sent to America were taken to the
23     station where we boarded a train. I peered out the
24     window, trying to find Mum and Dad, but I couldn't see
25     them. Many younger children thought it was a grand
26     adventure, but I wept as the train pulled away. I wept
27     again after we boarded the ship and as it sailed away
28     from Britain.

1    MARGIE: As soon as Shirley got here, I knew we had made
2        a mistake. Talk about Miss Prim and Proper. When
3        we were introduced, I started to hug her, but she got
4        stiff as a board and stepped back. We ended up
5        shaking hands.

6    SHIRLEY: The authorities called us "Vackies" because we
7        had been evacuated. I was sent to a town in Iowa. On
8        the way there, the train passed a field of large
9        animals, and I was frightened until I learned they
10      were cows. I had never seen a cow before.

11    MARGIE: I'd never had to share my room. Or my parents.

12    SHIRLEY: My American parents tried hard, but
13      everything was different here. The school children
14      had few rules. At home in England, the girls are not
15      allowed to talk to the boys. Here, the boys and the
16      girls sit together. Worst of all, the Yanks hardly knew
17      anything about the war. Instead of being worried
18      because London was being bombed, my classmates
19      talked about songs on the "Hit Parade."

20    MARGIE: I was in the sixth grade. Shirley said she was in
21      something called third form, but she was put in my
22      class. She mortified me on the very first day by
23      refusing to repeat the Pledge of Allegiance. Every
24      school day of my life, starting with kindergarten,
25      everyone in the class has stood at the beginning of
26      the day and repeated the Pledge of Allegiance out
27      loud. Once the war started, some of the kids said the
28      pledge extra loud because they had family members
29      in the army or navy.

30    SHIRLEY: The first day of school was terrible. The teacher,
31      Mrs. Ruston, expected me to repeat the Pledge of
32      Allegiance along with the rest of the class. I told her I
33      could not do that. She handed me a piece of paper
34      and said those were the words, and if I didn't know
35      them by heart yet, I could read them until I had them

1     memorized.

2   MARGIE: Mrs. Ruston even gave her the words, but she
3       still didn't say them.

4   SHIRLEY: I was sorry to make the other children angry
5       with me on my first day, but I am a British citizen,
6       and I cannot swear my loyalty to another country's
7       flag. My allegiance belongs to King George. I
8       explained this to Mrs. Ruston, who said as long as I
9       stood up and showed respect by placing my hand on
10      my heart, I didn't have to say the words.

11  MARGIE: After that, the other kids didn't want anything
12      to do with her, especially John and Julia, whose
13      brother got killed fighting in the war. A gold star
14      hangs in the window of their home, and everyone in
15      town is proud of their family's sacrifice.

16  SHIRLEY: The only good part was that my American hosts
17      had a cat. Johnny was a tabby cat with white feet that
18      looked a little bit like my Winston did. He let me pet
19      him the very first night, and when he purred, I
20      almost felt as if I were home with Winston.

21  MARGIE: As if it wasn't bad enough to have to share my
22      room, Shirley kept trying to hold my cat. Johnny
23      didn't seem to mind; in fact, he purred and settled on
24      her lap, but still, he was my cat and she shouldn't
25      have pretended that he belonged to her.

26  SHIRLEY: The worst part of leaving London, even worse
27      than saying goodbye to Mum and Dad, was taking
28      Winston to the veterinarian clinic to be put down.
29      There was a long line of other people with their
30      animals, all waiting to do the same thing. Tears
31      streamed down our faces as we told each other it was
32      the kindest thing to do for our puss. I was being sent
33      to America, Dad was called up for the Territorial
34      Army, and Mum hoped to stay in London, but she had
35      no way to protect Winston. He did not know what an

1    air raid siren meant, and animals weren't allowed in
2    the underground shelters.
3  MARGIE: When we went to bed that first night, I said what
4    Mom and Dad have always said to me: "Good night.
5    Sleep tight. Don't let the bedbugs bite." And do you
6    know what Shirley said? She said, "Oh, no! You have
7    them here too?" I've never seen a bedbug in my life,
8    but apparently where she came from they were
9    common. I hoped she hadn't brought any with her.
10  SHIRLEY: My new classmates and I were out on the
11    playground during recess one day when an airplane
12    flew over. I quickly dropped to the ground and
13    covered my head, as I had been taught to do. The
14    Yanks all gathered 'round and laughed at me.
15  MARGIE: I felt sorry for her when that airplane scared
16    her. I told the other kids they'd duck too if their
17    school had been bombed.
18  SHIRLEY: One morning in class, Mrs. Ruston asked if I
19    had seen that day's newspaper. I had not, so she
20    showed me the story. A ship, *City of Benares,* that was
21    part of the Children's Overseas Reception Board
22    program, had been torpedoed by a German U-boat,
23    and sunk. Of the ninety children aboard, only seven
24    survived. Instead of being kept safe until the war was
25    over, those eighty-three children died at sea. I burst
26    into tears.
27  MARGIE: Everyone felt sorry for Shirley when Mrs.
28    Ruston told us about the ship that sank. We all knew
29    it could have happened to her.
30  SHIRLEY: The Yanks asked me questions that day, about
31    what it had been like to leave home and sail across
32    the ocean. When I told them I had never ridden in a
33    vehicle of any kind until I boarded the train, they
34    were astonished.
35  MARGIE: Shirley had terrible nightmares at first. She

1    would wake up crying, and that woke me up too. If

2    Mom heard her, she would come in and sit on the

3    edge of Shirley's bed and sing softly to her. It seemed

4    strange to hear my mom singing "You Are My

5    Sunshine" to someone else. That's what she always

6    sang to me when I was sick.

7  SHIRLEY: I felt safe in my American town, but feeling safe

8    is not enough when the ones you love are not safe too.

9    Every day, I longed for a letter from home. I craved

10    news of the war, wondering if my dad was fighting

11    the Nazis, wondering if I would ever see him again.

12  MARGIE: Shirley could never relax and have fun. In the

13    middle of a game of Monopoly, she turned on the

14    radio to hear the war news. After the Japanese

15    attacked Pearl Harbor, Dad bought a map of Europe,

16    and every day he and Shirley located the places that

17    were in the news.

18  SHIRLEY: One Saturday afternoon, we went to the

19    movies. I was excited to see my first movie, but before

20    it began, the theater showed "The March of Time."

21    There were pictures of bombed-out buildings. The

22    reporter told of huge casualties.

23  MARGIE: She got hysterical in the theater, and we had to

24    leave without seeing *Dumbo.* I think that day was

25    when I finally understood what Shirley was going

26    through. I quit being disappointed that she wasn't

27    like me and started to see how brave she was, and

28    how lonely.

29  SHIRLEY: When December came that first year, I told

30    Margie about Father Christmas, and she told me

31    about Santa Claus. My gift from Father Christmas

32    the year before had been a fresh orange. Food was

33    rationed, and an orange was a wonderful treat.

34  MARGIE: My family isn't wealthy, but I realized how I

35    took plentiful food for granted. There had never

1       been a Christmas when my only gift was a piece of
2       fruit.
3 SHIRLEY: When I stepped away from Mum and Dad back
4       then to go to the train station, we all thought the war
5       would end soon. We thought I would return home in
6       less than a year. Instead, I stayed with my American
7       family for three years.
8 MARGIE: I was twelve when Shirley moved in. Now I am
9       fifteen, and she is leaving today. At first there were
10      times when I couldn't wait to get rid of her. Now, I'm
11      sorry to see her go.
12 SHIRLEY: Three long years. I'm afraid Mum and Dad
13      might not recognize me, but I know I'll recognize
14      them. I'm so grateful that they both survived. They
15      will be there to welcome me home.
16 MARGIE: *(Talks directly to SHIRLEY.)* Johnny is going to
17      miss you. He'll have to sleep on my bed now, like he
18      used to do before you came.
19 SHIRLEY: *(Talks directly to MARGIE.)* You must pet Johnny
20      every night and make him purr. If I'm allowed to
21      have another cat when I get home, I will get a girl cat
22      and name her Margie, after you.
23 MARGIE: Good-bye, Shirley. Be sure to write. I'll miss you.
24 SHIRLEY: I'll miss you too. *(MARGIE starts to extend her
25      hand, as if to shake hands. SHIRLEY smiles, throws her
26      arms around MARGIE, and the girls hug.)*

# 53. Backstage Pass

**Cast:** CAROLINE and SAMANTHA

**Setting:** A line outside a concert venue

**Props:** Two sweatshirts: Caroline's should have a likeness of an artist or logo on it, and Samantha's should be plain. A slip of paper cut to look like a ticket is in the pocket of the plain sweatshirt.

1 *(As scene opens, CAROLINE is standing facing one side of*
2 *the stage, bouncing impatiently on her toes and*
3 *ostensibly the first to line up for the concert. SAMANTHA*
4 *enters from the opposite side of the stage looking bored*
5 *and walks toward CAROLINE.)*
6 SAMANTHA: Caroline? Ew. What are you doing here?
7 CAROLINE: *(Turns to face SAMANTHA.)* Oh. Hi, Samantha! I
8     didn't know you were coming to this concert.
9 SAMANTHA: *(Rolls eyes.)* I didn't know *you'd* be here, or I
10     might not have.
11 CAROLINE: Of course I'm here! I'm so obsessed with Jeremy
12     Jefferson. Have you never noticed that I wear this Jer-
13     Jeff sweatshirt every day? I can't believe he's actually
14     playing a show in our city! I've never been this excited
15     for anything in my life. I spent every penny in my piggy
16     bank on this ticket. And I'll still be doing chores for my
17     mom and dad for a month. But this show is worth it.
18 SAMANTHA: You have a piggy bank? That's cute.
19 CAROLINE: Well ... *had* one. It's empty now.
20 SAMANTHA: Why are you here so early, anyway? The show
21     doesn't start until, like, seven o'clock.
22 CAROLINE: I have to be in the front row!
23 SAMANTHA: What a waste of your afternoon.
24 CAROLINE: What do you mean? You're here too!
25 SAMANTHA: Not for the concert. I probably won't even stay
26     for that.

1   CAROLINE: There's nothing else happening here tonight
2       except for Jeremy Jefferson.
3   SAMANTHA: I'm early 'cause I have a meet-and-greet pass.
4   CAROLINE: What?! How did you get that? I called into 95.5
5       for weeks trying to get a meet-and-greet pass! I
6       thought there was only one!
7   SAMANTHA: There is.
8   CAROLINE: But I was listening to the radio and calling in
9       when they chose the winner! It was a man's voice on
10      the phone line.
11  SAMANTHA: That was my dad.
12  CAROLINE: Your dad likes Jeremy Jefferson?
13  SAMANTHA: No, stupid. He was calling in for me. I told
14      him to. He got a few of our housekeepers to keep
15      calling in with him. They had the phone line pretty
16      tied up from what I understand.
17  CAROLINE: I didn't know you liked Jeremy Jefferson.
18  SAMANTHA: I don't like him that much.
19  CAROLINE: You can't be serious.
20  SAMANTHA: Yeah, he's pretty juvenile for me. I told my
21      dad to get me the ticket like forever ago, but now I'm
22      pretty much over it. I'm surprised you still listen to
23      him.
24  CAROLINE: Would you sell the ticket to me?
25  SAMANTHA: *(Snorts.)* No.
26  CAROLINE: Why not? You're not even excited!
27  SAMANTHA: I'm just going to snap a picture with him to
28      make everyone at school jealous. He is totally cute,
29      even if his music is lame. Besides, you just said you'd
30      spent all your money on a regular old ticket. There's
31      no way you could afford mine.
32  CAROLINE: I'm sure my parents would give me a loan.
33      They know how much this would mean to me. I can
34      call them right now — *(Begins to reach in pocket for*
35      *phone.)*

1 SAMANTHA: Stop it. This is embarrassing to watch. I'm
2     here, I've got the ticket, and I'm going to meet Jeremy
3     Jefferson myself. Honestly, I don't know why you'd
4     even want to make a fool of yourself in front of him.
5     It's lucky I'm a bit more mature than you.
6 CAROLINE: I wouldn't make a fool of myself. He'd
7     probably appreciate a real fan more than you acting
8     too cool for school. You don't even have any of his
9     merchandise on! I bet he won't smile in a picture
10     with you.
11 SAMANTHA: What, you really think he cares?
12 CAROLINE: I know he does! I've read every interview he's
13     ever done. In *Teen Vogue's* November issue, he said
14     fake fans are his number-one pet peeve.
15 SAMANTHA: *(Trying to look unperturbed)* Who even reads
16     *Teen Vogue* anymore?
17 CAROLINE: You know what? I bet you don't get a picture
18     with him at all. The meet-and-greet pass doesn't
19     necessarily include that. He only does it if he wants
20     to. I read the fine print on his website.
21 SAMANTHA: Whatever. You're just jealous.
22 CAROLINE: No, I'm serious.
23 SAMANTHA: Fine. Caroline, give me your sweatshirt.
24 CAROLINE: What? No!
25 SAMANTHA: Why not? Jeremy Jefferson's not even going
26     to see you. You'll be like an ant in the crowd. Besides,
27     if you don't, I'll tell everyone about the time you peed
28     your pants on the first day of middle school.
29 CAROLINE: What? That didn't happen!
30 SAMANTHA: So what? I'll say it did. Who are people going
31     to believe, you or me? Give me the sweatshirt.
32     *(CAROLINE reluctantly takes off her sweatshirt and*
33     *hands it to SAMANTHA, who sheds her own sweatshirt*
34     *and tosses it carelessly back at CAROLINE. Both put*
35     *their new sweatshirts on.)*

1    SAMANTHA: That's better! Jeremy Jefferson is going to
2        love me. Maybe I'll invite you to our wedding,
3        Caroline. But probably not.
4    CAROLINE: Oh! Here comes the security guard.
5        *(CAROLINE and SAMANTHA look up as if a security*
6        *guard has opened a door from Off-stage and spoken to*
7        *them.)*
8    SAMANTHA: *(Raises hand and smiles sweetly.)* I'm here for
9        the meet and greet. *(Pauses as if spoken to again.)* My
10        ticket? Yes, it's right here. *(Reaches hand into pants*
11        *pocket.)* Hold on, it's in here somewhere. *(Checks*
12        *other pocket, then back pockets.)* Oh, it must be in my
13        sweatshirt pocket. Caroline, look and see.
14    CAROLINE: *(She has been watching SAMANTHA search her*
15        *pockets. Now she reaches her hand slowly into her plain*
16        *sweatshirt pocket and removes ticket. She looks down at*
17        *it as it dawns on her what has happened. Looks up as if*
18        *to security guard and slowly holds ticket up as if*
19        *showing it to him.)* Here it is.
20    SAMANTHA: Caroline, give it here.
21    CAROLINE: *(Points Off-stage, looking to "security guard.")*
22        This way?
23    SAMANTHA: *Wait!* That's my ticket!
24    CAROLINE: *(Turns back to SAMANTHA.)* Do I need to have
25        security call someone about you? I think you've been
26        standing for too long in the hot sun. Honestly, some
27        fans just can't handle their excitement. *(She walks*
28        *Off-stage, as if through a door escorted by security.)*
29    SAMANTHA: *(Rushes forward after CAROLINE and begins*
30        *to bang and kick closed "door.")* **Caroline!** Get back
31        here! You nasty little thief! *Caroline!*

# 54. Two by Two

**Characters:** MOOLIE and WOOLY. Note that both characters
sing some of their lines.

**Setting:** No special set required.

**Props:** None

1 MOOLIE: Are you going to be in the *Noah's Ark* play?
2 WOOLY: Unfortunately, yes. I tried to get out of it, but I need
3      the class credit.
4 MOOLIE: So do I. When I signed up for drama class, I
5      thought we'd do *Romeo and Juliet* or *A Streetcar*
6      *Named Desire.* I never imagined that I'd be stuck
7      playing the part of a cow.
8 WOOLY: At least cows are proactive. I play one of the sheep.
9 MOOLIE: What's proactive about cows?
10 WOOLY: When it's milking time, they go home all by
11      themselves. Sheep never lead the way; they only follow.
12 MOOLIE: On the other hand, sheep frolic. Cows plod.
13 WOOLY: This part doesn't call for frolicking. In fact, there
14      isn't much action in the script. All we do is walk onto
15      the ark, two by two. Instead of looking sheepish, I'd like
16      to ram into something. Maybe butt heads with the
17      other sheep.
18 MOOLIE: You could add some stage business of your own.
19      That's what I plan to do. Even though it's a terrible
20      script, I want my performance to be the cream of the
21      crop.
22 WOOLY: What are you going to do?
23 MOOLIE: I call it the bovine ballet. *(MOOLIE does a few*
24      *quick dance steps, while singing)* **Moo, moo. Moo, moo,**
25      **m-moo. If there are any talent scouts in the audience,**
26      **my act will be an instant cash cow.**
27 WOOLY: What if the director says you can't dance?
28 MOOLIE: He wouldn't dairy.

1 WOOLY: He might worry that the horses will be jealous if
2     you're outstanding in your field.
3 MOOLIE: I refuse to be cowed by the director. When the
4     other animals see my dance, they'll butter me up.
5     They'll want to learn my smoooooth mooooves.
6 WOOLY: Is your family coming?
7 MOOLIE: I told them it's a cheesy play and to stay home,
8     but they'll be here with bells on. What about your
9     family? Were you able to stall them?
10 WOOLY: No. My parents are going to corral my siblings
11     and shepherd them over here.
12 MOOLIE: My sister is coming voluntarily. She's always
13     said I was born in a barn, and she thinks this
14     production proves it.
15 WOOLY: At least it will be easy credit since we don't have
16     any lines to memorize.
17 MOOLIE: I may add some lines. As long as I'm stuck
18     playing a cow, I intend to milk it for all it's worth.
19 WOOLY: What do you plan to say?
20 MOOLIE: I'm going to talk the person who plays the other
21     cow into using the name Gertrude. Then, when I see
22     her, I can say, "Yo, Gert!" Get it? Yogurt?
23 WOOLY: *(Groans.)* What other lines are you adding?
24 MOOLIE: I don't know yet.
25 WOOLY: You could recite a poem.
26 MOOLIE: "Little boy blue, come blow your horn. *(MOOLIE*
27     *gestures toward WOOLY.)* The sheep's in the meadow."
28 WOOLY: *(Gestures toward MOOLIE.)* "The cow's in the
29     corn."
30 MOOLIE: Perfect!
31 WOOLY: Maybe I could sing. *(Sings.)* "Baa, baa, black
32     sheep, have you any wool?"
33 MOOLIE: Sweet! You have to do that.
34 WOOLY: *(Sings.)* "Mary had a little lamb, little lamb, little
35     lamb."

1   MOOLIE: *(Applauds, and then recites.)* "Hey, diddle,
2      diddle, the cat and the fiddle, the cow jumped over
3      the moon." *(MOOLIE leaps in the air.)*
4   WOOLY: I'd like to sing "Ewe Are My Sunshine." You
5      know, E-W-E? Ewe? But I'm afraid the audience
6      wouldn't get it.
7   MOOLIE: Maybe you should stick to "Baa, Baa, Black
8      Sheep."
9   WOOLY: Why don't you sing too?
10  MOOLIE: I'm too much of a *cow*ard to sing in front of a
11     crowd.
12  WOOLY: You shouldn't keep your talent bottled up.
13  MOOLIE: There's an oldie called "*Cud*-dle up a Little
14     Closer."
15  WOOLY: My grandpa sings, "There's an Old Cow Hand."
16  MOOLIE: I know! Let's sing a duet! I won't be nervous if
17     we sing together. We could do "Home on the Range."
18  WOOLY: That's about deer and antelope, not cows and
19     sheep.
20  MOOLIE: We'll change the lyrics.
21  WOOLY: That might be an infringement of copyright.
22     That would be baaaad. You don't want to get thrown
23     in the pen.
24  MOOLIE: "Home on the Range" is probably in the public
25     domain. Come on! It be*hooves* us to do something
26     clever.
27  WOOLY: If we wear costumes, I'll be a black sheep.
28  MOOLIE: I can wear a jersey.
29  WOOLY: What if the director doesn't like our additions?
30     What if he kicks us out of the show?
31  MOOLIE: We won't sing or dance at the rehearsal. We'll
32     wait until the performance and surprise everyone.
33     We'll call them "certified organic" acts.
34  WOOLY: We're the last animals to enter. I hope our
35     families aren't *ashleep* by then.

1   MOOLIE: Make sure they have plenty of *calf*-eine before
2       the show.
3   WOOLY: Does my wool coat look OK? *(Turns in a circle.)*
4   MOOLIE: Yes. It's a perfect fit. What about my cowlick?
5       *(Points to forehead.)*
6   WOOLY: *(Looks at MOOLIE's head.)* As long as you don't
7       scowl, you look fine.
8   MOOLIE: It'll be a Grade A show!
9   WOOLY: It'll be shear delight!
10  MOOLIE: Let's do it!
11  WOOLY: Yes!
12  MOOLIE and WOOLY: *(Together, singing)* "Oh, give me a
13      home, where the animals roam,
14      Where the sheep and the dairy cows play."
15  MOOLIE: Too bad we don't get paid for this performance.
16      I could use some *moo*-lah.
17  WOOLY: At least they'll flock to get our *hoof*-ographs.
18  MOOLIE and WOOLY: *(Together, singing:)* "Where seldom
19      is heard a discouraging word,
20      And the students will all get an A."
21  MOOLIE: We are *udder*-ly amazing! *(They exit, singing*
22      *together, "Home, home on the range.")*

# About the Authors

PEG KEHRET has won numerous awards for her middle grade books, including more than fifty state Children's Choice Awards, the PEN Center West Award in Children's Literature, and the Golden Kite Award from the Society of Children's Book Writers & Illustrators. Her plays are widely produced, and her books of monologues are staples for speech competitions and drama classes. Her most recent book is a memoir, *Animals Welcome: A Life of Reading, Writing, and Rescue.* Peg lives in Washington State near Mt. Rainier National Park.

BRETT KONEN is a freelance journalist and graduate of Whitman College. She writes a weekly column for *Sip Northwest Magazine,* and her work has also appeared in the *Seattle Globalist* and *The Stranger.* This is her first book. When she isn't writing, Brett enjoys coffee, baking, dancing, cribbage, travel, and adventure. She lives in Seattle.

# Order Form

**Meriwether Publishing Ltd.**
PO Box 7710
Colorado Springs, CO 80933-7710
Phone: 800-937-5297  Fax: 719-594-9916
Website: www.meriwether.com

*Please send me the following books:*

_____ **Two Voices  #BK-B359**                                  $17.95
by Peg Kehret and Brett Konen
*54 original duologues for teens*

_____ **Tell It Like It Is  #BK-B295**                          $16.95
by Peg Kehret
*Fifty monologs for talented teens*

_____ **Winning Monologs for Young Actors**      $16.95
**#BK-B127**
by Peg Kehret
*Honest-to-life monologs for young actors*

_____ **Encore! More Winning Monologs**            $15.95
**for Young Actors  #BK-B144**
by Peg Kehret
*More honest-to-life monologs for young actors*

_____ **Acting Natural  #BK-B133**                            $15.95
by Peg Kehret
*Honest-to-life monologs, dialogs and playlets for teens*

_____ **102 Monologues for Middle School Actors** $17.95
**#BK-B327**
by Rebecca Young
*Including comedy and dramatic monologues*

_____ **103 Monologues for Middle School Actors** $17.95
**#BK-B355**
by Rebecca Young
*More winning comedy and dramatic characterizations*

**These and other fine Meriwether Publishing books are available at
your local bookstore or direct from the publisher. Prices subject to
change without notice. Check our website or call for current prices.**

Name: _____ email:_____

Organization name: _____

Address: _____

City: _____ State: _____

Zip: _____ Phone: _____

❑  **Check enclosed**

❑  **Visa / MasterCard / Discover / Am. Express #** _____

|  | *Expiration* | *CVV* |
|---|---|---|

*Signature:* _____ *date:* _____ / _____ *code:* _____
*(required for credit card orders)*

**Colorado residents:** Please add 3% sales tax.
**Shipping:** Include $3.95 for the first book and 75¢ for each additional book ordered.

❑  *Please send me a copy of your complete catalog of books and plays.*

# Order Form

**Meriwether Publishing Ltd.**
PO Box 7710
Colorado Springs, CO 80933-7710
Phone: 800-937-5297  Fax: 719-594-9916
Website: www.meriwether.com

*Please send me the following books:*

_____ **Two Voices  #BK-B359**                              $17.95
by Peg Kehret and Brett Konen
*54 original duologues for teens*

_____ **Tell It Like It Is  #BK-B295**                      $16.95
by Peg Kehret
*Fifty monologs for talented teens*

_____ **Winning Monologs for Young Actors**    $16.95
**#BK-B127**
by Peg Kehret
*Honest-to-life monologs for young actors*

_____ **Encore! More Winning Monologs**         $15.95
**for Young Actors  #BK-B144**
by Peg Kehret
*More honest-to-life monologs for young actors*

_____ **Acting Natural  #BK-B133**                          $15.95
by Peg Kehret
*Honest-to-life monologs, dialogs and playlets for teens*

_____ **102 Monologues for Middle School Actors** $17.95
**#BK-B327**
by Rebecca Young
*Including comedy and dramatic monologues*

_____ **103 Monologues for Middle School Actors** $17.95
**#BK-B355**
by Rebecca Young
*More winning comedy and dramatic characterizations*

**These and other fine Meriwether Publishing books are available at your local bookstore or direct from the publisher. Prices subject to change without notice. Check our website or call for current prices.**

Name: _____ email:_____

Organization name: _____

Address: _____

City: _____ State: _____

Zip: _____ Phone: _____

❑ **Check enclosed**

❑ **Visa / MasterCard / Discover / Am. Express #** _____

|  | Expiration | CVV |
Signature: _____ date: _____ / _____ code: _____
*(required for credit card orders)*

**Colorado residents:** Please add 3% sales tax.
**Shipping:** Include $3.95 for the first book and 75¢ for each additional book ordered.

❑ *Please send me a copy of your complete catalog of books and plays.*